D0585916

WST

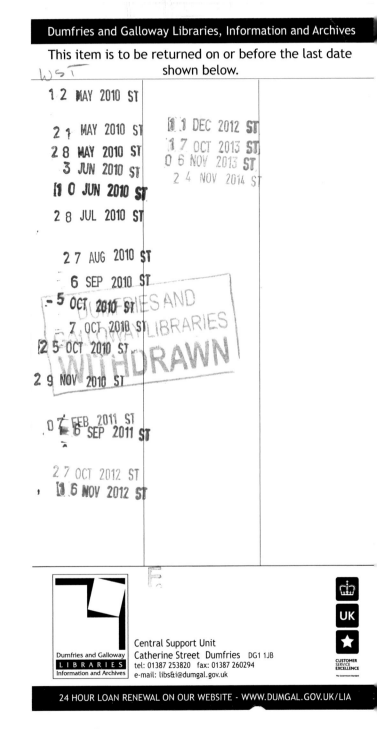

1 2 MAY 2010 ST

2 1 MAY 2010 ST
2 8 MAY 2010 ST
3 JUN 2010 ST
1 0 JUN 2010 ST
2 8 JUL 2010 ST

2 7 AUG 2010 ST
6 SEP 2010 ST
- 5 OCT 2010 ST
7 OCT 2010 ST
2 5 OCT 2010 ST
2 9 NOV 2010 ST

0 7 FEB 2011 ST
1 6 SEP 2011 ST

2 7 OCT 2012 ST
1 6 NOV 2012 ST

1 1 DEC 2012 ST
1 7 OCT 2013 ST
0 6 NOV 2013 ST
2 4 NOV 2014 ST

DUMFRIES AND GALLOWAY LIBRARIES

WITHDRAWN

Also by Christian Jacq

The Ramses Series
Volume 1: The Son of the Light
Volume 2: The Temple of a Million Years
Volume 3: The Battle of Kadesh
Volume 4: The Lady of Abu Simbel
Volume 5: Under the Western Acacia

The Stone of Light Series
Volume 1: Nefer the Silent
Volume 2: The Wise Woman
Volume 3: Paneb the Ardent
Volume 4: The Place of Truth

The Queen of Freedom Trilogy
Volume 1: The Empire of Darkness
Volume 2: The War of the Crowns
Volume 3: The Flaming Sword

The Judge of Eygpt Trilogy
Volume 1: Beneath the Pyramid
Volume 2: Secrets of the Desert
Volume 3: Shadow of the Sphinx

The Mysteries of Osiris Series
Volume 1: The Tree of Life
Volume 2: The Conspiracy of Evil
Volume 3: The Way of Fire
Volume 4: The Great Secret

The Count of Thebes Series
Volume 1: The Great Magician
Volume 2: Son of Light
Volume 3: The Brother of Fire
Volume 4: The Beloved of Isis

The Black Pharaoh
The Tutankhamun Affair
For the Love of Philae
Champollion the Egyptian
Master Hiram & King Solomon
The Living Wisdom of Ancient Egypt

About the Translator

Sue Dyson is a prolific author of both fiction and non-fiction,
including over thirty novels both contemporary and historical.
She has also translated a wide variety of French fiction.

The Great Magician

The Count of Thebes

Christian Jacq

Translated by Sue Dyson

SIMON & SCHUSTER

LONDON · NEW YORK · TORONTO · SYDNEY

First published in France by XO Editions under the title
Le Grand Magicien, 2006
First published in Great Britain by Simon & Schuster UK Ltd, 2010
A CBS COMPANY

1 3 5 7 9 10 8 6 4 2

Simon & Schuster UK Ltd
1st Floor
222 Gray's Inn Road
London WC1X 8HB

www.simonandschuster.co.uk

Simon & Schuster Australia
Sydney

A CIP catalogue record for this book is
available from the British Library

Hardback ISBN 978-0-74329-520-8
Trade Paperback ISBN 978-0-74329-519-2

Typeset by Rowland Phototypesetting Ltd,
Bury St Edmunds, Suffolk
Printed and bound in the UK by CPI Mackays, Chatham ME5 8TD

All the efforts we make to try and explain the very foundation of things became futile the day after Mozart appeared.

Goethe

A heart born for liberty never allows itself to be treated like a slave. And even when it has lost its freedom, it still retains the pride it had in it and laughs at the universe.

Mozart, Die Entführung aus dem Serail

Preface

Ever since I began to write, at the age of thirteen, Mozart has been with me. As I listened to him and discovered the civilization of ancient Egypt, I did not yet know just how much the two were linked. A few years later, I started a file entitled 'Mozart the Egyptian', the basis of the four-volume novel published today, to depict the spiritual adventure and secret life of one of history's greatest geniuses.

Above and beyond his Masonic involvement, Mozart was initiated into the mysteries of Isis and Osiris, as revealed in his Great Work, *Die Zauberflöte*.

In order to understand how this musician became the son and beloved of Isis the Great, whose universal message he passed on, we must go back to 342 B.C. The defeat of King Nectanebo II by the Persian Artaxerxes III marked the end of the thirtieth and final dynasty. From that moment on, the ancient land of the pharaohs was no longer independent and saw a succession of invaders and occupiers: Persians, Greeks, Romans, Byzantines and finally Arabs, who seized the country in A.D. 639 and imposed Islam upon it.

The death-agony was very long, since it lasted almost a millennium. Foreseeing the disappearance of their culture, Egyptian sages covered the walls of great temples like Edfu, Dendera, Kom-Ombo and Philae with writings, and wrote

numerous papyri. Giving up all hope of an impossible liberation, the brotherhoods confined their attentions to their
shrines.

In A.D. 383, Theodosius ordered the closure of all the temples
that were still active. The Christians either destroyed them or
transformed them into churches. The initiates were forced
to lead a clandestine life, then to leave Egypt, where passing
on the ancient Mysteries – already a difficult and dangerous
process – became impossible after the Arab conquest.

During the early centuries of Christianity, its principal
competitor was the cult of Isis, which was widespread in the
West and as far across Europe as Russia. So the expatriates
found a welcome in several places and – thanks to the brotherhoods of builders – prepared the way for the blossoming of
medieval art. To take just one significant example, episodes
from the Mysteries of Osiris are related on the door of Gniezen
Cathedral, in Poland.

Egyptian initiation did not come to an end with the
closure of the temples, for hieroglyphic thought, encapsulating
"the words of the gods" and the rituals in which they were
embodied, was passed on both orally and through coded texts.
See J. R. Harris (ed), *The Legacy of Egypt*, Oxford, 1971;
S. Morenz, *Die Zauberflöte*, Münster, 1952; E. Iverson, *The
Myth of Egypt and Its Hieroglyphs in European Tradition*,
Princeton, 1961; E. Hornung, *L'Egypte ésotérique*, Paris, 1999;
L'Egypte imaginaire de la Renaissance à Champollion, under the
direction of Chantal Grell, Paris, 2001; *Philosophers and
Hieroglyphs*, ed. L. Morra and C. Bazzanella, 2003.

The child of Thoth, master of sacred knowledge, hermeticism enriched the development of the builders' lodges. When
the era of the cathedrals came to an end, the descendants
of Egyptian initiates formed circles of alchemists, which gave
birth to one of the branches of Freemasonry. There, the ancient
Mysteries were celebrated in the form of three grades:

Apprentice, Companion and Master. The first revealed the creative elements of creation, the second the sacred geometry, and the third revived the myth of Osiris, now rebaptized as Hiram.

When Mozart was born, in 1756, the diverse Masonic movements were in crisis. Major aspects of the tradition of initiation had been disfigured, neglected, even lost. And it was while working on a project entitled *Thamos, König in Ägypten* ('Thamos, King of Egypt') that the musician, who was approached early on in his life by the Masons, came into contact with the universe of initiation. From that moment on, it became the most vital part of his life. His master, the Venerable Ignaz von Born, considered the Egyptian priests to be his true ancestors, and undertook research from which his disciple benefited.

After receiving the Light of initiation in December 1784, Mozart set himself an objective; to pass on what he had received. In reality, he was to go well beyond this by becoming the bridge between Egypt and symbolic Freemasonry. The apogee of his reasoning, *Die Zauberflöte*, opened up the way of the Royal Art, the marriage of Fire and Water, Man and Woman. This ritual opera casts light upon the Mysteries of Isis and Osiris, the key to the tradition of initiation. And Mozart's work traverses time, like a temple 'built from the beautiful stones of eternity'.

Christian Jacq

1

Upper Egypt, 1756

The ten Mamelukes bore down on their victim, determined to
slit the young monk's throat. Thamos was unarmed, so could
not possibly fight these professional assassins, henchmen of
a local petty tyrant who encouraged their acts of violence.
He took to his heels.

How could he ever have imagined that here, in the middle
of the desert, he would be attacked by a band of killers?
Ordinarily, he meditated facing the sunset, reminding himself
of the teachings of his venerable master, Abbot Hermes, an old
man of remarkable vitality. Time vanished beneath the sand of
the dunes, and a taste for eternity was born out of the silent
immensity, barely disturbed by the ibises' flight.

Thamos ran until he was out of breath. Since he had a
major advantage – his knowledge of the terrain – he took
full advantage of it. With a gazelle-like leap, he crossed the
dried-up bed of a wadi, then scrambled up the rocky slope of
a hill.

His pursuers were overweight, and sweating profusely.
One of them twisted an ankle and fell, dragging three of his
companions down with him. The others ran harder, yelling
insults at their accursed prey, and his seemingly inexhaustible
supply of breath.

Thamos ran along the edge of a patch of soft sand; two Mamelukes sank into it, and had to be helped by their comrades. But one man was too stubborn and too furious to give up the chase. When he saw that the young monk was getting away, he flung his sabre with vicious force. The weapon only just missed its target.

Thamos kept running for a long time, taking care not to head towards his monastery, for fear of endangering it. Eventually, badly out of breath, he stopped. He knelt at the foot of an acacia tree and gave thanks to God: without Him, he would not have escaped from those predators.

When his spirits had revived, the young man retraced his steps and checked that the Mamelukes had gone back the way they came. Accustomed to easy victories over mere men, they feared the demons of the desert and hated lingering there.

Not until nightfall did Thamos return to the fortified Monastery of St Mercury, where he had lived since childhood, together with eleven other Brothers, who were now all very old.

He knocked three times on the heavy wooden door. The doorkeeper appeared up above on the ramparts and, by the light of a torch, identified the new arrival.

'There you are, at last,' he said. 'What happened?'

'I escaped from a band of marauders.'

The doorkeeper came down from his observation post and opened the monastery door a little way. He took Thamos to Father Hermes, who was reading a papyrus covered with hieroglyphs. The old man was almost a hundred years old and rarely left his cell, which had been transformed into a library. The shelves were filled with writings dating from the era when the pharaohs ruled.

In those days Egypt had been prosperous and happy. But now, in these desolate times, it had fallen under the tyranny of the Ottoman Empire. Byzantium had been destroyed, and the

6

Ottomans had conquered the Near East and were threatening Europe. Since Islam was the absolute, final truth, they believed it should be imposed upon the entire world. The empire's military power would ensure that it triumphed.

Tortured, and crushed by taxation, Egypt was in its death throes. The Pasha gave a free hand to the beys of Cairo, exploiters who led armed militias which spent their time killing each other. At the moment the predominant one was composed of Mamelukes; it was merciless and well equipped. Poverty, famine and epidemics were strangling the Two Lands of Upper and Lower Egypt, and glorious Alexandria now contained no more than eight thousand inhabitants.

Since their invasion in the seventh century, the Arab barbarians had destroyed large numbers of ancient temples, imposed the veil upon women – who were now considered inferior beings – and torn up the grape vines. Fortunately, though, the Monastery of St Mercury seemed to have been forgotten. In this remote place, St Mercury protected the little community. Convinced that his two swords could descend from the heavens and slice open their throats, looters did not dare attack.

Choosing his words carefully, Thamos told the Father Abbot about his misadventure.

'The time is coming,' declared the old man. 'St Mercury cannot save us for very much longer.'

'Will we have to leave, father?'

'You, my son, will leave. We shall stay.'

'No! I'll defend you to my last drop of blood!'

'You are to carry out a much more important mission. Come with me to the laboratory.'

Since the massacre of the last community of Egyptian priests and priestesses, at Philae, the Isle of Isis, no hieroglyphic texts had been written. The secrets of the magic language of the pharaohs seemed lost for ever. However, they had been passed down from master to disciple, and Abbot Hermes formed the final link in the chain.

'They will kill us and burn down the monastery,' he predicted. 'Before that happens, we shall bury our treasures in the sand. And I am going to reveal to you the last phases of the Great Work, so that the tradition may continue, unbroken.'

The laboratory was a small room resembling the resurrection chamber in a pyramid of the Old Kingdom. On its walls, hieroglyphic inscriptions recalled how Isis had taught alchemy to Horus by bringing murdered Osiris back to life. Osiris was the primordial unity, reconstituted after its dispersal in matter; the triumph of light over darkness; the sun, reborn in the depths of the night.

'Barley can be transformed into gold,' said the abbot; 'the philosopher's stone is Osiris. Hieroglyphs give us an intuitive knowledge, capable of embracing all that is real, visible and invisible. Gaze upon the work of Isis.'

Thamos witnessed the end of the short way, the dazzle of a single moment in eternity, and the end of the long way, the marriage of the spirit and matter at the culmination of a long ritual process.

The young man engraved the words of power upon his heart.

'After one thousand five hundred years of waiting,' said Abbot Hermes, 'Osiris has permitted the Great Magician to be reborn and to take flesh in the body of a human being. But not here, in Egypt. His spirit has chosen the cold lands of the north. Wherever he appears, he will be destitute and deprived of the vital energy of our Great Mother. So you must pass on to him the wisdom of Isis and *The Book of Thoth*. You will help the Great Magician to build himself up until he is able, in turn, to pass on the secret of initiation and to light up the darkness.'

Thamos blanched. 'Father, I . . .'

'You have no choice, my son. Either you succeed, or the gods will depart from this land for ever and Osiris will never again be reborn. With the aid of alchemy, you will be able to travel, supply your needs, take care of yourself and speak in different languages.'

'I would much rather stay here, with you.'

'We shall pray together, one last time, and then you will leave. Find the Great Magician, Thamos, protect him and enable him to create the work which will give the world hope.

2

Salzburg, 27 January 1756

Leopold Mozart, a master of the violin, was braving the winter's cold. Not yet thirty-seven, he was a dynamic man with a military bearing. A native of Augsburg, the eldest son of a large and penniless family whose ancestors had been masons and stonecutters, he had learnt Greek and Latin, and taken courses in law and theology at the faculty in Salzburg, before opting for a career as a household musician, in the service of first the Count of Thurn and then the Prince-Archbishop of Salzburg.

A composer and performer, on 21 November 1747 he had married the lovely Anna Maria Pertl. Everyone agreed that they made the handsomest couple in Salzburg. Curious about everything, and the possessor of a microscope and an astronomical lens, Leopold Mozart was preparing to publish a reference work, *The Violin School*,* in order to pass on his technique and experience to future generations.

Soon to be the father of a seventh child, he hoped that it would be the second to survive, after his daughter Nannerl, aged four. One day, perhaps, science would explain why so many newborn children died. In the meantime, one

* Original title: *Versuch einer gründlichen Violin*.

must submit to the will of God and the fertility of mothers.

Leopold adored Salzburg, which was linked to Bavaria but was an independent ecclesiastical principality and the seat of an archibishopric. Here all was peace and tranquillity, while war was tearing Europe apart, setting the French, English and Prussians at one another's throats.

Salzburg – 'the fortress of salt' – boasted ten thousand inhabitants and was proud of its singularity. Traversed by the swift, tumultuous River Salzach, it stood within a circle of mountains and forests, and was proud of its seven hills and cultural heritage, which had earned it the nickname of 'the second Rome'.

Vast squares, narrow alleyways, churches, monasteries, castles, palaces and middle-class houses illustrated the opulence of this principality in which opera, imported from Venice, had been played for the first time in 1616.

Leopold served the powerful Count Sigismund Christoph von Schrattenbach, primate of Germany and the Pope's representative at the Diet of the Germanic Holy Roman Empire. Hostile to Protestantism in a city profoundly marked by the Benedictines, the count enjoyed music that was pleasant and in good taste. Salzburg life centred on his brilliant and cultured court, which was venerated by the petty nobility, by the well-off middle classes, city functionaries and the lower ranks of the clergy. This harmonious society suited Leopold perfectly; he was delighted to benefit from the favours of such a good prince.

Today, however, even contemplating his privileged situation did not dispel Leopold's main worry: would his dear wife give birth to a viable child, and would she recover from the birth? Born on Christmas Day 1720, Anna Maria was an excellent mistress of the household. Life without her would be unbearable.

But he must not give in to pessimism. The pregnancy had

passed without incident, and the family doctor was reassuring. Anna Maria's vigorous health and good appetite surely guaranteed a happy event . . .?

Lost in his thoughts, Leopold Mozart bumped into a small man dressed in grey.

'Forgive me,' he said. 'I am rather worried.'

'Nothing serious, I hope?'

'No, no . . . My wife is due to give birth shortly.'

'Congratulations. I wish you great happiness, Mr . . . I'm sorry, I do not know your name.'

'Mozart, musician at the court of the prince-archbishop.'

'Delighted to make your acquaintance. May fortune favour you.'

Leopold strode off. Struggling against the icy wind, he had not thought to ask the passer-by's name. But what importance could that have, on such a difficult day?

The little grey man was a young police officer, working for the Austrian crown. Josef Anton, Count of Pergen, suffered from an obsession: the growing influence of secret societies. In perfect agreement with Empress Maria Theresa, who detested Freemasons, Anton wanted to become the acknowledged expert on these disturbing forces – their unspoken goal was to overthrow the throne and win power by destroying religion, morality and society.

Very few ministers and dignitaries were aware of the danger. Some even considered Anton a maniac, but he cared nothing for such criticisms. Day after day, he added to his files and wove a network of informants capable of providing him with valuable information. Unfortunately, his superiors had placed an obstacle in his path. They did not believe there was a conspiracy, and considered the Freemasons and their ilk to be simple dreamers.

In fact, behind their rites and the symbols, the Masons concealed a formidable lust for power. If nobody barred their way, they would eventually triumph. Josef Anton would devote his life to combating them and preventing them from doing harm. He would have to climb yet higher in the administrative hierarchy, so as to have more resources made available to him. But he was patient and methodical, and he would succeed.

Anton enjoyed working both in the office and in the field, and he carried out the delicate investigations himself. That is why he was in Salzburg, where, according to a Jesuit who was generally well informed, conspirators belonging to the occult Rose-Cross movement, more or less linked to Freemasonry, were organizing an exceptional meeting.

Although they claimed to be Catholics, the Rosicrucians were suspected of practising suspect sciences, such as alchemy; they were said to obey Unknown Superiors, who hid behind pseudonyms. Anton was quite sure they did not confine themselves merely to smoky experiments in ramshackle laboratories.

Keeping watch on them posed serious problems, for Anton had not told the archbishop what he was planning. Salzburg was an independent principality, not part of Austria, and its overlord would have been less than pleased to see a Viennese policeman encroaching on his prerogatives, so Anton worked alone.

It was an uncomfortable situation, at risk of ending in failure, and the count saw a long road before him, strewn with obstacles. Only unfaltering resolution would enable him to prove to the authorities that his theory was well founded. Despite the absence of formal proof, Anton was convinced that the Rosicrucians were using the Freemasons whom the empress so despised. If the diverse factions succeeded in uniting under a true leader, their ability to do harm would become terrifying.

He gazed for a long time at the house under suspicion, an austere, imposing edifice. No windows were lit. Despite the cold and the snow, Anton kept watch. For more than an hour, nobody entered or came out. Curious, he went over to the building and, after a moment's hesitation, pushed the door open.

The interior was being rebuilt, and was uninhabitable. No meeting could be held here. At that moment, Josef Anton felt doubt. He doubted his informant, the existence of the Rosicrucians, the Freemasons' desire to harm the empire, and he doubted his own convictions. Frozen stiff, the little grey man left the house and set off back to Vienna.

Leopold was pacing up and down, back and forth, before a painting of St John Nepomucene, who was charged with protecting those faithful to him against malicious gossip. Beside it, on a chest of drawers, stood a wax figurine of the infant Jesus, blessed at the church of St Mary of Loreto. At that time, it was the best-known remedy for migraines.

'Is Mummy going to give me a little brother?' asked Nannerl, tugging her father's sleeve.

'God will decide.'

'Does He decide everything?'

'Of course.'

'Then I shall pray to Him.'

Leopold longed to have a son; but, whatever happened, this would be his last child. At thirty-six, his wife was running serious risks by giving birth for the seventh time. Edgily, he plucked at the strings of his favourite violin, as if the magic of the notes could help Anna Maria come safely through her ordeal.

At eight o'clock on the evening of 27 January 1756, the cries of a newborn child filled the apartment.

The midwife emerged from the bedroom, wreathed in smiles. 'Mother and child are doing well. It's a boy. There is just one small problem – nothing serious.'

'What is it?'

'He is missing the concha, the usual twist, on his left ear.

14

But it won't affect his hearing. Right, then, I shall go and take care of mother and baby. As the doctor advises, he is to be fed with water and most particularly not with milk.

Nannerl flung her arms round her father's neck. 'God and Mummy have given me a little brother!'

'He is to be called Johannes Chrysostomus Wolfgang Gottlieb,' Leopold decided.

He had wavered between the Latin Theophilus and the German Gottlieb, but the two names had the same meaning: 'Beloved of God'.

3

Salzburg, 1761

In his best handwriting, Leopold Mozart noted on the sheet music: 'This minuet and this trio were learned by Wolfgang in half an hour, on 26 January 1761, one day before his fifth year, at half past nine in the evening.'

Learning, learning, learning ... It was all the child ever thought about! And he could play music before he could read.

The official composer to the Salzburg court since 1757, Leopold had decided to undertake his son's education – and above all his musical training – himself. Fundamentally, composing interested him less than helping to mature this little prodigy, who was so different from other children. Sometimes he was just a little boy, sometimes the expression of a higher power, whose extent surprised his admiring but anxious father more with each day that passed.

To whom could he entrust him? The religious were wary of geniuses, who were sometimes inspired by the Devil, and Leopold did not earn enough to pay a private tutor. If Wolfgang's musical gifts were confirmed, wouldn't the court's foremost violinist be his best teacher?

Anna Maria did not ask herself questions like those. Happy to see her children growing, she made sure that the household ran smoothly. Thanks to her, they all had everything they needed.

The future looked very bright.

Vienna, March 1761

The five Freemasons met in a tavern. They had belonged to the Three Hearts Lodge, which had been wiped out after existing for only a year. Since 1743, Empress Maria Theresa had relentlessly pursued all manifestations of Freemasonry, which she considered contrary to good morals and incompatible with the natural superiority of the Church.

Braving her wrath, the five Brothers wanted to found a new lodge in Vienna. Each of them would have to swear to keep silent about its ritual activities.

'I have access to a discreet meeting-place,' said the eldest Mason, a penniless aristocrat.

'Which path are we to take?' asked a Brother who worked in the imperial stables.

'Let us put the emphasis on generosity. In the face of obscurantism, we must give the best of ourselves.'

Everyone agreed, and the group drew up a number of inspiring plans.

Suddenly, they became aware that the tavern was strangely silent. Apart from them, there were no customers. Absorbed in their discussion, they had not noticed the drinkers leaving, one by one.

A small man dresssed in grey crossed the poorly lit room and stopped beside them. 'You all belong to the Freemasons, do you not?' he said.

'Who are you?'

'A police officer charged with maintaining public order.'

'We're no threat to it.'

'I believe you are,' declared Josef Anton.

'That's a serious accusation. What evidence have you to support it?'

'Many indicators tally. I remind you that Her Majesty has no love for the stand you are making.'

'We are loyal subjects of Her Majesty, and we respect the laws of our land and are ready to defend it against all attackers.'

Josef Anton smiled. 'I am happy to hear that. Such words should reassure me.'

'Why do you say "should"?'

'Because a Freemason is first and foremost a Freemason, and his first loyalty is to his Order.'

'Are you calling us liars?'

'Your fine words don't deceive me, gentlemen. It's a long time since I was impressed by fiery declarations. Only my case files can be relied upon.'

The five Brothers stood up. 'We are free men and we are leaving this tavern freely.'

'I shan't stop you.'

'Then you have nothing to reproach us with!'

'Not yet. But don't try to found a new lodge without the explicit permission of the authorities,' Josef Anton advised sharply. 'You are all on file, and therefore suspect. If you put a foot wrong, the courts will deal with you. Be sensible and forget about your Freemasonry. In our country, it has no future.'

4

Prague, Easter 1761

A beautiful sun rose over the spring countryside. Near the eastern gate of the city, a middle-aged man in warm clothing was collecting plants.

Sensing someone's presence, he stopped and straightened up. Opposite him, about ten paces away, stood an elegant, well-made man with a solemn face and an intense gaze.

'Greetings, Brother,' said the stranger. 'I am from the Rose and the Gold.'

'And I am from the Cross.'

Together, they spoke the last words of the recognition code: 'Blessed be the Lord our God, who gave us our symbol.'

The stranger unfastened his jacket to reveal a piece of jewellery made up of a cross and a rose, suspended on a blue silk ribbon and pinned on the left side.

The plant-collector went closer and showed the newcomer a similar piece of jewellery, this time with a red ribbon. So the two men belonged to the same secret brotherhood of the Golden Rose-Cross.

'My name is Thamos, Count of Thebes,' said the stranger, 'and I ask to be received into your Lodge of the Black Rose.'

'How do you know about it?'

'It is founded on a book entitled *The True and Perfect Preparation of the Philosopher's Stone*, is it not?'

The plant-collector was impressed. 'Have you actually read it?'

'The book comes from Egypt, my homeland.'

The plant-collector was deeply suspicious. True, the stranger had known the recognition passwords, the date and place when they would be valid, and the exact title of the Brotherhood's secret book. But he might well be an impostor, sent by the police in Vienna.

'Do you doubt me?' asked Thamos.

'In the current situation, we must be extremely cautious.'

'I understand. But surely an initiate would rather die than reveal the secrets of the Great Work?'

Although disconcerted, the plant-collector took the stranger deep into the alchemists' quarter, the jewel of old Prague. Here, the imperial police had no informants. If the man was not genuine, nobody would come to his aid.

They entered a fine stone house, whose door closed soundlessly behind them. A guard immediately barred their way.

'This is Brother Thamos,' said the plant-collector.

'Has he been properly received into the Order?'

'I have experienced all the different degrees – Zealous Junior, Minor Philosopher, Major Philosopher, Major Adept, Exemplary Adept, Magister and Magus – of the Golden Rose-Cross,' said Thamos.

'Where does the supreme magus live?'

'In the visible and invisible world.'

'What is his number?'

'Seven.'

'If you have truly journeyed in spirit, show me the stone you possess in its oily form.'

'When a Brother moves from one place to another, the philosopher's stone must be reduced to powder.'*

'Can you exchange it for the treasure of our lodge?'

'I can give it to you, but neither sell it nor exchange it.'

So far, all the Egyptian's answers were correct.

'Where were you initiated?'

'In 1196, three Scottish brothers founded the Order of Eastern Architects, and their descendants settled in Egypt, where the sages preserve the secret of the words of power. It was there that I received the teaching.'

The guard stood aside.

A door opened, revealing a temple bathed in filtered light.

'After such a long journey, my Brother,' advised a gentle voice, 'slake your thirst at the spring.'

Six adepts of the Golden Rose-Cross handed their guest a palm frond, as a sign of peace, and each of them kissed him three times. Thamos swore to keep absolutely silent before being dressed in the 'pontifical costume' and kneeling before the Imperator, the Master of the Brotherhood, whose name remained unknown.

A ritualist cut seven locks of the Egyptian's hair and slipped them into seven sealed envelopes, offerings destined for the alchemical furnace.

Together, the initiates celebrated the rite of praising the Creator before drinking wine from the same cup and sharing bread.

'Brother of the Rose,' said the Imperator, a dark-eyed man of seventy, 'are you one of the Unknown Superiors appointed by Abbot Hermes?'

'He sent me out to seek the Great Magician,' said Thamos.

---

* God was considered the supreme alchemist, fulfilled via the Holy Spirit, the quintessence of the Work.

'Has he been . . . reborn?'

'That much is certain, but I don't know where or under what name, so I have come to ask for your help. Have you heard of any outstanding achievements by an exceptional man?'

The Imperator thought for a long time. 'The members of the Golden Rose-Cross are no ordinary men, but none of them has accomplished anything truly outstanding. We simply practise alchemy in great secrecy and celebrate our rites.'

'So the Great Magician is not among you.'

'I fear not.'

'Then I shall search in all the Masonic lodges, beginning with those in Vienna.'

'I strongly advise against it.'

'Why?'

'Empress Maria Theresa is extremely hostile to Free-masonry, whose most remarkable members have joined or will join our Order. You stand little or no chance of finding the Great Magician in Vienna.'

'Even if there's only the tiniest chance, I shall try,' said Thamos.

The Imperator's expression made it clear that he did not believe Thamos would succeed. 'These are dark times,' he said. 'Even if the Great Magician has been born, he will be snuffed out. And if the forces of destruction identify you as an Unknown Superior, they will annihilate you.'

5

Salzburg, January 1762

'Is that you playing, Herr Mozart?' asked the cook in surprise, abandoning her oven so as to hear the delightful music more clearly.

'No, it's Wolfgang,' replied Leopold. 'He has composed a minuet which is very nearly up to scratch.'

'You have produced a genius!'

'Kindly go back and prepare the dinner.'

'A genius,' the cook repeated, while Leopold noted down the child's first bars at the end of Nannerl's notebook.*

Clearly the education provided by Leopold was producing excellent results. Wolfgang adored mathematics, never balked at hard work, and thought of nothing but learning. Such talent deserved to be recognized.

When his two children were asleep, Leopold outlined his great plan to his wife.

'Wolfgang and Nannerl are ready,' he declared solemnly.

'Ready for what?'

---

* Minuet for piano in F major, K2. The 'K' stands for Köchel. Ludwig von Köchel (1800–1877) had the ambitious idea of drawing up a complete chronological and thematic catalogue of Mozart's works; the first edition appeared in 1862. Later musicological research has enabled several errors to be rectified, so that all the known compositions can be dated accurately.

'To travel.'

'To travel? Where to?'

'Munich. They will perform at Elector Maximilian's court and have a great success.'

'Don't you need the permission of the Archbishop of Salzburg?'

'Everything has been arranged.'

'But the cold, the bad roads, the children's health . . .'

'Don't worry, I shall take all the necessary remedies for colds, sore throats and earache – they won't hold out against our black powder or our elderflower tea. And then . . . Munich will only be the first step.'

'The first step? Where are you planning to go after that?'

'If all goes well in Munich, we'll move on to Vienna. When the empress and her court hear of the praise heaped on our two child prodigies, they're bound to want to hear them. Wolfgang's and Nannerl's careers will be launched, and we can conquer the whole of Europe!'

'The whole of Europe? Isn't that aiming a bit too high?'

Leopold took Anna Maria's hands tenderly. 'Trust me. The Mozart family is on the brink of a great future.'

Vienna, October 1762

Events unfolded according to Leopold's plan. The three weeks spent in Munich were crowned with great success, and word spread like wildfire.

The six-year-old Wolfgang would gladly have spent entire nights playing the piano and composing. Between March and September, several minuets for piano were born. Leopold noted that they were listenable, and particularly liked an Allegro comprising a theme, a development and variations on the first theme. Alert to the evolution of musical forms, he had taught his son a structure which was relatively new and unexplored. Besides being a good teacher, Leopold always paid careful attention to his colleagues' discoveries.

What pride he felt when, on 18 September, he and his two children climbed into a carriage destined for Vienna. Leopold sensed that this second journey would be a triumph which would open all doors to his offspring.

According to persistent rumours, the Viennese nobility was awaiting the two little prodigies impatiently. The children would undoubtedly play in the most exclusive salons, but Leopold cherished another ambition: to be received at Schönbrunn Castle, by the empress herself. Thanks to Lorenz Hagenauer, his rich patron and a believer in Wolfgang, Leopold had the money necessary for travelling expenses and lodgings. Now it would be all down to talent.

On 6 October 1762, Wolfgang had his first taste of Vienna, an imposing city of two hundred and ten thousand inhabitants. Its historic centre comprised five thousand, five hundred tall dwellings, sheltered behind fortifications which descended from the Glacis, a vast expanse of green where building was forbidden.

The magnificent Cathedral of St Stephen loomed over the city, whose main square, the Graben, was constantly buzzing with activity. More than four thousand coaches and carriages drove around the streets, where the passers-by liked to parade dressed in the latest fashions.

The Mozarts were immediately caught up in a social whirl. Moving from salon to salon, in the space of a few days Wolfgang and Nannerl became real stars who had to tear themselves away. And at the home of Vice-Chancellor Colloredo, the father of a man of the Church who seemed destined for a brilliant career, the hoped-for news was announced: the Mozarts were invited to Schönbrunn, at three o'clock in the afternoon of 13 October.

Vienna, 13 October 1762

With the music from Gluck's *Orfeo ed Euridice* still ringing in his ears after the first performance in Vienna on the 10th,* Leopold encountered Schönbrunn, whose name meant 'Beautiful Fountain'. With its tree-lined avenues, its gardens, arbours and fountains, the estate was reminiscent of Versailles.

Empress Maria Theresa prided herself on having improved the park and the castle, which now boasted a menagerie, a botanical garden and a new theatre. However, unlike in France there was no frivolity, for her co-regent, Josef II, detested luxury and pointless spending – it was whispered that his horses enjoyed better accommodation than he himself did. At Schönbrunn there were very few courtiers. People there did not enjoy themselves; they worked. Nevertheless, concerts were part of Viennese culture, and the court was not indifferent to new talents.

As skilled at playing with his hands covered with a cloth as he was at sight-reading a difficult piece of sheet music, Wolfgang charmed his audience. He surprised them when he complained about an archduke who played the violin badly, and aroused their sympathy when he slipped on the waxed parquet floor and was picked up by Princess Marie-Antoinette, to whom he declared: 'I shall marry you when I'm grown up!'

Embracing the little boy, who had jumped on to her lap, Maria Theresa asked him why he wanted to marry the princess.

'To reward her,' Wolfgang explained seriously, 'because she was nice to me.'

By the end of the audience, at six o'clock, Leopold Mozart's son had conquered the Viennese court.

---

* Christoph Willibald Gluck (1714–1787) had been based in Vienna since 1754.

6

Vienna, 21 October 1762

'Hurry up, Wolfgang! We're going to be late.'

'I don't feel well, Papa.'

'It's an important concert, you know. You're not going to crack now, are you?'

'I really don't feel very well . . . I hurt all over.'

Leopold laid his hand on the child's forehead. It was burning hot. With a fever like that, he wouldn't be able to display his usual virtuosity. Nannerl was in good health, so she would have to perform instead.

A fashionable – and extremely expensive – doctor was summoned urgently, and he diagnosed scarlet fever and poor general health, due to exhaustion. It was essential for the boy to have several weeks' rest. Although vexed, Leopold agreed.

The treatment cost him the considerable sum of fifty ducats,* in addition to the loss of earnings because of the cancellation of several concerts. 'Happiness is as fragile as glass,' he grumbled.

Lavishing apologies on the lofty individuals who were disappointed not to have their private concerts, Leopold pushed Nannerl forward, but she did not have her brother's magic. With him, she shone; without him, she became dull.

* 1 ducat = 4½ florins; 1 florin = a little less than 20 euros.

Leopold actively cared for Wolfgang and did not rush his convalescence. Fearing a relapse which might be fatal, he waited until the boy had recovered completely.

That recovery was accompanied, in December, by an extraordinary event.

Still aged only six, Wolfgang composed an entirely original minuet for piano.* It was neither a schoolboy's exercise nor an uninteresting little piece, but a real first work, based on the development of a single phrase.

Although overwhelmed, Leopold did not show his feelings. However, it was at that moment that he took one of the major decisions in his life: to devote himself entirely to the career of the genius who was his son. That dedication implied that he must give up his own ambitions as a composer. True, he would still write music for special occasions when commissioned to do so, but he could not surpass or equal the radiance hidden in the notes of the child's first work.

Now that Wolfgang was well again, Leopold resumed contact with the Viennese nobility in order to plan a new series of concerts. To his great surprise, he met with only a lukewarm welcome, even indifference. Now that their disappointment had passed, the Viennese were looking for other amusements as the end-of-year celebrations drew near.

In order to avoid additional accommodation expenses, Leopold limited himself to a few performances. They led to nothing further, so he decided to return to Salzburg.

Munich, late December 1762

Thamos was continuing his search. He never had a flicker of doubt, for Abbot Hermes could not have been mistaken. The hardest thing to bear was the cold. Thanks to the alchemical

* Minuet in G major, K1.

elixir, he avoided falling ill. And when his money was on the brink of running out, he used one of the Rose-Cross's laboratories to make gold.

During a concert at a salon in Munich, he looked into the eyes of a man who was different from the others. He had a lively gaze, and was uninterested in the easy music that an uninspired pianist was playing; he gazed constantly at the Egyptian.

At the end of the concert, he came over to Thamos and introduced himself. 'Tobias Philippe von Gebler. I do not have the honour of knowing you.'

'Thamos, Count of Thebes.'

'Thebes . . . Where is that principality?'

'In the East.'

'Are you enjoying your visit to this beautiful city, despite the rigours of winter?'

'Except when it rains, as it is at the moment.'

Outside, a beautiful day was nearing its end. The setting sun created pink haloes round the few clouds in the sky.

Gebler's expression changed. 'Let us leave here, my Brother, and walk a little. No indiscreet ears will be able to hear us.'

After bidding farewell to their host, the two men entered a quiet alleyway where it would be easy to spot anyone following them.

'Where are you from?' asked Gebler.

'From a Lodge of St John.'*

'Welcome, my Brother. All the lodges are open to you, but we must be very careful. In Vienna Maria Theresa hates Freemasonry. Here in Munich, great upheavals are in the offing. We shall soon free ourselves from the English influence

---

* This is one of the major questions/answers enabling two Freemasons to recognize each other as such. It refers to the esoteric tradition passed on by John the Evangelist.

and deepen our rituals, developing our own genius. What is the situation in the East?'

'Islam reigns and wishes to extend its empire over the whole world.'

'I am one of the few who think that war with the Turks is inevitable, but nobody listens to me. Do you need somewhere to stay?'

'No, thank you. I have a mission to fulfil: to find an exceptional person who could pass on the light of the East to humanity.'

Tobias von Gebler stopped in his tracks. 'Are you serious?'

'Very serious.'

'Then you must belong to the Order of Eastern Architects. But everyone believes it has vanished!'

'Its Numbers are known to me.'

'That is ... that is extraordinary news. But I don't think the person you seek is within our lodges. We are trying with great difficulty to rebuild a rather modest structure, and no architect of genius has come to inspire us.'

'But he does exist. He will accomplish remarkable things which will reveal his true nature.'

'The only recent remarkable thing I can think of is the concert given at Schönbrunn by a six-year-old boy, in the presence of the empress. Vienna talked about him for two months.'

'What is his name?'

'Wolfgang Mozart. His father is a musician in Salzburg, in the service of the archbishop.'

'And he's remarkable, you say.'

'Definitely. According to those who know, the child's virtuosity is exceptional. He has even composed a few short works worthy of respect. However, his father, Leopold, is suspected of exaggerating, and of having composed most of the works himself. Poor child! Leopold uses him like a wise monkey, and the day will come when he'll be too old to charm a curious audience. The poor little boy seems to me to be doomed to a most cruel fate and is certainly not the Great Magician.'

Von Gebler was probably right. Would Abbot Hermes have omitted to say that the Great Magician was a child? In speaking of the need to build up the person who was going to pass on the Light, had he been referring to the boy's young age?

'Give me your address,' von Gebler said, 'and I'll inform you of the date of our next Gathering. My Brothers will have many questions to ask you.'

7

Salzburg, January 1763

When he arrived home on 5 January, Leopold was still fulminating. Yes, Wolfgang's talent had dazzled Vienna, but for such a short time! He was still convinced that his son was much more than a mere fashionable phenomenon. But how was he to reconquer the imperial court?

First, by working relentlessly. So Leopold put his son back to work, notably by making him learn the violin. Despite his extraordinary gifts, it would take several years for him to reach an acceptable standard.

Despite the rigours of the exercise, Wolfgang practised counterpoint with an ease which was all the more surprising because he amused himself by combining three voices he called 'the Duke of Bass', 'the Marquis of Tenor' and 'Mr Alto'.

Before finalizing new contracts in Vienna, Leopold awaited an important promotion in Salzburg. He was sure his experience and skills destined him for the highest post in the corporation of musicians. When the decision was made, his disappointment was bitter: the archbishop appointed Francesco Lolli to be his new Kapellmeister. Leopold Mozart must be content with the position of Deputy.

'It's a steady, well-paid position,' said Anna Maria, happy to see her husband recognized as an excellent professional.

'You're right, I know. All the same . . .'

'You're thinking of Wolfgang's future, aren't you? Don't worry. He will also enter the archbishop's service and lead a peaceful, happy life.'

'Perhaps. Perhaps. Go and make us a good meal.'

Salzburg, February 1763

The good news spread like lightning across the whole of Europe: the Seven Years' War was over! There was an end to the colonial rivalries between France and England, Austria and Prussia. By abandoning Silesia to Prussia, Maria Theresa had re-established peace. At last people could travel without the fear of being murdered.

For Leopold, the future was opening up. 'We're going to conquer Europe,' he decreed again.

Salzburg, 9 June 1763

Leopold, Anna Maria, Nannerl and Wolfgang climbed into a carriage whose wheels had been checked by the head of the family. Drawn up with care, the itinerary took in Munich, Frankfurt, Cologne and Brussels, the capital of the Austrian Netherlands, before reaching Paris, where Wolfgang and Nannerl's international glory would be born. When they played at Versailles, their fame would know no limits . . .

The deputy Kapellmeister had hidden nothing of his plans from his august patron, the debonair and broad-minded Sigismund von Schrattenbach, Prince-Archbishop of Salzburg. The prince had not opposed the long journey, for any success would reflect upon his city.

Despite his unshakeable determination, Leopold's heart was in his boots. Far from cherishing any illusions, he knew very well that nobody was expecting his two children. They would have to force open many doors, persuade the aristocrats to take them in, organize concerts, most of which would not bring in much money, and win fame by the sweat of their brow.

Just before they left, Wolfgang had composed the start of his first slow movement, displaying a degree of seriousness unexpected in a child of seven. And there were more surprises in store for Leopold. During the first recital of this long tour, in Munich, in the presence of the elector, Wolfgang played the violin like a professional. In a mere five months, he had mastered this tremendously difficult instrument.

Frankfurt, 25 August 1763

At the end of a successful concert, a fourteen-year-old youth approached the seven-year-old pianist. He would have liked to congratulate him and thank him for the moments of happiness he had just given him. But Goethe was so nervous that he was unable to voice a single compliment, afraid that he would utter ridiculous words which would not do justice to the genius of this remarkable musician. Instead, he moved away, wondering if the miracle would be a lasting one and if the child Mozart would survive the rigours of time.

As he climbed back into his carriage and prepared to set off again, Wolfgang decided to escape to Rücken, the 'hinterland kingdom', an imaginary land which enabled him to forget the monotony and fatigue of the journey. Sebastian Winter, the family servant, had drawn a map of this territory; Wolfgang was its king, and its citizens knew how to make children good and kind.

Alas, Winter had lost the precious map. The little boy was on the verge of tears, so his father and mother set to work looking for it.

Through the open carriage door, Wolfgang saw a man dressed like a valet approaching.

The man smiled and asked, 'Is this what you're looking for?'
Wolfgang seized his treasure. 'Where did you find it?'
'On the ground, beside one of the horses.'
'Who are you?'
'I am from Rücken.'
'Do you really . . . really exist?'
'Yes, really.'
'Are you going to come with me?'
'Of course. But now you must rest.'
The man from Rücken disappeared. Wolfgang called his parents over and showed them the map, without mentioning that one of his subjects had brought it to him. It would be his secret.

As he watched the carriage draw away, bearing the Mozart family to its next stop, Thamos ceased to doubt. By the expression in the boy's eyes, the light in his soul, and the radiance of his personality, the Egyptian knew he had identified the Great Magician.

His discovery was accompanied by a thousand and one questions, for dark forces were prowling around the child. Would he succeed in overcoming them? Would he become a mere virtuoso, wrapped up in his own success? Would he be capable of experiencing real initiation? Would he succumb to the siren-calls of the outside world? Would he draw back when faced with the immensity of the task that Thamos would entrust to him?

The Egyptian's mission, which consisted also of passing on the Tradition to Masonic lodges which were suffering doubts, seemed impossible. He prayed to his master, Abbot Hermes, to give him the strength he needed.

8

Paris, 18 November 1763

The weather was execrable, the streets dirty, and the people not at all welcoming. But the Mozarts had at last reached Paris, the goal of their journey.

'How I miss Salzburg,' murmured Anna Maria. 'Will we have decent lodgings and suitable food?'

'Don't worry,' replied Leopold. 'I have planned everything.'

Nannerl was dozing, while Wolfgang was travelling in Rücken, where he kept seeing the kindly subject who had given him back the map. Surely this proved that if you sincerely experienced something in your mind, it could become reality? The world of the mind, like that of music, was not imaginary. All you had to do in order to bring it into being was to want it very much.

Unlike a visionary, Leopold had not struck out into the wilds without a few landmarks. The Count of Arco, grand chamberlain at the Salzburg court, had given him a letter of recommendation intended for his son-in-law, the Count von Eyck. Von Eyck received the Mozarts in his Beauvais home and wished them an excellent stay.

Once polite formalities had been exchanged, Leopold addressed the main question.

'Can you help us to arrange some concerts? My son and

daughter are true child prodigies. They have already charmed the German and Austrian nobility. Here, they will be enormously successful.'

The Count seemed embarrassed. 'Parisians are difficult and capricious. Moreover, music is not one of their main interests. However, I can introduce you into two or three noted salons.'

'And . . . Versailles?'

'Don't be too optimistic. The court welcomes none but celebrities.'

'My children have been applauded in Vienna, Munich, Frankfurt—'

'But not in Paris.'

Leopold's optimism was shaken. If this stay amounted to only a few salon successes, it would be a disaster.

Paris, 20 November 1763

'Where do you come from?' the Venerable Master of the lodge asked Thamos.

'From the East. I have come to search for what was lost and must be found.'

Knowing the secret of the Mastery, the Egyptian was enclosed in a cardboard tower seven feet tall, then freed and admitted to a room where the Venerable One, taking on the role of King Cyrus, dubbed him a Knight of the East by striking his shoulders with the flat of a sword-blade before embracing him.

This threadbare ritual revealed to Thamos the pitiful state of French Freemasonry. Amateurish and inconstant, it dreamt of egalitarianism and whispered muffled criticisms of royalty and the Church. The lodges willingly admitted those who were merely curious, or who wished to cement relations with those in high places and amuse themselves at drunken dinner parties.

During the meal, the Egyptian tried to obtain the information he sought. 'How can a young foreign musician succeed in Paris?'

'He needs the approval of the small group of authorized intellectuals who decide everything,' replied his neighbour at the table. 'They make and destroy careers, deliver final judgements without ever creating anything themselves, and don't allow anyone to encroach on their territory. Until this coterie has given a favourable opinion of the artist, he doesn't exist.'

'Has the group an overall leader, to whose views they defer?'

'Indeed they have: Baron Grimm.* He's a friend of the Encyclopedists, secretary to the Duc d'Orléans and absolute judge of intellectual and artistic life. He wears so much make-up that his nickname is "the White Tyrant".'

Paris, 25 November 1763

A native of Ratisbonne, Friedrich Melchior von Grimm was forty years old and full of his own importance. Although incapable of producing anything himself, he never doubted his own judgement. His small smile revealed a prickly, even cruel nature, and an assurance untouched by doubt. The baron reigned over Parisian culture, halfway between the sometimes extreme tendencies of the Encyclopedists and the established powers.

'The Count of Thebes requests an audience,' announced his private secretary.

Grimm frowned. 'Never heard of him. What does he look like?'

'Expensive clothes in the latest fashion, and a good deal of *ton*. He undoubtedly has a sizeable fortune.'

---

* No connection to the Brothers Grimm, authors of the famous *Fairy Tales*.

The baron could be as mercenary as the next man. 'Show him into the small drawing room and bring us some coffee.'

Thamos's appearance much impressed him. One rarely encountered a gaze of such intensity.

'Thank you for receiving me, Monsieur le baron. I am very aware of the honour you do me. I come from the East and am exploring this magnificent city, the capital of arts and letters. Paris owes its fame in large part to you.'

'You mustn't exaggerate,' protested Grimm, flattered.

'I am not! As soon as one mentions philosophy, literature, music or painting, your name is on everyone's lips – no talent escapes you. Alas, I do not have your clear-sightedness and I shan't be able to form my own judgement of the phenomenon that has just arrived in Paris.'

Grimm's curiosity was at once aroused. 'A phenomenon, you say? Who is this phenomenon?'

'A little Salzburg boy, Wolfgang Mozart, who has come to give concerts with his elder sister. The boy is also a composer, it seems. But is he a performing monkey or an authentic prodigy? You alone can distinguish the real from the false.'

The baron agreed with a nod.

On 1 December 1763, he published in his famous *Correspondance littéraire, philosophe et critique* an article which had enormous repercussions all over Paris. In part it said:

True prodigies are so rare that one should not omit to mention them when one has the opportunity to see one ... Wolfgang Mozart is a phenomenon so extraordinary that one can scarcely believe the evidence of one's own eyes and ears ... What is incredible is to see this child play from memory for an hour, non-stop, and then abandon himself to the inspiration of his genius ... He writes and composes with wondrous facility.

Leopold reread the text a dozen times. The very next morning the invitations came pouring in. Just before Christmas, he received the most treasured of all presents: an invitation to Versailles.

9

Versailles, 1 January 1764

Eight-year-old Wolfgang Mozart brought forth marvellous sounds from the organ in the royal chapel at Versailles. Then the little Salzburg family was received at the *grand couvert*, a ceremonial meal during which the Queen of France spoke German with the child prodigy.

Leopold was in heaven. At last, his efforts had been crowned with success! And it was not just a question of the fine sum of 1,200 livres offered for the concert. Above all, his son's fame was established.

A meeting with the composer Johann Schobert, a thirty-four-year-old Silesian, hardly enchanted Leopold, who thought him apt to flatter you to your face and insult you behind your back. Schobert showed some of his pieces to Wolfgang, who liked them and very quickly assimilated their substance. 'This man changes his religion according to the fashion of the day,' thought Leopold, and he determined to keep his distance from the composer.

Leopold did not like Paris. Everything was very expensive, with the sole exception of wine, and the repulsively elegant women looked like painted dolls from Berchtesgaden. One had only to come home from church or walk along a street, and either a tramp or someone blind, paralytic or lame would appear.

But what a joy it was when Wolfgang took his first official steps as a composer, with two sonatas for harpsichord with violin accompaniment, dedicated to Madame Victoire, daughter of Louis XV! They summarized elements of his former work and took account of several months' professional work. The little boy was already working on two new sonatas, for Madame de Tessé.

Paris, 9 March 1764

On a cold, shivery morning, Leopold and his sons were walking near the sinister Place de Grève, where people sentenced to death were hanged almost every day.

An unshaven man with an unsavoury smile accosted them. 'Do you want to see a fine spectacle, my fine sirs? I can offer you a place in the front row. They're going to hang a chambermaid, a cook and a coachman who robbed a rich blind man.'

'Here, that is necessary,' said Leopold, 'or nobody would be safe. Stand aside, my friend.'

'You don't understand, my good sir. You must attend this spectacle and pay me in accordance with my services. Give me your purse, immediately! Or else . . .' The man brandished a knife. 'Hurry up. I'm not joking.'

A gentleman's walking stick struck the ruffian's forearm hard and disarmed him. Immediately he took to his heels.

'I don't know how to thank you,' declared Leopold, much relieved.

'In future,' advised Thamos, 'avoid unsavoury districts. Paris is a dangerous city.' With that, their saviour disappeared.

Wolfgang had instantly recognized the man from Rücken who had first appeared dressed as a valet and now reappeared in the guise of a nobleman. Protected like this, the boy would never again be afraid of anything.

The Great Magician

London, April 1764

'Not another journey, Papa!' Wolfgang had protested.

'It is necessary. Paris has become too small for you. Your reputation has reached the English court, and you must perform in London.'

The child had sighed and accepted his fate. Provided he was allowed to play and to compose . . .

As soon as they arrived in London, Leopold handed Wolfgang a new notebook, in which he was to note down his composition exercises. The publication of the apprentice composer's first works did not exempt him from continuing his studies and developing a style different from the one practised in Salzburg.

Thamos easily found the most influential Masonic lodge and, after making himself known as a noble Brother, of good fortune and morals, was able to whisper a few words in the ear of one of the king's ministers. Consequently the young George III, a Hanoverian, and his wife, Charlotte of Mecklenburg-Strelitz, received the Mozarts on 27 April 1764, at six o'clock in the evening. Both George and Charlotte were great lovers of music – the king adored the organ, and the queen sang.

Wolfgang's talent instantly won them over, and they were happy to see that a famous musician who was nearing the age of thirty, Johann Christian Bach, was taking the prodigy under his wing. The son of Johann Sebastian, who was now almost completely forgotten, Johann Christian initiated Wolfgang into the light, romantic style prized by the English public. He opened all the doors of British high society to the Mozart family and spent long hours playing the harpsichord with the little boy, who was still as eager as ever to learn.

'Do you really know, dear Leopold,' asked Bach, 'what your son is planning?'

'Nothing bad, I hope.'

'Oh no, not at all. It's astonishing, quite astonishing. At his age, he's already thinking of composing an opera.'

'It's too soon, much too soon.'

'Given his emerging genius, why not? We must take him to everything in London that's worth hearing, particularly my own works.'

Bach's attitude reassured Thamos. Although not a composer of the first rank, he was genuinely interested in Wolfgang and wished only to help him.

On 19 May, King George granted the boy another audience, and was as enthusiastic as at the previous one. The Mozarts, murmured members of the court, would soon become intimate acquaintances of the ruling family. On 28 May, in St James's Park, the king even ordered his coachman to stop, opened his door and joyfully hailed Wolfgang, who was out walking with his parents.

On 5 June, Wolfgang and Nannerl gave their first public concert in the great hall of the Spring Garden, near St James's Park. And on 29 June Wolfgang played an organ concerto at Ranelagh, during a charitable concert to raise the funds needed to build a new hospital. This generous act enchanted the English, and Wolfgang would have remained a popular sensation if, in August, Leopold had not fallen ill. For reasons of health he decided to move to Chelsea, a charming suburb removed from the bustle of the capital.

Wolfgang took advantage of the respite to tackle a new genre: the symphony. Putting several instruments together and making them sing: what an adventure!

Thamos made discreet enquiries and was reassured that Leopold would soon recover. When, therefore, he received a message from von Gebler, entreating him to come to Germany as quickly as possible in order to meet Baron de Hund, he left England, knowing that Wolfgang was in no danger.

10

Kittlitz, December 1764

At the age of forty Charles, Baron de Hund, hereditary lord of Lipse, in Haute-Lusace, had seen his most ardent dream come true. At Kittlitz, a little under forty miles from Dresden, he had set up the Mother Lodge, the Lodge of the Three Pillars, based on a new Rite whose future looked exceptional.

The great adventure had taken flesh on 24 June 1751, when the baron and a few Brothers met in an alchemical laboratory deep in a cave near Naumburg.

The new Order comprised true higher levels, and was based on an esoteric tradition. Born in Egypt, initiation had been passed on to the first Christians by the Essenes, then noted down by the canons of St Sepulchre, based in Jerusalem. Wishing to re-establish the ancient Order, early in the twelfth century they had formed the Order of the Poor Knights of Christ and the Temple of Solomon by conferring supreme initiation on a few deserving men.

During that century and the next the Knights Templar thrived, gaining great wealth and temporal power. But they had not been sufficiently wary of the greed of the French king, Philippe IV, nor of the cowardice of Pope Clement V, and the Order was all but destroyed.* Before being executed, the Grand Master, Jacques de Molay, had handed his nephew, the Comte de Beaujeu, the Templars' treasures, the crown of the kings of Jerusalem, the seven-branched candelabrum, the relics, annals and rituals of initiation.

Escaping Philippe's assassins, Beaujeu mingled his blood with that of nine knights, raised to the rank of Perfect Architects, and ordered them to take the path of exile in order to pass on the secrets of the Order. They found refuge in Scotland, and there created lodges which were entered only by a few initiates, chosen with great care. They performed rituals dealing with the Mysteries of the Temple of Jerusalem and the hieroglyphs carved in ancient shrines.

Baron de Hund wanted to give back life and power to this tradition by creating a system of high grades which would extend to the whole of European Freemasonry. It was Germany's task to restore the Order of the Temple and to make the authorities recognize it.

The new Masonic system took the name of Strict Templar Observance and its symbolic birth was fixed on 11 March 1314, the date of Jacques de Molay's assassination. Of course, estates must be acquired, schools opened and salaries offered to directors so that they would work hard to develop the Order.

For more than four years, the baron had devoted his time and fortune to perfecting the statutes and rituals, along with committed Brothers. But the terrible Seven Years' War, which began in 1756, had halted this initial progress. Almost all the new Templars were army officers, so had left for the battlefields. His lands ravaged, threatened by the Prussians, Baron de Hund had taken refuge in Bohemia.

As soon as peace was proclaimed at Hubertsburg, he had

---

* Philippe forced Clement to suppress the Templars in 1312, and seized much of their money and property.

returned to work and, by 1764, many Freemasons wanted to adhere to Strict Templar Observance.

Hund was unbending when it came to principles and discipline. Every Brother wishing to 'rectify' himself in relation to conventional Masonry must sign a deed of submission and swear obedience to the Unknown Superiors, of whom the baron admitted he was not one.*

The baron hoped to recruit as many wealthy aristocrats as possible, for their financial participation would be vital to the Order's reconstruction, so when his secretary informed him that the Count of Thebes wished to see him he immediately agreed.

A huge, stiff-backed man with an oval face and a thick neck, Charles de Hund was not a tolerant person and ordinarily he exercised immediate ascendancy over others. Thamos was the first noble to impress him. The visitor single-handedly filled the large salon with his presence and imposed a solemn atmosphere.

'What can I do for you, Monsieur le comte?' the baron asked.

'I have climbed the seven steps of the forecourt and seen the nine stars, the nine founders of the Order of the Temple. The three doors of the lodge are continence, poverty and obedience. The tools found there are such as the set square, the compass, the hammer or the trowel, because the knights had to work as craftsmen in order to survive.'

It was clear that the Count of Thebes had been initiated into a lodge which, in addition to following the classical rituals, had added notions that belonged to the Templar Rite! Nevertheless, Baron de Hund was not expecting his subsequent words.

'The stages of which I have just spoken are, in your eyes, merely a preparation for two high degrees. The first is that of

---

* The eight provinces of the Order reproduced the administrative divisions of the Templars, and covered the entire continent of Europe, plus Russia.

novice, during which the initiate drinks a bitter cup in order to remember the misfortunes of the Order of the Temple, whose origins are revealed to him. The second is the vital one. It alone gives access to the interior Order, where the knight receives a Latin name.'

The baron swayed on his feet. 'How do you know this? Only the Brothers closest to me are working on drawing up this degree.'

'Think,' Thamos advised him.

'You . . . Are you one of the Unknown Superiors?'

'I have come from Egypt to fulfil a vital mission: to enable the Great Magician to shine forth and to offer his Light to our world. Also he must benefit from vital support, or he may be destined to preach in the desert and yield to despair.'

'Am I . . . Am I to be one of those supports?'

'You plan to restore a Templar Freemasonry which will give back meaning to the whole of Europe, do you not?'

'There is no other way to prevent our societies from becoming the slaves of materialism,' Hund replied.

'But is there not a risk of coming into conflict with the authorities?'

'They will understand the need for the Order. It will oppose neither kings nor princes – on the contrary, it will help them to govern better.'

'You will need time, patience and the commitment of many lodges.'

'I shall find all those things – even the Seven Years' War did not discourage me. And today here you are! Does that not prove that my course of action is well founded?'

'Persevere, Baron. The road promises to be long and difficult.'

'I am not afraid of difficulties. But tell me, sir, is this your first and last appearance, or shall we meet again?'

'Destiny will decide.'

Few Freemasons could boast of having met one of the nine Unknown Superiors who traversed time and the ordeals of humanity to restore strength and vigour to initiation at the opportune moment. Baron de Hund did not venture to ask the name of the Great Magician, but this unhoped-for appearance proved to him that he was following the right path.

11

London, December 1764

Leopold had fully recovered from his illness, but his morale was as dismal as the weather. True, on 25 October the Mozarts had been received for a third time at court, but the young prodigy and his sister were no longer novelties, and the public's curiosity was waning.

Expenses were mounting up, particularly for the printing of six new sonatas by Wolfgang, dedicated to Queen Charlotte. Leopold noted the influence of the hypocritical Schobert and of the Italian-style musicians in London, foremost among whom was J. C. Bach. Despite his extraordinary gifts and his faculty of assimilation, Wolfgang worked hard, and each day he discovered again how immensely difficult it was to become a true composer, who would not drown in the crowd of anonymity.

With Bach's help, Wolfgang learnt the art of the Italian aria and bel canto. He listened to the works of his mentor, other operas and oratorios by Handel, whose majesty dazzled him.

It was a studious winter, with little contact with high society, during which Wolfgang finished several symphonies, which were light and sparkling. Although happy to see his son blossoming so well, Leopold could not forget the financial problems. If he tried hard, could he contrive to organize some concerts?

Back in London, meanwhile, Thamos observed the Mozart family from afar. He approved of the child's serious attitude and was glad to see him composing rather than performing like an educated monkey. Assuming he reached maturity, the Great Magician must be a creator, not a travelling entertainer in search of applause. How much longer would his father leave him in peace?

Hamburg, January 1765

Received as a Freemason at the Absalom Lodge, Hamburg, in 1761, Johann Joachim Christoph Bode was proud to become a Knight of the Strict Templar Observance movement,* for which he would be an ardent propagandist. Born on 16 January 1730, Bode had been an oboist in the military orchestra of the duchy of Brunswick, then a teacher of music and foreign languages in Hamburg, a bookseller and printer, as well as translating Italian, French and English plays, humorous British books and Montaigne's *Essays*.

All these activities were mere amusements compared to his true passion: the struggle against the occult influence of the Jesuits, who he believed were solely responsible for the decadence and corruption that had plunged the whole of Europe into decay.

An outspoken depressive, Bode preferred to ignore his failed marriages and the deaths of his children at a young age. Since nobody took his diagnosis seriously, he must take action himself and persuade the Brothers to help him.

With the appearance of Templar Freemasonry a new hope was born. If its followers really wanted to combat the Pope, they would also have to attack his protégés, the Jesuits. In adhering to the Strict Templar Observance, Bode was not

* Under the name of *a Lilio Convallium*.

planning to remain a dormant Brother, bogged down in stifling discipline. Being a knight gave him rights, which he was planning to make use of by denouncing the Jesuits' stranglehold over English and French Freemasonry. Fortunately, Germany appeared to be reawakening and following a different path. Were the Templars not ferocious warriors?

No great dignitary would silence Bode. And his tribune's voice would eventually draw all Masons into an attack on the clerical fortress.

London, June 1765

Leopold mulled over his resentment of the English, who were entirely Godless. And what an accursed damp fog, the cause of persistent colds! On 21 February, the concert given by his children had brought in only a moderate sum; since the concert on 13 May, there had been no more definite engagements.

Though still dreaming of opera, Wolfgang had just composed a bravura aria for tenor and also a motet for four-part choir, to the words of Psalm 46. Leopold had generously decided to offer them to the new British Museum.*

In the immediate future, a taxing day awaited the young prodigy. An English lawyer, Daines Barrington, who was also an antiquary and naturalist, wished to examine him and put his talents to the test. Unwilling to antagonize this influential and eminent man, Leopold consented to the examination.

'Mr Mozart?'

'The same.'

'Barrington. May I see Wolfgang?'

'He is working at the moment.'

'Excellent. It is precisely this surprising juvenile work which

* The aria was '*Val dal furor portata*', K21, and the motet was 'God is our refuge', K20.

52

interests me. I wrote to Salzburg to obtain confirmation regarding his age: it is nine, and not eight, as you would have people believe.'

'Sir . . .'

'If he really is the author of the works he has signed, what a phenomenon he is! But scientific rigour obliges me to check.'

'As you wish.'

Amused, Wolfgang submitted to the tests imposed upon him by the austere visitor. He sight-read a complex piece of sheet music without a single error, composed a love song on the word '*affeto*', an enraged aria on the term '*perfido*', and played his latest work, which Barrington judged to be incredibly inventive.

An interruption by a cat brought the test to a halt. The little boy, who adored animals, left his piano, played with the cat, then picked up a stick, bestrode it as though it were a horse, and proceeded to gallop across the room.

Satisfied by what he had seen and heard, the lawyer did not continue with his examination.

'I shall make an official report to the Royal Society,' he informed Leopold. 'You are not lying, Mr Mozart. Your son is a genuine prodigy.'

London, July 1765

Composing was fun, too. Wolfgang dreamt up a harpsichord sonata for four hands, which he played with Nannerl. The piece displayed their virtuosity, notably when Nannerl's left hand, which was playing the lower notes, crossed over her little brother's right hand, which was playing the upper part.

Leopold had little interest in these childish pursuits. Although Wolfgang had received a remarkable and intensive artistic training during his stay in London, the financial consequences were catastrophic. Since nobody was offering him any concerts, they must pack up their belongings again and set off to conquer another land.

At last Leopold received a reply to one of his numerous enquiries: the Dutch ambassador informed him that the Netherlands awaited with interest the arrival of the Mozart children.

12

When they arrived in the Netherlands in August, Wolfgang was sure he saw the man from Rücken. This time he was wearing a fine suit and riding a white horse, but his benevolent smile was just the same – there was no other like it. Between them there was total complicity, sealed by silence and secrecy. Wolfgang would never reveal the Rückener's existence, not to his father or mother, not even to Nannerl.

One grave concern was troubling the Mozart family.

'How is Nannerl?' asked Wolfgang.

'Very ill,' replied Leopold.

'The doctor will make her better, won't he?'

Leopold did not answer. He was beginning to loathe this country, despite the fact that everything there ought to be smiling upon him.

A great admirer of Flemish painting, especially Rubens, Leopold had taken great pleasure in exploring the Netherlands' artistic treasures. Wolfgang had played many fine organs, and at the end of September he and his sister had given a highly successful concert.

But Nannerl was cross and sulking. Misfortunes never came singly, and she had fallen seriously ill with a congestion of the lungs for which no cure was known.

It was not to a doctor that Leopold opened his door, but to a priest. He was to administer the last rites to Nannerl.

Leopold tried to comfort his tearful wife, and Wolfgang declared, 'Don't worry, Mama. Nannerl will get better.'

Anna Maria kissed her son.

'I am not saying so to make you feel better,' he explained. 'I had a vision, and she was playing the piano again. So she will get better. All we have to do is believe very hard.'

Wolfgang was right. Despite the doctors' pessimistic prognoses, Nannerl gradually regained her strength, got up, ate with a good appetite and was eventually able to breathe properly again.

Just when it was certain that she would recover fully, Wolfgang became feverish and took to his bed. The round of doctors began again.

The seriousness of the attack left little room for hope. In despair at seeing his son fading away from one day to the next, Leopold agreed to receive a doctor who was very different from the others.

'Wolfgang is asleep,' he told the doctor. 'He has stopped eating.'

'Don't wake him, and try to persuade him to take liquids.'

'But . . . don't you want to examine him?'

'There is no need.' The doctor handed Leopold a small glass bottle. 'He is to take ten drops of this each evening, for one week. After that, his body will fight the disease by itself.'

'What is this medicine?'

'An energy potion manufactured in the East.'

'It must be very expensive . . .'

'Allow me to make a gift of it to you. I am an admirer of your son and I guarantee that he will recover.'

Leopold would have liked to ask more questions, but the doctor was already leaving.

Although sceptical, Leopold administered the treatment –

though he took the precaution of writing to his patron, Lorenz Hagenauer, asking him to have a series of masses said, asking Heaven for Wolfgang's recovery. Masses had also been said for Nannerl, but not so many.

There was no flesh left on Wolfgang's bones, and he seemed destined for the grave. But on 10 December Leopold thought he looked a little less pale, and from then on death slowly receded. Was the miracle the result of divine intervention, wondered Leopold, of Dutch medicine or of the Eastern potion?

On 20 December, despite his weak condition, the little boy began to compose again – a symphony. It was both gay and serious, and the slow movement, in G minor, gave pride of place to the wind instruments.

Wolfgang took advantage of his convalescence to compose several works, consolidating what he had learnt and assimilated in Paris and London. Never complaining about his illness or this enforced cerebration, he continued to make good progress.

Vienna, December 1765

Because of his serious temperament and absolute loyalty, Josef Anton had been authorized by Empress Maria Theresa to set up a secret service to track the development of Masonic lodges.

He set to work with alacrity, and set up a small team of discreet and skilful colleagues. Their first task was to extend the network of informants, if need be by paying the necessary price. Of course, Anton was also counting on traitors, and those who were disappointed or embittered; men who, having been dismissed from their lodges, would have plenty of confidential information to offer.

This morning, he had opened a new file, marked 'Strict Templar Observance'. According to several reports, this new

Order was beginning to conquer important towns and cities such as Berlin, Hamburg, Leipzig, Rostock, Brunswick and even Copenhagen.

Josef Anton summoned his right-hand man, Geytrand, a curious fellow who was both indolent and virulent, and who hated Freemasonry for an excellent reason: despite his manoeuvres, he had been refused the office of Venerable Master. Draping himself in a non-existent dignity, Geytrand had slammed the door of the temple behind him, swearing to have his revenge. He had been a petty official, vegetating quietly, when Josef Anton spotted him. Now Geytrand was willing to work day and night for his new superior.

Anton asked, 'Do we know who the leaders of the Strict Templar Observance are?'

'There's only one worth paying attention to,' said Geytrand, 'and that's Baron de Hund. He has the remnants of a fortune, and he's a member of the old nobility and a convinced Freemason. This new Rite is his work; he's been devoting all his time to it.'

'A skilful propagandist, it seems.'

'More a believer who's convinced that his mission's important.'

'And what exactly does that consist of?'

'To restore the Order of the Knights Templar.'

Josef Anton knitted his brows. 'You're joking!'

'Unfortunately, sir, I'm not.'

'The Order was utterly destroyed in the fourteenth century.'

'Not according to Baron de Hund. A few Templars survived, and he's gathered their treasures together and is continuing their work.'

'Why can't he and his followers be content with their grotesque ceremonies, in which they pretend they're medieval knights?'

'The baron wants to re-create Freemasonry, to instil the

necessary discipline and create a new chivalry, capable of ruling Europe. The Templars were formidable warriors, don't forget. If the Strict Observance movement gets big enough, it might even attack governments.'

'Aren't you exaggerating the danger?'

'Everyone who meets Hund can see his determination,' said Geytrand. 'Far from being a dreamer or a mere mystic lost in his own fantasies, he behaves like an experienced administrator. According to my initial checks, several wealthy nobles and a few rich merchants have recently adopted his hazy theories. In other words, he's amassing a war-chest.'

The gravity of the situation was not lost on Josef Anton. His intuition was right.

'I want a list of all Strict Templar Observance lodges,' he said, 'and of all the Brothers who belong to them.'

'That will be difficult, sir, but not impossible.'

'Your efforts will be well rewarded.'

Geytrand bowed, delighted.

Josef Anton spent a sleepless night. From a more or less secret society, in which more or less subversive ideas circulated, Freemasonry was threatening to become a political force, aiming to seize power with both hands.

He realized that his role was going to be pivotal. It was up to him to fight fiercely and ruthlessly against a formidable foe.

13

The Hague, March 1766

Wolfgang had fully recovered and was amusing himself by
writing a work of 'musical gibberish' on popular themes, rich in
burlesque effects, to mark the enthronement of William V,
Prince of Orange. The Mozarts were back in the Dutch capital
after two concerts by ten-year-old Wolfgang and Nannerl,
who was now fourteen, in Amsterdam on 29 January and
24 February. There, the little boy had played his recent
compositions, variations for harpsichord and violin, and
sonatas for piano and violin dedicated to the Princess of
Nassau-Weilburg. Strongly influenced by the style of Johann
Christian Bach, these little works demonstrated the child's
return to creative life after his recent brush with death.

On 16 April, Wolfgang was to play for the last time in
Holland. Health problems had spoilt the family's time there
and prevented the children from achieving a brilliant success.
It was impossible to make up the lost time. Better to forget
these bad times and set off again for more favourable shores.

'Are we going to travel again, Papa?' asked Wolfgang.

'Holland's a small country, and we've exhausted its possibilities.'

'Where are we going?'

'Versailles was a triumph, so we shall go back to France.

You've made such great progress that you'll astound your audiences.'

Hanover, March 1766

The Strict Templar Observance movement now had twenty-five lodges and was gaining a firm foothold in Brunswick. This didn't yet represent the success they were hoping for, but they must not give up, in spite of facing two serious problems.

The first one was spiritual. Some Freemasons were not satisfied with the knightly nature of the new rituals. If the Templars had inherited an immemorial wisdom, they believed, they owed this to the clerics, who were experts in the occult sciences, but the clerics' teaching did not feature strongly enough in the progression to the highest degrees. So the dissenters had suggested to Hund that there should be three rituals forming a separate system and giving a better account of Templar thought. It involved a forty-day retreat, a novitiate period and the reading of numerous Christian writings in order to re-establish real contact with the divine mystery.

The baron hesitated. Should he add the rank of Canon to that of Knight? Or would that risk directing the Order towards a mysticism which was too far removed from reality and from the conquests it must undertake?

The second problem, which was altogether material, concerned the financing of the movement. So far, despite the movement's growing number of lodges, subscriptions were not coming in. The main burden of expenses therefore rested on the shoulders of the baron alone. No longer able to offer an open house to twenty knights and pay them large salaries, Charles de Hund had been obliged to sell his lands and incur debts by giving his possessions to bankers, in exchange for a lifelong annuity. From now on, he would have to live on the small Lipse estate.

Here in Hanover, he tried to persuade his staff to set the Order's finances on a healthy footing at last. Since the baron could no longer provide for all its needs, the lodges and the Brothers must pay their vital contributions to the Provincial Grand Masters.

The future of Strict Templar Observance depended upon it.

Paris, 12 June 1766

'It's finished, Papa.'

Leopold examined the sheet music. 'Religious music?'

'It's a Kyrie for four voices. When we get home the archbishop is sure to commission a mass from me, so I'm starting it in good time.'

Leopold did not oppose this new departure.

The return to Paris, where they had lodgings in the rue Traversière, courtesy of Baron Grimm, had been a bitter disappointment. Despite giving several concerts, one of them at Versailles, they had met with little success.

Leopold waited impatiently for the meeting with Grimm – the baron had been promising him one for days. Although extremely busy, the arbiter of Parisian cultural life eventually received him.

'Are you enjoying your second stay in our beautiful capital, Monsieur Mozart?'

'Worries about the future prevent me from doing so, Baron.'

'Why is that?'

'My son is growing up. I must think of his career and find him a permanent position with a proper salary.'

Grimm seemed annoyed. 'Here in Paris?'

'I would be honoured and delighted.'

'Your son is an exceptional musician, but he is much too young to lay claim to the kind of post you are hoping for.'

'You know that he composes and—'

'Yes, I know, I know! You must simply be patient, Monsieur Mozart, very patient, if you want to conquer Paris. I shall write another article, which will inform people in even more glowing terms about your marvellous son. He must continue to work, and his reward will come.'

As he emerged from Grimm's residence, Leopold realized he had failed. Wolfgang was destined to play in less and less exclusive salons until he ended up being completely unfashionable. He made a vital decision: to forget his French, English and Dutch dreams, and return to Salzburg.

On 9 July, the Mozarts left Paris. On the 15th, Grimm's second article appeared. 'Wolfgang Mozart, that miraculous child,' it said, 'has made miraculous progress in music ... The most amazing aspect of all is the profound understanding of harmony and its most hidden passages, which he possesses to a supreme degree.'

Switzerland, September 1766

One concert in Dijon in July, another at Lyon in August, and then Geneva in September. To Leopold's great chagrin Voltaire refused to receive his son. The atheistic and pretentious philosopher lacked even the most elementary courtesy.

Summoned to Lausanne, Wolfgang performed successfully there at the end of September, before a journey across Switzerland, punctuated by several concerts in Bern, Zurich and Schaffhouse. They spent a very taxing time in Donaueschingen: nine musical evenings in twelve days! The prince paid twenty-four gold louis to Leopold, who was happy to fill his purse.

Munich, 9 November 1766

For the third time in his young career, Wolfgang played before Elector Maximilian, who was delighted to hear him again.

At the end of the concert, the little boy was exhausted and unsteady on his feet.

'He's ill!' exclaimed Leopold anxiously. 'He must lie down.'

A room was immediately placed at the Mozarts' disposal and a doctor was called.

While Leopold ran to fetch water, Thamos entered the room. Wolfgang was conscious, but having difficulty breathing. The Egyptian gave him a small golden pill to swallow.

As soon as he had taken it, the child felt much better and wanted to talk to the man from Rücken about his secret kingdom, but he had already disappeared.

On 30 November 1766, the Mozart family returned to Salzburg after an absence of almost three years. With the fees from the final tour, Leopold had brought back capital of 7,000 florins, a reassuringly substantial sum which would make a good war-chest.

Yet he was still worried: how would his employer, the archbishop, greet him?

14

Salzburg, 1 December 1766

'Your travels have been interminable!' grumbled the archbishop. 'Did you at least derive some satisfaction from them?'

'My son was applauded throughout Europe, Your Grace.
The kings of France and England received him at court, and his
first compositions were greatly admired.'

'Excellent, excellent! His growing fame will reflect well
upon our dear Salzburg. But I should like to verify our young
prodigy's gifts for myself. Would you agree to a programme of
composition for my palace?'

Leopold could only bow.

After a few days of relative rest, Wolfgang was overwhelmed
with work. At the end of the year, the archbishop would enjoy
his *licenza* for tenor, a work designed to honour the master of
the city during his presence at a concert.

January 1767 saw the birth of a symphony in four movements which synthesized all that the eleven-year-old composer
had learned during his travels. Shedding J. C. Bach's Italianate
style, he immersed himself in German music by listening to
famous composers who were highly esteemed by the critics.

Salzburg, February 1767

Anton Weiser was a rich man and one of the most visible of Salzburg's prominent citizens, a supplier of fabrics to the archbishop's palace and the principal noble families. But he did not believe that merely making money was all that life held. Convinced he owed his wealth to divine benevolence, he read and re-read the Bible, and never forgot to offer daily thanks to God, thanks which he tried to express in verse.

A tall, dignified, extremely elegant man entered the shop. Weiser did not know him but he was clearly an aristocrat of high lineage.

'May I help you, my lord?'

'Certainly.'

'Not even in Munich and Vienna will you find finer fabrics. Do you wish to decorate your residence?'

'Indeed. The old building requires a great deal of work, and I like brightly coloured fabrics.'

'I have everything you will need.'

'Then I shall award you the commission. But first I have a request to make of you.'

Anton Weiser's ears pricked up. 'I am at your service, my lord.'

'I have heard that you produce remarkable writings dealing with the greatness of God and the need to respect His commandments.'

The merchant blushed. 'It is true, I confess . . . It is only right that I should give thanks to my Creator for all His gifts.'

'Letting your works go unread would be regrettable. Could one of them not be set to music?'

Weiser gaped. 'But which composer would be interested?'

'I know at least three: Michael Haydn,* who is an

---

* 1737–1806, brother of Josef Haydn.

experienced technician; Aldgasser, the court organist; and little Wolfgang Mozart, who has just returned from a triumphant European tour. They can give your prose a brilliance that will enchant you.'

The merchant looked down at his feet. 'There is one text that means a great deal to me ... Would you be willing to read it?'

'Gladly.'

'And could you pass it on to the right person?'

'Very easily.'

It was no masterpiece, but it was the kind of solemn, rather pontificating work that Thamos needed. It was time to put the Great Magician to the test and see if he could express a thought in music. The hour had come to leave Rücken, the wondrous imaginary kingdom, and confront reality.

Salzburg, March 1767

The offertory for four voices composed by Wolfgang on the occasion of the festival of St Benoit and dedicated to a priest who was a friend of the Mozart family slightly offended the priest, for its style was close to that of a comic opera. On the other hand, the seriousness of the music illustrating the first part of the *Duty of the First Commandment*, a sacred drama by Anton Weiser, astonished the audience at the Benedictine University of Salzburg.

In it appeared a Christian who was so lukewarm in his faith that he fell asleep in a flowery bush. Divine Justice punished the wicked and rewarded the virtuous, and this Justice harkened to the Christian Spirit, which was extremely discontented with the lukewarm attitude of most humans. How were they ever to be made to see clearly, if not by opening their eyes to the punishments that lay in store for the damned, condemned to Hell?

Alas, the half-hearted sleeping Christian was in danger of listening to the pernicious Spirit of the World and giving himself up to a thousand and one forbidden pleasures. It was the task of Justice to awaken him, and of the Christian Spirit to guide him.

And the miracle happened: no more half-heartedness! At last aware of his duties, the awakened Christian received Justice and Mercy, and respected the precept written in Chapter 12, Verse 30 of St Mark's gospel: 'You must love the Lord your God with all your heart, with all your soul, with all your mind and with all your strength.'

Astonishingly for an eleven-year-old, Wolfgang used this text as the basis of a funeral cantata, or *Grabmusik*, which was played on Good Friday, 7 April. It depicted the Soul and the Angel, sung by bass and soprano soloists respectively, debating before a tomb – the Angel was of course from the life after death. It was clear that, shattering many childish dreams, death had burst into the musician's thoughts.

Despite the flaws and the naivety of the music, Thamos was reassured about the Great Magician's abilities. He had succeeded in grasping set words and giving them a touch of life. The moment of his first contact with initiation was approaching.

When he returned home, the Egyptian was confronted by two men with inscrutable expressions.

'You are to come with us. Someone important wishes to see you,' declared the elder man.

'I never yield to force.'

'It would be a pity to waste time, my Brother. The Rose-Cross demands our constant devotion, and it would be an unpardonable insult to make the Imperator wait.'

'Does he live in Salzburg?'

'Follow us, my Brother. There should be no violence between us.'

Thamos could easily have got rid of the two Rosicrucians. But they were probably not alone, and he had been expecting a new confrontation with the head of the Order.

15

Salzburg, April 1767

The Imperator's face had changed, and now showed not a trace of amiability or brotherly affection remained. Indeed, it was openly hostile.

'We have just taken an important decision,' he informed Thamos. 'We shall infiltrate as many Masonic lodges as possible, by grafting our high degrees on to theirs. Our followers will easily integrate with the various rites practised and, beyond the degree of Master, will accomplish them through our teachings. The Strict Templar Observance movement seems an excellent breeding ground. Grand Master Jacques de Molay of the Templars was murdered by a tyrant: he is our common hero, is he not?

'But before I tell you any more, there is a serious question to be answered. Several of our Brothers regard you as an Unknown Superior. I, on the other hand, believe you are an impostor.'

'Your founder, Christian Rosenkreuz,' said Thamos, 'lived in Egypt, where the secrets of initiation were revealed to him so that he could pass them on to the West, where he died in 1494 at the age of a hundred and six. His alchemical texts nurtured the Knights of the Golden Stone, from which you derive.'

Disconcerted, the Imperator let fly his final arrow. 'If you really are the disciple of Abbot Hermes, you must know the true name of Elie Artiste, our protecting genius and our guide.'

'He is the alchemist Schmidt of Sonnenburg, born in Bohemia,' declared Thamos with emphasis. 'It was he who decided that a part of the initiation tradition should be taught within the framework of the Golden Rose-Cross.'

'Then you really are an Unknown Superior,' conceded the Imperator, much moved. 'I can now share with you my deep conviction: the Great Magician is among us. And it is you who will initiate him, this very night, by taking him through all the degrees in a single breath.'

'It is much too soon. A child could not bear it.'

'You are wrong about the identity of the Great Magician. He is not a child but an alchemist, who has reached the end of his personal practice and who must be raised to the summit of our Mysteries. He is here, and I entrust him to you.'

On one hand, the Imperator was submitting Thamos to a difficult ordeal, to find out if he really knew all the rituals of the Golden Rose-Cross and if he was capable of directing them; on the other, if the Egyptian was sincere, he might perhaps have discovered the real Great Magician . . .

The alchemist who claimed to be the Great Magician was tall, stern and contemplative. A Freemason and 'Scottish Master', he answered all Thamos's questions correctly, in the presence of six Gold Rose-Crosses. Then the Egyptian moved on to start the actual alchemical work. First, the man manufactured silver. Little by little, radiation from the sulphur, the philosophical sun, appeared.

He lost ground, however, when Thamos presented him with the red-hot stone. Its brilliance died, and it became sterile. And he proved unable to bring forth the true philosopher's stone, which enabled a member of the Golden Rose-Cross to converse with the Spirit by means of the creative fire.

No, this second-rate alchemist was not the Great Magician.

Salzburg, 13 May 1767

In the great hall of the university, the atmosphere was effervescent. A troupe of gifted amateurs was presenting *Apollo et Hyacinthus*, a dramatic cantata for five performers, comprising nine main pieces and a chorus. For Leopold, who was both proud and anxious, this was no less than a first attempt at the opera Wolfgang had been dreaming of since his encounter with Johann Christian Bach. But how, at the age of eleven, could he master such a complex art?

Based on Book X of Ovid's *Metamorphoses* and works by other ancient authors, the plot appealed greatly to the audience. The abominable Zephyrus, who was in love with pretty Melia, Apollo's betrothed, killed the unfortunate Hyacinthus and accused Apollo of the murder. As he died, Hyacinthus succeeded in shouting the truth, thus ruining the murderer's scheme. Apollo consoled those who loved his brave friend by transforming him into a beautiful flower.

'The child already knows how to compose some pretty little arias,' observed one aristocrat.

'And he's very good at description,' added his wife, who had been charmed by the piece. 'When the words mention a lion, the orchestra roars; if they talk of sleep, it yawns; for storms and furious seas, its full power is unleashed. I understood all of it.'

Leopold had a modest triumph on his hands. He was not satisfied with the cantata's technical side, but the work's reception by the elite of Salzburg reassured him. Perhaps his son was beginning the enviable career of an opera composer . . . However, there would have to be more consistent works to be certain that it was so.

As for Wolfgang, he joked with his fourteen-year-old best friend, Anton Stadler. Although destined for studies in moral theology, Anton preferred music and had had a wonderful time singing a part in *Apollo*.

Leopold was not opposed to his sons having a few distractions, provided they were brief. Because of a new plan he had just devised, his son must set to work again.

<h1 align="center">16</h1>

Salzburg, 11 September 1767

With a heavy heart, Anna Maria finished packing. 'I have not the slightest desire to go to Vienna, Leopold. The city's so big that it frightens me – and here in Salzburg the autumn's so pleasant.'

'We have no choice. You know as well as I do that Archduchess Maria Josefa, the empress's daughter, is to be married to King Ferdinando of Naples. Can't you imagine the tremendous celebrations? We mustn't miss them.'

'But we haven't been invited!'

'There will be many concerts, Wolfgang will far outstrip all his competitors, and we'll be summoned to court. Once there, he's certain to obtain a permanent, well-paid post.

'Are you sure, my dear husband?'

'As sure as one can be.'

As they got into the carriage for Vienna, the Mozarts did not realize that this was to be the last journey made by all four members of their little family.

Vienna, 16 September 1767

It was a sinister city, with a heavy atmosphere and the weight of sadness upon it.

74

Leopold did not recognize Vienna. Why was the great city not rejoicing at the approach of such a joyful event?

'Since Emperor Franz's death three years ago,' explained the coachman, 'Her Majesty has withdrawn into her grief and has banned overt celebrations in Schönbrunn. As for her co-regent, Josef II, there are only two words on his lips: economy and austerity. According to him, that's what's needed to maintain Austria's prosperity. It doesn't go down well with people who'd like to celebrate.'

'All the same, this betrothal . . .'

'Despite everything, we're hoping for a few good moments. A little gaiety would do Viennese morale a world of good.'

Leopold did his best to raise the morale of his own family. Not only were Wolfgang and Nannerl going to shine in a succession of concerts, but they would also be received at court, which they were going to conquer all over again.

Berlin, October 1767

Unlike Leopold, Thamos was expecting nothing from the Mozart family's second trip to Vienna, for Wolfgang's continual public appearances were holding back his progress as a composer. But he understood the anxiety of a father who, paradoxically, was making his son live the life of a circus performer in order to secure him a stable future by acquiring a permanent, well-paid post in one of the great courts of Europe.

The Imperator of the Rosicrucians had admitted his mistake. Only an Unknown Superior could identify the Great Magician. All the circles of the Golden Rose-Cross were now open to Thamos, who had access, in Vienna and in Salzburg, to alchemical laboratories where he produced the metals necessary to assume the role of the Count of Thebes.

A message from his Brother von Gebler had alerted him to an event which might be extremely important: in Berlin, the

Rite of African – that is, Egyptian – Architects had appeared, at the instigation of Friedrich von Köppen, a thirty-three-year-old officer in the Prussian army. Was this a flash in the pan, or a promising development? Thamos was determined to neglect nothing. Which Masonic plan should serve as a framework for the future initiation training of the Great Magician? Thamos would employ the best one, after a detailed examination of them all.

Right in the heart of Berlin, he was surprised to find an official building furnished with a temple, a library, a natural-history room and a laboratory.

Friedrich von Köppen received him in a well-appointed office, which was dominated by an impressive quantity of manuscripts and books devoted to the hermetic sciences and to Christianity.

The creator of the new Rite was a squarely built man, open and direct. For the third time, he examined his visitor's calling card. 'Count of Thebes ... Don't tell me you come from Egypt?'

'The name which you give to the Great Architect of the Universe and which is also the secret word of your first degree, Disciple of the Egyptians, is Amon, the god of ancient Thebes.*

The Prussian stood up very straight. 'I shall immediately hand over to you the key to this office and leadership of the Order.'

'It is for you, and only you, to develop your new Rite. I have brought you some documents which you are to study at your leisure and from which you will produce a publication. The resurrection of the Egyptian Mysteries is a vital task.'

Von Köppen's hands trembled as he accepted the precious manuscript.

* The other planned degrees were Initiate into the Aegean Mysteries, Cosmopolitan, Christian Philosopher, and Knight of Silence.

'This magnificent building surprises me,' admitted Thamos. 'It would seem that you benefit from the support of the ruling power.'

'Our great King Friedrich encourages me to pursue intensive research and has provided vital material support.'

'Aren't you worried that he may reverse that policy?'

'He is rather unpredictable, I admit, but he knows all about my project and doesn't see anything in it that might endanger his throne. Actually,' confessed von Köppen, 'the rituals interest me less than the pure research. We must study the ancient writings, rediscover all the myriad aspects of the lost wisdom, carry out alchemical experiments and unravel the secrets of nature. The followers of my Order will work night and day.'

'I wish you success.'

'Would . . . would you be prepared to help me a little?'

'Gladly.'

'Then let us set to work.'

Vienna, 1 October 1767

Geytrand placed a slim folder on Josef Anton's desk. Inside were a few pages concerning the organization and aims of the Order of African Architects.

'So they're authorized and protected by King Friedrich. That's annoying. They'll have to be handled with care.'

'Don't worry too much,' advised Geytrand. 'The king sometimes changes his mind without warning. Besides, the founder of the Order won't get very far.'

'Why such optimism?'

'Because his programme demands long hours of research every day. Already, one discontented Brother, who complains that he had to work too hard for insignificant results, has returned to his former lodge, where he can doze peacefully.

This fine fellow will help me present a damning picture of von Köppen. No Freemason will take him or his Order seriously.'

'Excellent. Nevertheless, we must keep the Order under observation.'

'Just like all the others, sir.'

17

Vienna, 15 October 1767

Distraught, Anna Maria woke Leopold. 'It is horrible, dreadful, unimaginable!' she cried.

'Calm down! I know we haven't yet given a single concert, but I shall eventually set one up.'

'This has nothing to do with music. Archduchess Maria Josefa has died of smallpox. This time, people aren't talking about just a few cases. It's a real epidemic and there'll be hundreds or even thousands of deaths. We must leave the city right away!'

'Let's keep calm; rumours are often misleading. I shall go to Schönbrunn and find out the truth.'

Although the archduchess's death was confirmed, the court asked the population not to panic and requested that musicians remain in Vienna, with a view to new ceremonies once a new fiancée had been found for the King of Naples – one was already being actively sought.

Leopold tried to reassure his wife, but could not soothe her fears. Every day she begged him to leave Vienna before it was too late.

When Archduchess Elisabeth also died of smallpox, there was panic everywhere.

'We are leaving immediately,' decided Leopold on 26 October.

Berlin, 26 October 1767

Friedrich von Köppen was in seventh heaven. Thamos was opening up unknown horizons and enabling him to enrich his Order's rites in ways he had never dreamt of.

A letter his secretary handed him brought him abruptly down to earth.

'Bad news from Vienna,' he told Thamos.

'What has happened?'

'A smallpox epidemic. Several well-known people have already died, and many of the Viennese are leaving for Moravia, which is so far free of the disease.'

Thamos felt a cold shiver. Wolfgang's life was in danger. 'Is there a local doctor capable of treating this sickness?'

'Yes, and he's a Brother. His medical reputation is second to none.'

'Go on with your research, I must leave.'

'Already? But—'

'Give me the doctor's name and address.'

Olmütz, Moravia, 28 October 1767

Deeply relieved, Anna Maria Mozart held her children's hands tightly. It had taken only two days to reach this little town, which was beyond the reach of the epidemic.

At dinner, Wolfgang wasn't hungry. At ten o'clock that evening he complained of a bad headache.

His mother examined him and, to her horror, found pustules. 'Smallpox!'

Leopold rushed to one of his son's admirers, Count Podstatsky, to ask for help. Despite the risks involved, the count did not abandon the child: on the contrary, he immediately offered to provide the family with food and lodgings.

That night Wolfgang had a high fever and became delirious,

with swollen, painful eyes. He muttered words which were incomprehensible except for 'Rücken', the name of the realm where his soul was wandering, little by little detaching itself from the earth.

When Doctor Wolff arrived to see the child, he thought of the strange encounter that had brought him to Olmütz. A Brother Mason, impressively tall and with a magnetic gaze, had given him a large sum of money for his moving expenses and professional fees. In exchange, the doctor was to devote himself exclusively to the little musician, and to the recognized remedies he was to add a potion based on Eastern plants. At first reluctant, he had been assured that the potion was in no way harmful.

Olmütz, early December 1767

'How do you feel this morning?' asked Doctor Wolff.

'Much better,' replied Wolfgang with a smile.

'The fever has disappeared, and so have the pustules.'

'Will I be scarred?'

'Hardly at all. Heaven is clearly protecting you.'

'Am I really cured?'

'Yes, really.'

'Then I can play the piano?'

'I would be happy to hear you.'

Wolfgang did not need to be asked twice. At first stiff and hesitant, his fingers soon rediscovered the magical ways of the keyboard, and the notes sang out with surprising strength. The serious illness had not affected the boy's gifts.

'Would you do me a great favour?' asked Doctor Wolff.

'You saved my life. Of course I will.'

'My daughter has a pretty voice, and I would be the happiest of fathers if I could present her with a song written and signed by Wolfgang Mozart.'

Christian Jacq

'Do you have a suitable text?

'Yes, this short poem: "O joy, queen of the sages, who, with flowers about their heads, address praises to her on their golden lyres, which are silent when wickedness holds sway: hear me from your throne on high."'*

At first merely dutiful, but then won over, Wolfgang set to work, wiping out the memory of all those long, empty, feverish days. He did not suspect that he was, for the first time, setting to music a Masonic text passed on by Thamos and provided by Brother Wolff. This prayer to serene joy, one of the goals of initiation, was formulated in flowery terms which would not attract the attention of outsiders. Nevertheless, as Thamos had hoped, they touched Wolfgang's soul, opening up new horizons to him.

On 23 December, the Mozart family returned to Vienna, where the smallpox epidemic was at last over. En route they stayed with the brother of the Archbishop of Salzburg for the celebrations, before continuing on their way.

Still obsessed by the desire to obtain a post at court, Leopold ordered his son to compose a duet for two sopranos, a lament on the premature death of Archduchess Josefa.† Leopold hoped it would demonstrate the Mozarts' attachment to the ruling family. But they had yet to be received at court.

* *An die Freude* by J. P. Uz, K53.
† *'Ach, was müssen wir erfahren'*, K43a.

18

Baron de Hund ought to have been jubilant. Strict Templar Observance now had some forty lodges, spread through Austria, Germany, Switzerland, Poland, Hungary and Denmark. However, despite this success there was discontent among his troops, for the promised economic recovery had not materialized. True, subscriptions were coming in a little more satisfactorily, but many Brothers were hoping for a rich, powerful Order from which they themselves, like the Templar knights of the Middle Ages, would derive substantial advantages. The baron and his counsellors had explored several ways to create wealth, but none had come to fruition.

There were other worries, too. Many Brothers complained about the poverty of the rituals. Moreover, a fearsome predator was hunting in the baron's territory: a thirty-seven-year-old Prussian army doctor who went by the name of Zinnendorf.* He had introduced into Germany a new Rite, the Swedish Rite, which was hostile to Strict Templar Observance, despite the fact that the traitor had previously belonged to it. The Swedish rite aimed to put its followers' spirits in touch with divinity, while waiting for the reappearance of their patron saint, John

---

* His real name was Jean-Guillaume Ellenberg.

the Evangelist. By conjuring up the invisible powers, the Brothers planned to obtain inner illumination.

This course of action was too mystical, and displeased Charles de Hund. However, he took his opponent seriously. He was being attacked on several fronts, and would have loved to see again the Unknown Superior whose wisdom he missed very much.

Vienna, 9 January 1768

A new file lay on Josef Anton's desk: 'Swedish Rite. Zinnendorf.' The doctor, head of the Prussian army's health services, was an interesting man. Determined to have his revenge on Strict Templar Observance and on Baron de Hund, he talked freely and had told everything he knew to Geytrand, who was as sympathetic and understanding as he could wish. He was a most valuable – and free! – recruit to the Viennese secret service.

'Is the attack on the Templars really serious?' asked Josef Anton.

'Possibly,' replied Geytrand. 'Zinnendorf seems very determined, and he controls a far from negligible branch of Freemasonry. Moreover, the Strict Observance movement's financial problems are by no means resolved, and there's even talk of internal conflict.'

'Excellent! If the Freemasons destroy each other, they'll save us a great deal of work. But will the baron hold out against this storm?'

'The Templar Order is his life's work. No matter what it costs him, he won't give up.'

The Great Magician

Four lean months of illness, numerous expenses, and no receipts. Leopold had to face the facts. Wolfgang would soon be twelve, and could no longer be shown off as a child prodigy; his career was stagnating. Was he a future composer? That was not certain. His first attempts were encouraging, certainly, but it was particularly difficult to make one's mark in this milieu, which was full of pitfalls and fierce rivalries. Would Wolfgang become a virtuoso? Nothing was less certain. At sixteen, although she was somewhat colourless, and definitely no genius, Nannerl displayed greater virtuosity.

These days Wolfgang seemed fragile and dreamy, too remote from a reality whose pitiless, sordid aspects Leopold knew only too well. How was he to make the boy understand that reality could not be reduced to an imaginary kingdom?

Who was in favour at the moment, in Vienna? Above all, Gluck and Haydn, both experienced composers who fell in with the demands of the powerful and were sufficiently masters of their art to adapt to circumstances, without losing their personalities. Wolfgang was still floundering a thousand leagues behind these two musicians, and yet it was vital to strike a great blow, pleasing the Viennese, who were much taken with lightness and disliked the serious and the intellectual.

Leopold was searching, and Leopold would find.

As for Wolfgang, he listened to a great deal of music, notably that of Haydn, to which he proved particularly receptive. He behaved not like a passive listener but like a creator who quenched his thirst with others' work in order, little by little, to fashion his own language. On 16 January, he finished a symphony in D major, in the style of Haydn. His father approvingly noted the technical prowess, but Wolfgang would not achieve prominence with this kind of imitation.

Leaving his son to his artistic experiments, Leopold did the rounds of all his contacts and all Wolfgang's admirers in order to obtain an audience at court, the only event that could unblock the situation and put Wolfgang back on the path to celebrity. As the days passed, Leopold had difficulty sleeping, lost his appetite and became irritable. Had he really lost all his persuasive abilities?

At last, he received the news he had so hoped for: the Mozarts were summoned to court, at three o'clock on the afternoon of 19 January.

19

To Leopold's astonishment, it was the co-regent, Josef II himself, who came to greet his guests in the anteroom. The master of the Austrian Empire had a long, stern face empty of expression or vitality, was simply dressed and hardly inspired gaiety. Despite sad, reclusive Maria Theresa's increasing inactivity, he had urged her to undertake vital reforms, such as liberalizing the penal code, which was too repressive. Also, he wanted to economize more and more, reducing the state's expenditure before it collapsed.

Never had Leopold dreamt he would be shown into one of Schönbrunn's salons by such a great man!

The second surprise was that there was no piano and no string instruments.

'Be seated,' ordered Josef sharply.

Wolfgang gazed around, while Leopold adopted a submissive posture.

'Majesty, do you wish my son to play you his latest work?'

'Not today. I simply wish to talk to you about music. Despite the terrible smallpox epidemic and the deaths that have afflicted us, the Viennese court must hold its own as the artistic capital of Europe. I would not wish the reputation of London or Paris to surpass our own.'

'Knowing those two cities, Majesty, it is highly unlikely.'

'Governing is all about foresight, Herr Mozart. The empress and I must take charge of all areas of social life, including music. My Viennese subjects are rather frivolous, but I am determined to give them works of quality.'

'That is to Your Majesty's great honour.'

'I am told that your son is a composer.'

'He works night and day, and his first works augur well. I am not speaking as a father, Majesty, but as a demanding and objective musician.'

'Very good, Herr Mozart. I think Vienna would appreciate a brand-new opera. Is such a young boy capable of composing one?'

'Wolfgang has already demonstrated his abilities with *Apollo et Hyacinthus*, which was presented in Salzburg. Since then, he has made such progress that he will give you complete satisfaction.'

'Since this is an official commission, a proper contract will be drawn up and signed. Young Wolfgang must set to work immediately. I wish to have this opera by the end of April, at the latest.'

'Your wish is our desire, Majesty. May I . . . may I ask you a question?'

'Pray do so.'

'Gluck is the most famous composer in Vienna. Will he not be opposed to such a young musician?'

'However great he may be, Gluck is in my service.'

Leopold regretted having raised this delicate point. Josef's reply was hardly reassuring for, despite his determination to control everything, he could not unravel the tangled web of musical quarrels.

All the same, as he left Schönbrunn Leopold felt like dancing. The emperor himself commissioning an opera from Wolfgang! It was beyond his wildest dreams.

Almost indifferent to the situation, the boy whistled a merry tune.

'Note it down,' advised his father. 'This very evening, you must set to work.'

Vienna, late January 1768

In the presence of the young Baron van Swieten, son of Empress Maria Theresa's personal physician, Gluck had told Leopold Mozart that he saw no problem in his young son composing an opera in the Italian taste, *La finta semplice* ('The False Innocent'), to a libretto by Goldoni. The contract was therefore drawn up with an intermediary, Affligio, in exchange for one hundred ducats, a fine sum which made Wolfgang Mozart officially a professional.

La finta semplice was to be a comic opera in three acts. The convoluted plot did not much interest the boy but, since he was being given a chance to make characters live musically, he found the necessary enthusiasm for his arduous task.

There are two brothers, who are both miserly, starchy and cantankerous. Their young sister is charming and cheerful, and she dreams of a great love. Along comes an officer with his sister, who is pretty and alluring. They stay with the two misers. The officer falls in love with the sister of these grouches, whom the false innocent (the officer's sister) seduces one after the other. The intrigue ends well, since the misers' sister marries the officer.

It was typical Goldoni, and Leopold did not bat an eyelid. Wolfgang must adapt, and he would do so.

Vienna, 2 February 1768

Brotherhood was not just a word between von Gebler and Thamos. The former sensed that the latter was to play an

Christian Jacq

essential role in the development of Freemasonry, and was eager to inform him of those major events of which he was aware, so he told him about Baron de Hund's problems and the upheavals within the Strict Templar Observance movement.

'I am not sure,' he ended, 'that he will succeed in restoring the Order of the Temple. Nostalgia is not always a good counsellor, and wanting to revive things that are past and gone may lead to a dead end. But tell me, has the Great Magician's training begun?'

'He has taken his first steps but still does not know his true nature. Perhaps he will never discover it.'

'Why are you so pessimistic?'

'There are many, many obstacles in his way.'

'If you see life in such dark colours, how can the Light shine again in our lodges?'

'Don't worry, I am not admitting defeat.'

'Two of our Brothers could give you valuable help, but neither is easy to handle. The first is called Mesmer, and he's a doctor, a musician, and a wealthy man. The second is Baron van Swieten, who seems destined for a brilliant diplomatic career in the service of the Austrian state. I am almost the only person who knows that he was initiated in Germany – that secret must be jealously guarded. Although he appears hostile to Freemasonry, van Swieten wants to protect it, notably in Vienna, so he won't attend any lodges there. The authorities must not on any account learn of his true commitment.'

'Thank you for confiding in me.'

'Be extremely cautious. Sooner or later, you will be in danger. And if something bad were to happen to you, the Great Magician could not flourish.'

20

Vienna, 3 February 1768

Thamos was completing a transmutation in his alchemical laboratory when an unexpected sound alerted him, a sound like boot-heels striking the paving stones in the courtyard. In the middle of the night, it broke the usual silence of a peaceful house whose only occupants were an old aristocratic couple and the Egyptian.

Trusting his instinct, Thamos knew he must escape at once. He poured a red liquid on to the molten stone, put on a thick cloak and slipped out by a hidden door just as the police burst in.

This was the first sizeable operation under Josef Anton's leadership. The empress had ordered him to arrest alchemists, destroy their equipment and burn their work. In this case, the policemen were spared the trouble, for the furnace exploded in their faces.

As he walked calmly away, Thamos realized he must have been denounced either by a good Brother or by a neighbour. From now on, he must be even more cautious and conceal his secret activities even more carefully.

Vienna, late March 1768

Formerly a minister at the court of Louis XV, forty-seven-year-old Prince Dimitri Galitzin had been Russian ambassador to Vienna since 1762, and he played a key role in diplomatic relations between Austria and Russia. He belonged to a family of seventeen children, of whom he was unquestionably the most talented.

He had not remarried since losing his wife in 1761, but nevertheless led a luxurious life, welcoming the Viennese nobility to his Krugerstrasse palace with its eleven main rooms. Fourteen carriages, eleven horses, numerous servants, a summer residence with grottos, fountains and false ruins: the prince loved luxury and beauty.

'Has he arrived?' he asked his butler impatiently.

'Not yet, Highness.'

'Is everything ready?'

'Down to the smallest detail.'

At last the young prodigy arrived. Prince Galitzin had long heard talk of this astonishing musician and wanted to hear him in his home, one to one. The well-dressed and well-educated Wolfgang impressed him. The boy was leaving childhood behind, though he was still a long way from being a man, and an unusually serious light shone in his eyes.

As soon as Wolfgang played one of his own piano sonatas, even though it was inferior to those of Haydn the prince sensed that this young lad was moved by an incomparable genius. One day, if necessary, he would help him to become one of the most prominent men in Viennese society and to conquer the artistic capital of Europe.

Vienna, April 1768

Leopold was furious. The performance of *La finta semplice* had been postponed again. Affligio, the impresario, was behaving like a crook, unable to obtain a theatre. And Josef II was in Hungary, on the border of the Turkish Empire, whose warlike spirit alarmed him. They must await his return in order to resolve this frightful situation: an opera completely ready, an official commission fulfilled by the planned date, and neither a cast nor a stage!

Wolfgang did not sit idle. Benefiting from the assistance of and his relationship with Prince Galitzin, he gave concerts in the salons of the Viennese nobility, where his reputation was spreading. Above all, he continued to listen to a great deal of music, which he assimilated as he composed and thus incorporated into his own writing.

'When are we going home?' Anna Maria asked her husband. She much preferred the calm of Salzburg to the bustle of Vienna.

'As soon as *La finta semplice* has been performed. Its success will confirm him as a composer and open all kinds of doors to him.'

As usual, Anna Maria gave in. Her husband must be right, since he always acted in the best interests of the family.

A worrying official letter had just reached Leopold from Salzburg. He had been away from his court post for six months, and Prince-Archbishop Sigismund von Schrattenbach would not pay him indefinitely for doing nothing. The letter was not as bad as it might have been: his employer was not sacking him, nor even ordering him back to Salzburg immediately. But from 31 March he would no longer pay Leopold a salary.

True, thanks to Wolfgang's earnings, the Mozarts were able to fund their stay in Vienna, and there was still the

little war-chest from the European tour. But it was out of
the question for Leopold to lose his comfortable position at
the archbishop's court. Torn between the need to return
to Salzburg without undue delay and the possibility that
Wolfgang might meet success in Vienna, Leopold prevaricated.

21

Vienna, July 1768

The Dutch-born Baron Gottfried van Swieten was pursuing a successful diplomatic career, which had taken him to Brussels, Paris and London. He was hoping for a much-coveted post in Berlin.

However, his mind was occupied by another ideal: Freemasonry. In a Europe torn apart by many upheavals, and whose future was worrying, he relished the atmosphere of certain lodges where speech was still free. There, enlightened minds insisted on the need for urgent reforms, as well as providing a spiritual dynamism beyond dogmas and beliefs. They formed only a small group, whose voice was in danger of being stifled.

Because of Maria Theresa's hostility to Freemasonry, van Swieten did not frequent any of the few Viennese lodges, which were extremely discreet. On the contrary, he took care to show disdain and contempt for the movement, which he described as vaguely subversive and entirely sterile. Restoring initiation in Vienna would be be extremely arduous, perhaps even impossible. But van Swieten was patient and resolute.

Back in Vienna for a few weeks, he resumed contact with friends and relations. The day's first visitor was unknown to him: the Count of Thebes.

The stranger's bearing and compelling gaze were impressive. He said, 'I have a request to make of you, Herr Baron.'

'I am listening.'

'You may know that the young musician Wolfgang Mozart has finished an opera commissioned by the emperor. But because of the incompetence and mismanagement of a crook named Affligio, it is impossible to stage the work. Can you help?'

'Why are you interested in the boy?'

'Because he is the Great Magician.'

Van Swieten was silent for a long time. Eventually, he said, 'Count of Thebes . . . Who are you really?'

'A Brother who has come from Egypt to ensure that the initiation you care about so much is reborn. Have no fear: your secret is well guarded and will remain so. But the Great Magician has need of your help.'

Perturbed, van Swieten knew he ought to ask this strange visitor a hundred questions, but he let him leave without asking any of them.

A few days later, he summoned to his home Wolfgang Mozart, his father and some musicians and singers to listen to *La finta semplice*. Neither the libretto nor the music greatly impressed him, but here and there he detected flashes of a talent which merited consideration.

At the end of the performance, Leopold asked the baron what he thought of the piece.

'Interesting, coming from a boy of that age. However, this performance is liable to be the first and last.'

'But . . . it was commissioned by the emperor!'

'I have learnt, Herr Mozart, that the court musicians do not wish to see a young lad succeed; it would offend them. You would do well to return to Salzburg.'

Leopold was stubborn. 'I wish to speak with the emperor.

Since you have heard the opera, could you obtain an audience for me?'

'I will try.'

Vienna, 20 September 1768

During the summer, Leopold had worked hard writing a Memoir narrating the misadventures suffered by Wolfgang and *La finta semplice*. '*Musical hell in its entirety,*' he wrote, '*has been unleashed so that a child's talent may not be recognized.*'

At last, on the verge of autumn, Josef agreed to receive him.

'This is the truth, Majesty! My son has worked hard, met his deadlines and provided a work worthy of being heard. But a corrupt go-between and jealous colleagues have condemned us to unjust failure.'

Josef remained expressionless. Leopold was afraid he might have angered the emperor by speaking so frankly, but Josef said, 'I find you correct on all points. A court case will put an end to this man Affligio's dealings.'

A broad smile spread across Leopold's anxious face. 'Am I to understand, Majesty, that Wolfgang's opera will at last be played on a stage in Vienna?'

'No, Herr Mozart. The right moment has unfortunately passed, and I now have other preoccupations. Ensure that your son continues to work, and fortune will favour him.'

On emerging from the palace, Leopold went to drink beer in a tavern. Not only was *La finta semplice* condemned to oblivion, but Josef had not commissioned any new works, even unofficially. To think that they had been so close to success . . .

Should he plan a new series of concerts in Vienna, or return home to Salzburg? The second solution was the obvious one. Better to retain an official, well-paid post than to hang on to a dream.

Scarcely had he opened the door of his apartment when

Anna Maria rushed to meet him. 'A doctor's here, and he wants to see Wolfgang right away. He's gravely ill and you've kept it from me, haven't you?'

'Of course not!'

'But a doctor . . .'

'What is his name?'

'Mesmer. His valet will come and fetch Wolfgang tomorrow morning and take him for lunch at his master's house.'

Still reeling from his dreadfully disappointing audience with Josef, and befuddled by the beer, Leopold sank into an armchair. Tomorrow was another day.

22

Vienna, 21 September 1768

Born in Swabia in 1734, and based in Vienna since 1759, Franz Anton Mesmer had studied medicine under van Swieten *père*. His thesis had dealt with the influence of the stars on living bodies, and he had obtained his physician's diploma in 1766. Married to a very rich woman, Mesmer was a tenor, pianist and cellist, and had been initiated at the Viennese lodge called Truth and Union. He had just had a long conversation with his friend Gottfried van Swieten.

Yielding to the baron's arguments, he had immediately invited young Mozart to his table. He found the boy immensely interesting, and there was an immediate rapport between them. Leopold, on the other hand, he found surly and suspicious. Mesmer reassured him, providing him with an excellent lunch in the luxuriant garden of his house.

'Music is an extremely important art,' declared Mesmer. 'Like all creation, it feeds on the universal fire that all life depends on.'

'Even the life of plants and stones?' asked Wolfgang.

'Of course. And we humans are endowed with a special sense which puts us in touch with the whole universe. People must become more conscious of it and develop it.'

'For example, by composing?'

'Yes, for a musician can spread positive energies. You see, my boy, all bodies are sensitive to the universal force of attraction, to gravity, to the fluid that serves as a vehicle between bodies. In our world, it acts through either repulsion or attraction, and it maintains the general balance.'

'There are notes which love each other and create harmony,' observed Wolfgang.

'Respecting it and preserving the circulation of positive energy contribute to maintaining our health,' the doctor went on, 'which is why I study magnetism. This treatment causes a movement of fluids inside the patient, which dispels disturbances.'

'What do you do?'

'I haven't yet perfected a technique which can be used on a large number of people at once. But magnetism's effectiveness is easy to judge. Do you have any pain anywhere?'

'A little, in my left elbow – I banged it this morning.'

Mesmer laid his right hand on the painful spot. Almost immediately, Wolfgang felt a gentle heat, then every hint of pain disappeared.

'It is possible to re-establish the circulation of fluids in a weakened organism,' said Mesmer. 'This science comes from ancient Egypt, and I wish to adapt it for our times.'

'Neither I nor my son is ill,' interrupted Leopold, who did not much care for the doctor's words. 'Why did you want to see Wolfgang?'

'To commission a short work from him,' replied the magnetizer with a smile. 'I shall pay well and it will be played right here, in this garden.'

'What kind of work?' asked Wolfgang eagerly.

'A little story I would like set to music, a *Singspiel* as they call it in Germany. A young girl, Bastienne, is in love with Bastien and fears he is unfaithful, so she asks for help from the village seer. 'Pretend you aren't interested in him any more', he advises her. And then the seer tells Bastien that Bastienne has found a new lover. Fearing they are going to lose each other, the two young people unite and live in perfect happiness.'

The story appealed to Wolfgang. The young girl took the initiative, and the drama finished well. As soon as he left Mesmer's house, he set to work.

Vienna, October 1768

A beautiful late afternoon, a garden bedecked in the colours of autumn, an audience made up of people of quality: perfect conditions for the performance of *Bastien und Bastienne*, Wolfgang Mozart's *Singspiel*. He had worked very quickly, with all the dedication of a true professional.

'Are you pleased, Count?' Mesmer asked Thamos, who was standing aside from the admirers.

'Thank you for your welcome, my Brother.'

'That boy astonishes me,' admitted the doctor. 'At times, one would swear he is not of this world. In a society as mediocre as ours, how will he find his path?'

'By creating.'

Vienna, December 1768

A first *opera seria*, *Apollo et Hyacinthus*; a first *opera buffa*, *La finta semplice*, and a first *Singspiel*, *Bastien und Bastienne*: in a year and a half, a young lad had just created three vocal works in three different styles. Leopold could not help but admire, but a good teacher should not show such feelings in front of his pupil.

It was with great satisfaction that he had received a commission from a Jesuit for a mass to inaugurate the chapel of an orphanage under the lofty protection of Josef II. Writing the piece would enable Wolfgang to improve his command of religious music.

On 7 December, it was performed under the direction of the twelve-year-old composer in the brand-new building, in the presence of the court. His precision in leading the orchestra was rewarded with great applause and admiration. How right Leopold had been to persevere and stay in Vienna. This was the second time Wolfgang had given the emperor complete satisfaction, thus proving he was a serious composer whom the Church – and therefore Maria Theresa – could trust.

Now in full flow, Wolfgang wrote a short mass for vocal quartet, string quartet and organ, and on 13 December finished a symphony influenced by the style of Haydn.

There was only one cloud on the horizon, but it was an invasive one: there was still not a single offer of a fixed post. Josef might hold Wolfgang in high esteem but the court musicians, led, by Gluck, were barring his way. According to Leopold, there was a conspiracy against a composer who was so greatly gifted that he would eclipse them all.

How could he, a modest deputy Kapellmeister from Salzburg, succeed in defeating such a powerful clique? Besides, there was always the risk that the archbishop would run out of patience and dismiss his employee. From mediocre, the results of the stay in Vienna would become catastrophic. Very well, then, since Vienna was closed to them, they must return to Salzburg.

But Leopold had already come up with another plan.

23

Vienna, February 1769

Maria Theresa's proposal had stunned Baron de Hund. She was the Church's prime supporter and the sworn enemy of Freemasonry; he was the founder of Strict Templar Observance. And yet she had put his name forward for high office in Vienna.

A trap ... it must be a trap. The empress wanted to neutralize him, lock him up in an official job which would prevent him from pursuing his Masonic dream. He, one of the empress's counsellors of state and a close adviser of the emperor? The honorary titles, yes. The gilded prison of the court, never.

Using the most respectful words, Baron de Hund declined Maria Theresa's offer. The future of Strict Templar Observance would continue to occupy all his time.

Vienna, March 1769

At Tobias von Gebler's side, Thamos had participated in the foundation of the Viennese lodge called To Hope. Hope was a fine virtue in these difficult times when the Brothers confined themselves to brief ceremonies and forbore to utter the slightest criticism of the ruling power.

'Our Freemasonry is marking time,' commented von Gebler,

'and, despite his convictions and his commitment, Baron de Hund cannot give it back the necessary status.

'Is Strict Templar Observance in difficulty?' asked Thamos.

'It is making progress, but in too formal a way. The fundamental basis is lacking, and I am not certain that the Templar reference is entirely justified. And then there are internal disputes, competition with other ritual systems ... Hund has not yet conquered Europe. Alas, Vienna doesn't seem to be a favourable environment for the blossoming of the Great Magician. Unless you can supply To Hope or another lodge with the rituals that would make them fit for conducting his initiation ...?'

Thamos did not reply. It was too soon. Much too soon.

Salzburg, spring 1769

Now thirteen, Wolfgang escaped from time to time to play, joke and chat with his friend Anton Stadler. The court, the cathedral, the salons of the nobility and the middle classes ... Salzburg's space had grown smaller. Masses, promenades, society games and concerts offered the archbishop's subjects distractions which satisfied most of them.

As for Leopold, he demanded work and more work. Since his return, on 5 January, to the city of his birth, Wolfgang had been composing constantly.

The austerity of the old German masters, the *galant* style, sonata forms from North and South, counterpoint, *opera seria*, *opera buffa*, the techniques of Schobert and Johann Christian Bach: Wolfgang tried out all of these means of expression and used them as he pleased. Speaking Italian fluently and French correctly, he read a great deal, including authors said to be serious, including the German poet Christian Gellert, the Swiss writer Salomon Gessner, and the French ecclesiastic and writer François Fénelon.

Masses, minuets for dancing, cassations made up of a suite of small pieces played at official banquets, wedding feasts and solemn sessions at the university: the commissions came thick and fast. As he wrote his first serenade, a piece more elegant and more distinguished than a cassation, Wolfgang knew that it would be played only once, in the open air and at the end of the evening, to the glory of the person who had commissioned it. A Salzburg notable wanted some music of his own, which had never been heard before and which could be consumed like a tasty dish. Afterwards, it would vanish. Having it played a second time would have profoundly annoyed the buyer and discredited the composer.

This hard work obliged Wolfgang to work quickly, while mastering many facets of musical discourse. It also had a sad consequence: he tore up the map of Rücken, for that imaginary realm had disappeared. The reality of Salzburg banished dreams.

Berlin, summer 1769

The tension between Austria and Prussia was becoming dangerous. At stake was the possible partition of Poland. Therefore, after dismantling a number of monasteries in Austria to use their possessions for charitable works and educational projects, Emperor Josef decided to meet the redoubtable Friedrich II, who had ruled Prussia since 1740.

A man who spoke French to human beings and German to animals, an admirer of the Encyclopedists and Voltaire, and a Freemason, Friedrich never hesitated to use his army, demanding from his soldiers the 'discipline of a corpse'.

Josef wanted to avoid a new conflict, which would deal a fatal blow to the peace obtained with such difficulty at the end of the Seven Years' War. So the Prussian menace must be dispelled in order to attend to the real peril, Turkish expansion.

While negotiations began, the designated successor to the Prussian throne, Friedrich Wilhelm, was exploring the occult sciences. Worldly, superficial Freemasonry bored him. On the other hand, a specialist who had just settled in Berlin interested him, and he decided to make his life easier by giving him a post as a curator at the library.

His new protégé, Dom Antoine-Joseph Pernety, born at Roanne on 13 February 1716, was no ordinary man. Former chaplain to the navigator Bougainville, defender of the Indians, he had left the Benedictine Order to indulge his interest in Freemasonry, the Kabbalah, hermeticism and alchemy. In his books *Egyptian Fables* and the *Dictionary of Myths and Hermeticism*, he claimed to decipher the teachings of the ancients. He had had to leave Avignon because he was under investigation by the police, who were becoming more and more of a threat.

Here in Germany he could develop his Hermetic Rite in complete freedom, in the hope of contacting the spirits who would reveal to him the technique for manufacturing alchemical gold. He would teach initiates how to question the Holy Word and how to interpret its enigmatic declarations using Hebraic numerology. In his lodge, the Persecuted Virtue, he would go beyond conventional Freemasonry by celebrating two higher degrees, Novice and Enlightened One.

Thamos had been informed by von Gebler of Dom Pernety's arrival, and hoped the newcomer would prove equal to his ambitions.

At their first meeting, Pernety was on the defensive. He was nervous of the charismatic Egyptian, but thought his origins and his knowledge of the Eastern Mysteries might be useful, so he agreed to initiate him into the Hermetic Rite. The ceremony began with the celebration of a mass. Next, he consecrated the new follower at the top of a hill where stood an 'altar of power', at the centre of a circle drawn on the ground.

Thamos was instructed that for nine days he must gaze upon the sunrise at this point and burn incense on the altar. It was for God to recognize the new initiate, by manifesting himself in the form of an angel, who would henceforth act as his guide and with whom he could converse.

When Thamos went back down the hill for the ninth time, Dom Pernety knew that he had survived the ordeal, and therefore revealed to him the extent of his plans.

'By following the right way, the real Freemason will become a Knight of the Golden Key. He will relive the journey of the Argonauts and discover the Golden Fleece. Raised to the rank of Knight of the Sun, he will read mythological legends with an alchemist's eye. And when the philosopher's stone shines forth, the initiate will worship the Most Holy Virgin.'

It would take Dom Pernety months, even years, to compose the whole of his Hermetic Rite, assuming King Friedrich tolerated his presence and Friedrich Wilhelm continued to protect him. Would all this hard work yield convincing results? As he travelled along the road to Salzburg, Thamos wanted to hope so.

24

Salzburg, 5 November 1769

As he entered the office of Prince-Archbishop Sigismund von Schrattenbach, Leopold Mozart was still thinking about the blunder committed by his son. On 15 October, at the Church of St Peter, his solemn mass had been sung in honour of the ordination and first celebration of the Reverend Father Cajetan Hagenauer. An almost dull commission – if one of the solos of the Kyrie had not begun in waltz rhythm! Wolfgang saw nothing wrong in it. Why must religious music be boring?

Fortunately, this grave mistake had escaped the attention of the authorities and, on 27 October, Wolfgang had been appointed court Konzertmeister ('concert master'), an honorary and unsalaried post. This was not enough to make Leopold alter the plan that he had been mulling over for almost a year.

'Is there a problem, Herr Mozart? asked the archbishop.

'No, Your Grace. It's just that . . .'

'Yes?'

'I have a request to make of you.'

'Regarding your son, I assume?'

'That is so.'

'But I have granted him a title which ought to delight such a young musician.'

'Wolfgang is already a remarkable technician, but he still lacks some essential elements if he is to become a great composer whose renown would add to that of our dear principality.'

'Are you asking permission to leave on another journey?'

'Indeed, Your Grace.'

'What is your destination this time?'

'Italy. Its tradition and its musical treasures will complete my son's training.'

Heart in mouth, Leopold awaited the archbishop's decision.

'Very well, Herr Mozart. But during your absence, no salary will be paid to you.'

Salzburg, 11 December 1769

'When will you be back?' Anton Stadler asked Wolfgang.

'In a few months. Everything will depend on the success of the concerts.'

'On one hand, I hope they're a triumph; on the other, I'd like to see you again as soon as possible.'

'My father will decide, as usual.'

'Don't you sometimes feel like rebelling?'

'Next in line after God there's Papa. Without him, I wouldn't be a musician. And Italy – how wonderful!'

The two friends parted, and Wolfgang returned home. There he embraced his mother and sister, who were staying at home this time. Now eighteen, Nannerl was no longer a child prodigy, did not compose and did not have sufficient personality to make her way as a soloist. On the other hand, she would be a good piano teacher and would be able to help her mother look after the family home.

Wolfgang found a carriage equipped with boards, an inkwell and music manuscript paper. There was no longer any question of dreaming about an imaginary kingdom. During this journey, he would be creating musical pieces destined for his forthcoming concerts in Italy.

As soon as the wheels began turning, he started work. Four charming symphonies were born during the journey.

Mantua, 16 January 1770

During a marathon concert, Wolfgang had played fourteen works, some of them his own. He was exhausted, and all he wanted to do was sleep, but Leopold was exulting in his son's success and in the money taken.

'Bravo, my boy! Our Italian campaign has got off to the best possible start. And, believe me, this is only a beginning. I don't much like this name Amadeus which the Verona *Gazette* has landed you with. It may be a translation of Gottlieb, 'beloved of God', but I prefer the original. Amadeus doesn't sound serious – more like an Italian joke. Remember that our name, Mozart, comes from the Old High German *muot-harti* and means "courageous" or "determined".'

Milan, 23 January 1770

Count Karl von Firmian was governor-general of Lombardy and nephew to the former Archbishop of Salzburg. He greeted the Mozarts warmly and offered them comfortable lodgings within his palace.

'Milan is a wealthy city, and fond of music. You will enjoy yourself very much here, particularly as the carnival is just beginning. As a welcoming gift, here are nine books containing all the opera libretti of the great Metastasio.'

Leopold thanked him effusively.

'Of course,' added the governor, 'you will give several concerts here and you will hear beautiful music, notably that of Piccinni and Sammartini.'

Wolfgang's gaiety charmed his famous colleagues, who swallowed their jealousy and even murmured vague compliments.

On 3 February, a few days after celebrating his birthday, the fourteen-year-old boy composed an aria on Latin words from the Gospel, designed to be sung by a castrato of his own age. With sly irony, he made sure to emphasize the phrase: 'Seek the things of above and not those of below.'

After a grand concert given on 23 February, father and son sampled the eccentricities of the Milan carnival. On the last day of the festivities, 3 March, numerous decorated carts processed along the streets of the city, which were thronged with people in masks.

One of them asked Wolfgang, 'Are you enjoying yourself?

'It's a bit noisy, but the colours are magnificent and I do like late winter.'

'Are you pleased with your latest compositions?'

'The Italians like them.'

'You don't seem to have understood my question.'

Wolfgang suddenly recognized the voice. 'You're the man from Rücken, aren't you?'

'It's just a mask . . .'

'Rücken no longer exists. I destroyed the map of it.'

'I know, Wolfgang. That is why I am asking you to think about my question.'

Milan, 12 March 1770

During the farewell concert given at Count von Firmian's palace, several arias by Wolfgang, to texts by Metastasio, were performed. Like the other technical experts who attended, Leopold noted definite progress. His son was beginning to learn how to handle the voice, that most exceptional of instruments.

Amazed by the young German's performance, the count

drew Leopold aside. 'Magnificent, Herr Mozart, quite magnificent! Your son has conquered Milan. You must continue your journey – I understand that and applaud it – but you must come back. I am going to give you a good reason to do so: an opera.'

'You mean . . . a commission?'

'Given Wolfgang's gifts, it is a genre which should suit him. The Italians are crazy about it! Does the idea appeal to you?'

'Of course, of course! What would the subject be?'

'The story of King Mithridates, written by a professional librettist, Vittorio Cigna-Santi, after a rather dull play by Racine, a French dramatist. I am convinced that Wolfgang will be able to get the best from this sombre story.'

'Is the opera needed urgently?'

'Don't worry. Explore Bologna, Rome and Naples, admire Italy's thousand marvels, and then come back to us. You shall have the libretto at an opportune moment.'

Almost drunk with excitement, Leopold thanked the all-powerful count. This journey promised to be filled with successes.

25

Lodi, 15 March 1770

During a halt on the road between Parma and Bologna, Wolfgang thought and thought about the masked man's question. Eventually, he understood.

After dinner, he shut himself in his room and scribbled strange notes on paper.

When Leopold woke his son, early in the morning, he examined the composition. 'What on earth is this?'

The boy rubbed his eyes. 'A string quartet.'

'It's a most peculiar one, and not very interesting – certainly not suitable for a concert.'

'I wasn't thinking of that.'

'Then what were you thinking of?'

'Of composing for myself, free from all obligation, just to make music. This quartet's only a way of entertaining myself; I'm sure I can do better.'

'Get ready quickly. We're leaving in an hour.'

Leopold attributed this oddity to the whims of adolescence, which would probably lead to nothing. After all, a professional musician must always satisfy the demands of his audience.

Christian Jacq

Bologna, 26 March 1770

During the grand concert staged at Count Pallavicini's house, a remarkable thing happened, attracting the attention of the audience as much as did the young German's performance.

The renowned scholar Padre Martini, from the Monastery of San Francesco, came to hear the foreign prodigy. As far back as the people of Bologna could remember, the scholar had rarely attended concerts. This Mozart lad must interest him enormously if he had temporarily abandoned his research.

The sixty-five-year-old monk never left the city, and had even turned down a post as choir master at St Peter's in Rome; he confined himself strictly to his monastic duties. Musicians from all over Europe came to consult him for, through his work on a monumental *History of Music*, whose first two volumes had recently been published, he had acquired unequalled knowledge. His library contained unique pieces of sheet music, some dating from the sixteenth century.

When Padre Martini approached Wolfgang, Leopold feared he was about to criticize or remonstrate with him. But the monk showed no trace of animosity, and invited the youth to come and see him at the monastery.

Wolfgang jumped at the chance. During two conversations with the illustrious scholar, he learned to perfect his command of counterpoint and of opera recitatives. In record time, he constructed a fugue which his teacher would have taken a whole day to compose.

Wolfgang was sorry to leave the peaceful monastery, which was dedicated to scholarship, and he promised Padre Martini to return.

114

Rome, 11 April 1770

After a stop in Florence, the Mozarts reached Rome at noon and rushed to St Peter's Basilica, not because of any religious impulse, but in order to admire the great monument.

It was there that the boy heard Allegri's *Miserere*, whose score never left the Sistine Chapel. Despite the work's complexity, Wolfgang memorized every note and later wrote it down, thus stealing one of the Eternal City's secrets.

'Is this etiquette really necessary in order to know God?' Wolfgang asked as he observed the ballet of Church dignitaries.

'Rome is a theatre,' replied Leopold. 'This ostentatious devotion doesn't guarantee a good and healthy faith.'

Wolfgang made a point of trying out the tourists' favourite experience and wrote immediately to his sister:

I had the honour to kiss Saint Peter's foot, in Saint Peter's Church, but as I have the misfortune to be too small, I, the old prankster Wolfgang Mozart, had to be lifted up to him!

The young lad, who liked to call himself 'the friend of the League of Numbers', because he enjoyed mathematical games so much, asked Nannerl to send him the rules of arithmetic, along with numerous examples, which he had mislaid.

Scarcely had the letter left for Salzburg when in the street Wolfgang and his father encountered a gentleman whom Leopold, to his astonishment, recognized.

After greeting them, Thamos said, 'I believe you lost this document.'

Wolfgang examined it immediately: it was the rules of arithmetic. They were accompanied by another booklet, dealing with Divine Proportion and the Golden Number, with a few examples of their use in musical rhythm.

'Aren't you the gentleman who came to our rescue in Paris?' asked Leopold.

Thamos smiled. 'I think Rome is safer than Paris, but beware of thieves. May God protect you.'

Leopold would have liked to converse longer, but did not dare detain the gentleman. As for Wolfgang, he did not reveal that he had known this envoy from another world for a long time.

In this month of November, Wolfgang had not only strolled through the streets of Rome: he had also produced a Kyrie for five sopranos, some quadrilles destined for Salzburg, two arias for soprano and a symphony in D major.

Despite the riches of the great city, Leopold wanted to continue their journey and discover what southern Italy had to offer.

Vienna, April 1770

Archduchess Marie-Antoinette, born in Vienna in 1755, was the much-cosseted younger daughter of François I of Lorraine and Maria Theresa. However, because of decisions made by her mother and Josef, her life took a demanding turn.

On 19 April Marie-Antoinette was married by proxy to the Dauphin of France, who had remained at Versailles. The marriage would put an end to the incessant wars between the Habsburgs and the Bourbons, thereby consolidating peace in Europe.

These bright prospects did not make Josef happy. The young Archduchess had both charm and intelligence, but she was frivolous and quite unaware of the difficulties of her task. She would have to leave the cocoon of Vienna and conquer a land which was not fond of foreigners – let alone Austrians. Moreover, France was in the grip of dangerous intellectuals

116

who were calling into question the secular bases of power, religion and society.

Marie-Antoinette dreamt of an easy life of excess, at the head of a brilliant court. She foresaw spending most of her time enjoying herself and sampling a thousand and one pleasures. She did not foresee the base acts, the jealousies, or the hatred; or that when she was alone there, so far from Vienna, nobody would come to her aid.

26

The Road to Naples, 12 May 1770

A burning sun made Leopold and Wolfgang's journey extremely arduous. Their carriage was stifling.

Suddenly, it halted. There was an animated conversation, shouts, and then a cry of pain.

Three hairy men, armed with knives, opened the door.

'Get out,' ordered the brigand chief. 'If you give us everything you possess, we may let you live.'

A shot rang out. One of the attackers howled, his shoulder covered with blood. A second bullet whistled past the chief's ear.

'Run!' he ordered.

The trio disappeared into a wheatfield.

'Don't move, Wolfgang. I shall go and see.' Leopold got down from the carriage and checked the surroundings.

There was nobody to be seen. Who had saved them? Fortunately, the coachman had only been knocked out. He recovered consciousness and felt capable of driving to the next stopping-place.

Hidden behind an old acacia tree, Thamos watched the carriage move away, reloaded his pistol, patted his horse and continued to follow his protégés.

Naples, 15 May 1770

Dirty, noisy and dangerous, Naples was not to the Mozarts' liking. And the court, which was as crowded as it was un-distinguished, did not improve their opinion. Nevertheless, they must charm a new audience, and Wolfgang dressed in a stage costume of flame-coloured watered silk, decorated with silver lace and with a sky-blue lining.

After the first piece he played, in which his virtuosity amazed even the most sceptical listeners, a member of the audience shouted, 'The boy is a sorcerer! And I know who is responsible for his power: the Evil One! His ring – his magic is contained in his ring. Make him take it off, and then let's see if he can still master the keyboard.'

The boy removed the ring and attacked a second piece, which was even more difficult than the first.

Penaud, his accuser, was the first to applaud, shouting: 'Amadeo, Amadeo!' It was not the Devil who gave power to the boy's fingers, but God.

Versailles, 16 May 1770

The court celebrated the marriage of the Dauphin to Marie-Antoinette, who officially became the Dauphine. Their union ushered in a peace which everyone had longed for but few had really believed could happen.

Countless rumours were circulating. According to some, the foreign princess was stupid, capricious and unbearable; others said she was calculating, authoritarian and merciless. Dull and ordinary, observed her opponents; fascinating and beautiful, declared her supporters. Would she consent to live at Versailles, or would she prefer Vienna?

Forgetting the controversial personality of the future Queen of France, thousands of revellers attended a gigantic fireworks display. Alas, the drunken and delirious crowd trampled upon one hundred and thirty-two unfortunates, who suffocated to death.

People prophesied a sinister reign for the Austrian princess, who was already to blame for a catastrophe.

Pompeii, 13 June 1770

The guardian of the ruins was astonished. 'You want to visit Pompeii?'

'If possible,' replied Leopold.

'It isn't very safe ... And your son seems very young to be interested in antiquities.'

'Don't deceive yourself,' retorted Wolfgang in annoyance. 'Show us around, if you please.'

'As you wish. But I warn you, it isn't pretty, and it's difficult to get around because of the holes. A lot of people turn back.'

'Come on,' persisted Wolfgang.

By the light of torches, the Mozarts explored the grottoes of the Sibyl of Cumes. Leopold soon grew tired and wanted to stop.

'I'm going on,' decided Wolfgang.

'Very well, but be careful. I'll wait for you here.'

The depth of the underground passages amazed the boy. He sensed a sacred atmosphere, imbued with the world beyond. Probably the gallery led to the invisible world, the source of all things.

Before a carving depicting the initiation of a woman into the Mysteries of Isis sat Thamos the Egyptian. Wolfgang felt an intense surge of wellbeing, as if he were gaining access to the heart of his imaginary realm.

'Have you studied the documents I gave you?' asked Thamos.

'Yes, and even experimented with them. With the aid of Divine Proportion, the notes harmonize better and the phrases come together without conflicting with one another.'

'May that proportion live in your heart and in your hand. If not, it would be only an inert technique. As you breathe Italy's air and are nourished by its sun, you will pass through a new stage. But the goal is still a long way off.'

'What is it?'

'Look at this carving. After a long probationary period, the woman is leaving the secular world in order to explore the world of the Great Mysteries. You are progressing along this path, but will you have the courage to explore the unknown without selling your soul?'

'I will!'

'The gods hear you, Wolfgang.'

'Who are you, and why do you protect me?'

'I shall see you again soon.'

Thamos disappeared into a gallery which, despite Wolfgang's entreaties, the guide refused to enter.

'It's too risky,' he decreed. 'And your father must be getting impatient.'

Rome, 5 July 1770

The Mozarts happily left the court of Naples and returned to Rome. A symphony, a *miserere* for three voices, canons, minuets, a short mass: Leopold was not displeased with the summer's tally. Whatever the circumstances, his son continued to compose.

On this sunny day, dressed in their finest clothes, father and son honoured an invitation to lunch from Cardinal Pallavicini at the palace of Quirinal. In addition to the excellent food there were two surprises, which the prelate announced with great dignity.

'First, I am to hand you a decree from His Holiness Pope Clement XIV, appointing Wolfgang Mozart a Knight of the Gold Spur.'

121

Leopold thought he had misheard. 'Your Eminence . . .'

'It is a very high distinction, which crowns a young talent about which His Holiness has heard great things. The Church is expecting your son to produce many religious works to its glory.'

'I shall ensure that he does, Eminence.'

'Next,' continued the cardinal, 'you are to be received in a private audience on 8 July by His Holiness at the palace of Santa Maria Maggiore.'

Bologna, 20 July 1770

The audience, which was very formal, bored Wolfgang to tears. How taken up these religious men were with their own importance! Representing God and possessing the absolute truth hadn't given them any sense of humour. Living among them, in their suffocating palaces, must render the most fecund creator sterile.

On the road from Rome to Bologna, on the other hand, the boy had enjoyed himself reading an Italian translation of a book of episodic tales, *The Thousand and One Nights*, a gift from his mysterious protector. Magic and fairyland would feed his imagination, and he glimpsed a series of characters worthy of featuring in an opera.

As soon as he arrived at Count Pallavicini's country house, Wolfgang was delighted to receive the libretto of *Mitridate, rè di Ponto*, which he could not wait to set to music. Starting work on this arduous commission did not prevent him going on donkey rides with one of the young boys of the family, who was the same age as he was.

Waited on hand and foot, Leopold finally took the time to have an unpleasant leg wound treated. And Wolfgang pursued his Italian dream.

27

Prague, August 1770

The rebirth of a Prague lodge, the Lodge of the Three Crowned Pillars, determined to question itself about the meaning of symbols, gave back a little hope to Ignaz von Born.

Born in 1742, in Transylvania, he had studied with the Jesuits before going on to study philosophy, law, the natural sciences and mineralogy at the University of Prague. Very early on, he had become interested in alchemy, and his research had led him towards Freemasonry, in which he hoped to discover the keys to knowledge.

It had proved a relative disappointment, because most of the Brothers were unimpressive and the rituals were feeble. But it had also confirmed his premonitions: beneath its mediocre façade, Freemasonry was the contemporary form of initiation into the Mysteries born in ancient Egypt. He must therefore trace it back to its source.

With tireless perseverance, Ignaz von Born followed the trail leading to the forgotten treasure. A great reader of ancient initiates such as Plutarch and Apulaeus,* and of treatises on

---

* The treatise *On Isis and Osiris* by the Greek Plutarch (A.D. 46–120) and the novel *The Golden Ass* by the Roman Apulaeus (A.D. 125–180) contain essential information about Egyptian initiations.

alchemy and hermetic texts which had come from Egypt and been known in the West since the eleventh century, he had pored over Horapollon's *Hieroglyphica*, translated into German in the sixteenth century. The author, whose name was drawn from the names of Horus and Apollo, two sun-gods, passed on a small part of the sacred science and revealed that hieroglyphs were a vehicle for esoteric knowledge of the utmost importance. Thus, Osiris appeared as the soul of the universe and the source of wisdom. And several works published during the seventeenth century provided von Born with valuable information.*

There was a new development in 1732: the translation into German of the novel *Séthos*, written the previous year by Abbé Jean Terrasson, professor of Greek and Latin philosophy at the Collège de France. The abbé mixed erudition with romantic elements, and the novel was said to be 'a work in which one finds described initiations into the Egyptian Mysteries'.

But all this was not enough. Convinced that the oral transmission of information had never been interrupted, von Born wondered if he would one day have the good fortune to encounter one of its guardians, the Unknown Superiors.

Three things were certain: first, without initiation the world would subside into chaos; next, initiation came from ancient Egypt and gave access to knowledge; finally, Freemasonry could serve as a crucible, a link with the past and a means of transmission for the present and the future.

Ignaz von Born's health was poor, because he had been seriously poisoned in the depths of a mine in Chemnitz, where he fulfilled the role of technical adviser; and he also suffered

* For example, the first collection of hieroglyphic inscriptions brought together by Horwarth von Hohenbourg in 1606; the revelation of the alchemical content of the hieroglyphs by Michel Maier in 1622; and the four volumes of *Oedipus aegyptiacus*, by Athanasius Kircher, which appeared between 1652 and 1654.

from chronic sciatica. Despite this handicap, he imposed a punishing work-rate on himself. Despising worldly things, and lacking any interest in success in his career, he lived frugally and shared his time between working as a mineralogist and his commitment to Freemasonry.

The majority of the lodges were just ticking over. The one that had just been reawakened in Prague, a city of alchemists, was to be a research centre, welcoming Brothers who wished to break out of this torpor and direct themselves towards the Mysteries of Isis and Osiris. Together, they would closely examine the symbols and rites, in order to discern their deep meaning.

The rebuilding of the temple was beginning.

28

Bologna, 10 October 1770

The members of the austere Accademia Filarmonica had gathered in solemn session to examine an application for membership. The severity of their judgement struck fear into even the most experienced musicians, and many preferred to give up rather than risk a humiliating rejection.

So several academicians were stunned to see that Padre Martini was accompanied by a fourteen-year-old boy, whom he introduced to them as a future colleague. Some were shocked, while others laughed behind their hands.

Wolfgang Mozart was shut away in a small room, and given a piece of Gregorian chant to transcribe for four voices. He had three hours in which to do it. Thirty minutes later, the candidate emerged from the room and, to everyone's surprise, presented his finished work to the learned assembly.

After it had been examined, the vote was unanimous: 'Satisfactory'.* Wolfgang became a member of the Accademia, and Padre Martini handed him a sort of certificate: 'I found Mozart well versed in all aspects of the musical art. What is more, he supplied me with proof, notably on the harpsichord,

* According to C. de Nys, Padre Martini had corrected Mozart's work, which he considered too original.

where I gave him several themes which he immediately developed in a masterly fashion, according to the rules.'

Milan, 20 October 1770

Wolfgang's fingers were sore after writing the recitatives for his opera. And he still had all the arias to compose. Perhaps this time the task was beyond him?

At times, his tiredness brought him to the verge of despair. But when he thought of the chance destiny was offering him, he set to work again, forgetting both amusements and rest.

As Leopold confided to his wife, 'Wolfgang is now dealing with serious things, which make him very serious himself.'

At the start of November, his son rebelled. 'I can just about cope with producing arias to measure for singers who are imposed on me. But being unable to alter the libretto in any way: that I cannot bear. And I don't like the story.'

'Calm yourself,' advised Leopold. 'That's the law of the genre: a librettist on one side, a composer on the other.'

'It's a bad law, and it ought to be changed.'

'Custom is custom, Wolfgang. Adapt to this subject.'

'A father and a son both in love with the same woman, a king who dies during an attack by the Romans and forgives his son for falling in love with another woman, and then grants the hand of his beloved to another son . . . It's difficult to recognize oneself in such an imbroglio, or to take any interest in it. It should be remodelled and cut, the principal characters should be given more depth, their actions should be better—'

'There isn't time for that. And you must learn to bow to the demands of your profession.'

Christian Jacq

Milan, 26 December 1770

At the first performance of *Mitridate, rè di Ponto* a spectator shouted: '*Viva el maestrino!*' and applause rang out. Enthroned as *signore cavaliere filarmonico*, Wolfgang spent a happy winter: twenty performances of his opera, a concert at Count von Firmian's house, and a few days' rest in Turin. He wrote a light symphony, the first in a series of six, which he ended with an exclamation: 'Finished, thanks be to God!'

At the end of this exhausting period, Wolfgang thought again about the question his mysterious friend had asked him. Was he really ready to write for himself, detaching himself from all outside influences?

The difficulty was like a mountain with an unattainable summit. But he would not give up trying to climb it.

Berlin, 27 December 1770

Thamos was not present at the first performance of *Mitridate*, because a letter from von Gebler had summoned him to Berlin, where Masonic events were gathering pace. It was the Egyptian's task to assess their importance and detect any positive aspects for the future of the Great Magician.

Thamos was greeted by Baron Gottfried van Swieten, who had been appointed ambassador to the court of King Friedrich. This high-ranking post enabled the baron to research the scores of a forgotten musician, Johann Sebastian Bach, and to take part – with extreme discretion – in Masonic life.

'What brings you to Berlin, Count of Thebes?'
'I hope to find out what is really happening.'
'Today Germany's Masonic Grand Lodge is born.'
'In your opinion, will it be favourable to the blossoming of thought regarding initiation?'

128

'I scarcely think so. Are you thinking of intervening in some way?'

'Not yet.'

Vienna, 31 December 1770

The freezing weather did not bother Josef Anton. Indifferent to the snowstorm raging outside, he was filing his paperwork when Geytrand arrived to give his report. The latter also loved the winter, and loathed the summer and its heat. A big eater, who never caught a cold, he took great pleasure in relentlessly tracking down the Freemasons.

'There's good news and bad news, Herr Count.'

'Let's begin with the good.'

'The Masonic Grand Lodge of Germany has just come into being. This rigid structure will make it easier to identify and control Freemasons. The king likes order and wants a well-structured administrative organization which he can control easily. Of course, he has excluded from managerial posts all individuals who are suspect or disliked by the powers that be, like Baron de Hund and the declared supporters of Strict Templar Observance. The victor is called Zinnendorf, and he's been appointed deputy Grand Master. He will place greater emphasis upon the Swedish Rite, which is already practised by several German lodges.

'Does the king favour the Swedish Rite?'

'He doesn't dislike it. His designated successor, Friedrich Wilhelm, is fascinated by the Golden Rose-Cross. He surrounds himself with a group made up of Brothers who belong to that Order, and strengthens Lutheranism in order to combat the rationalism and scientism that are flooding across Europe. The struggles for influence will be fierce. Fortunately, King Friedrich has a firm hand on the tiller and will not allow anyone to wander from the mainstream. Prussian discipline is not just a word: if he has to kill parasites and those who get in his way, he won't hesitate.'

'And what is the bad news?''

'A new lodge, the Lodge of the Three Eagles, was opened in Vienna yesterday.'

'Which Rite?'

'Strict Templar Observance.'

'Do you think it's dangerous?'

'All the founders are on file. They're good Christians, who belong to the petty nobility and the prosperous middle classes. They should prove respectful towards the law and the authorities. Besides, like so many others this lodge may not last long.'

'All the same we must be wary of it. The restoration of the Order of the Temple remains a fact, and I do not want to see that madness spread in Austria. Fill in a detailed file card on each new Brother and continue to develop our network of informers.'

29

Milan, 31 January 1771

The celebrations at the end of the year provided the Mozarts with a pleasant moment of relaxation. Of course, it pained them to be separated from Anna Maria and Nannerl, but the warm hospitality of their Milanese hosts at least partly compensated for their absence.

If Leopold was dragging his feet a little before heading back to Salzburg, it was not without reason. *Mitridate*'s success had attracted the attention of Italy's music-lovers and proved to them that the young lad from Salzburg had no lack of talent. Logically, they ought not to leave it at that.

Leopold's predictions proved correct: Milan commissioned a new opera from Wolfgang for the opening of the 1772–1773 season. To their great joy, father and son were able to leave Italy in the certainty that they would soon be returning to charm a vast public.

Venice, 20 February 1771

Reaching the city of the Doges on 10 February, Shrove Tuesday, the Mozarts decided to enjoy themselves for a few days. They attended receptions and went to several concerts – but only in the audience. They made sure to conform to the local custom of going everywhere by gondola. The first few nights, when Wolfgang was sleeping he felt as though his bed was swaying.

One day, when he was enjoying having a small gondola all to himself, he hummed an aria from his forthcoming opera.

'Light and sparkling,' observed the gondolier.

Wolfgang recognized the voice instantly. 'It's you! Have you have moved to Venice?'

'Like you,' said Thamos, 'I travel a great deal.'

'I haven't forgotten your question, but I rarely have a minute to myself. I am overwhelmed with commissions, and my father allows me very little leisure. Venice is an exception.'

'I was not asking you to respond soon. Don't let yourself be deceived either by success or by failure, and attach no value to the world's noise. Attempting to charm it will lead you nowhere, for it is not the world that will create you. And you have not yet seen the light of day, Wolfgang.'

'But . . . but I've been born. In Salzburg.'

'That was your physical birth. Next you were born to music, then to composition. As you die to childhood, and soon to adolescence, you will be born to manhood. And all these stages may perhaps lead you to spiritual birth.'

'What do you mean?'

'Here we are. Your father is waiting for you on the quayside.'

Padua, 12 March 1771

After a grand concert in Venice on 5 March, the Mozarts set off back to Salzburg. The nobility of Venice had been much taken with Wolfgang, though they disliked his father, whom they considered to be perpetually discontented. Cantankerous Leopold would never return to this damp and pretentious city.

During a day spent in Padua, Wolfgang gave a series of small concerts and received a commission to write a Lenten oratorio. On 17 March, the day after a stop in Verona, Leopold received excellent news: Milan had confirmed its request for a new opera, and the Viennese court wanted a work for the occasion of Archduke Ferdinand of Austria's marriage to an Italian princess.

Everything was happening for the best in the best of all worlds.

Salzburg, 28 March 1771

Anna Maria kissed Wolfgang tenderly, and threw her arms round her husband's neck; he had been away for fifteen months. Nannerl had become a little woman, and showed greater reserve. Deep down, she hadn't missed her brother so very much.

Wolfgang found himself back in the family home without any particular joy. His boyhood room seemed rather cramped after his various stays in sumptuous palaces.

That evening, he saw his friend Anton Stadler and told him all about his exploration of Italy.

'Well, here you are,' said Anton, 'a Knight of the Golden Spur – and that's not exactly nothing.'

'I'm afraid so,' replied Wolfgang.

'Such a high honour at your age! The whole principality will be throwing itself at your feet.'

'I'm afraid not.'

'And what about the Pope? Did you like him?'

'No, he was too starchy. You'd swear great prelates swallow an overdose of vanity every day.'

'Don't say things like that in Salzburg! You could land yourself in serious difficulties.'

'Don't worry, I shan't say them to anyone but you.'

Knowing he would soon see Italy again, Wolfgang took

advantage of this interlude in Salzburg to compose church music the archbishop would like, but also light, cheerful symphonies intended for future concerts in Italy.

Prague, April 1771

After closing the lodge's session, Ignaz von Born invited the visiting Brother, the Count of Thebes, to explore his library.

With his long face, expansive forehead, dark, shining eyes and slight smile, the mineralogist was nothing like the other Freemasons Thamos had met. This time, he detected a true depth, an inner fire of rare intensity and a burning desire to experience the great Mysteries.

'Are you really from Egypt?' asked von Born.

'From the monastery of Abbot Hermes, the master who taught me everything.'

Thamos was reading the titles of the books collected by his host. 'Our own library contained this knowledge, and much more besides. From his predecessors, Abbot Hermes had received manuscripts revealing the wisdom of the initiates of ancient Egypt.'

Von Born dug his fingernails into his palms to assure himself that he was not dreaming. Never had he hoped to hear such a clear declaration, the crown of long years' research.

'Would you be willing to pass on this secret knowledge?'

'My mission is exactly that. According to Abbot Hermes, the tradition of initiation is to be reborn here, in Europe.'

'Won't Freemasonry be its channel?'

'One of the channels,' Thamos corrected him, 'as long as a few lodges choose the path of initiation. Following our fathers' example, we must formulate, transmit and reveal without betraying. And then there is the Great Magician. He will have the power to create a new form of expression, capable of giving birth to a new horizon.'

'Does such a person really exist?'

'He is fifteen years old and his name is Wolfgang Mozart. Despite a career as a child prodigy in Vienna, Paris and London, which could well have broken him, he is building up his true nature little by little. The road will still be a long one before he becomes fully aware, and makes Light the main material for his work. Without him, we can achieve only poor results. You and I must therefore devote ourselves to the full flowering of Mozart, who will radiate far beyond his own existence and his own time.'

The gravity of Thamos's tone and the scope of his prediction impressed von Born.

'In what way can I help you?'

'Develop your research lodge in Prague, with the aid of the parts of *The Book of Thoth* that I shall entrust to you. Deepen the rituals, awaken the perceptions of your Brothers, incline them towards knowledge. Sooner or later you will go to Vienna, and there you will play a determining part. It is your task to build a temple where the soul of the Great Magician will take flight. For my part, I shall protect him by trying to remove as many obstacles as possible from his path and ensuring that he avoids dangerous snares. But only the gods and Mozart himself hold the keys to his destiny.'

After Thamos had left, von Born remained motionless for many hours in the darkness. Would he be worthy of carrying out his new duties?

30

Salzburg, 24 June 1771

While writing two works for ceremonies in honour of the Virgin, Wolfgang had experienced a real mystical surge, even if his music, sometimes close to opera, was moving noticeably away from the usual. On this St John's day, his new religious composition was being performed, an Offertory for four voices, in which a touching fervour was expressed.

As the composer was leaving the church Johann Baptiste, a monk at the monastery of Seeon, stopped him.

'We are friends, my dear Wolfgang, and I want to offer you my sincere congratulations. How happy I am to see that you are still a faithful believer, particularly devoted to the cult of Mary. A few evil tongues have accused you of handling some of your masses in a light-hearted manner, but I don't believe a word of it. On the other hand, writing too many operas and symphonies carries the risk of distorting your inspiration.'

'Er . . . why?'

'Because light music moves people further away from God.'

'Doesn't He like opera?'

'Wolfgang! How dare you ask such a question?'

'And what about you? How dare you attempt to indoctrinate me and restrict my freedom in the name of a belief?'

'A belief? A belief? But this is religion, my friend, the truth!'

'Go back to your monastery. I'm going to write an oratorio for Italy.'

Angrily, the monk turned on his heel.

Wolfgang was already thinking about *La Betulia liberata*, the tragic subject he was to set to music for Padua. The libretto was again by the celebrated Metastasio – the young musician secretly considered his poetry rather mediocre, though he would take care to keep that opinion to himself. It was up to Wolfgang to glorify the character of Judith, victor over the Assyrians. The instrument of God's will, she killed the tyrant Holophernes and carried back his head to Betulia, thus freeing that oppressed land.

Milan, 31 August 1771

Delighted to be making their second trip to Italy, Leopold and Wolfgang had reached Milan on 20 August. The marriage of Archduke Ferdinand of Austria was planned for the middle of October, so Wolfgang must once again climb a steep-sided mountain and accomplish a titanic task.

He composed day and night in a vast house full of musicians who were always tuning their instruments, rehearsing, sight-reading and humming. Despite the continual noise Wolfgang managed to concentrate, and he encountered only one obstacle: his fingers were soon tired with so much writing. His sole entertainment consisted of talking in signs with their host's son, a deaf mute. The two adolescents got on wonderfully well, and their infectious gaiety relaxed the atmosphere.

Leopold was still anxious. There was so little time left in which to finish the opera! And when Venice also requested one, he was forced to decline the offer.

His son tried to reassure him. 'I promise you I'll be ready in time.'

'I have every confidence in you, but there are the others, all

137

the others. And so many incompetents and jealous people . . . If evil attacks people from both sides, it brings great danger.'

'We'll overcome it.'

Milan, 17 October 1771

The music of *Ascanio in Alba* was finished on 23 September, the rehearsals began on the 28th, and the premiere of this 'theatrical serenade' in two acts took place on the planned day, that of the wedding of Archduke Ferdinand of Austria to Maria Beatrice Ricciardia d'Este of Modena.

Once again, Wolfgang had produced a miracle. With each new achievement, Leopold was astonished by his son's creative abilities. How far back would he push his limits?

The author of the libretto, Giuseppe Parini, had produced one of those convoluted texts with which the musician had to struggle manfully. The goddess Venus wanted her son, Ascanio, to marry Silvia. An easy marriage? No, for first she must be put to the test. So Cupid brought Silvia to Ascanio, whom she did not know, and whose name was not revealed to her. Instantly she fell in love. Unfortunately, the young woman was promised to a certain . . . Ascanio. Faithful to her growing love, she swore that she would reject this unknown stranger. And so she passed the test. Ascanio married Silvia under the protection of Venus.

The spectators at the ducal Teatro Regio in Milan hailed the music of the German *maestrino* as a triumph. The most enthusiastic was Archduke Ferdinand, who applauded for all he was worth and was the first to congratulate the young composer and his father.

'Herr Mozart, your son will have a great career! I shall write to my mother, the empress, asking her to grant him a permanent post at the Viennese court.'

No words could have been sweeter to Leopold's ears.

The Great Magician

Milan, 2 November 1771

After finishing a symphony in F major, Wolfgang wrote to his sister:

> *Today is the performance of* Ruggiero, *Hasse's opera; but as Papa doesn't go out, I can't go. Fortunately I know all the arias by heart; so I can see and hear everything at home.*

The reason why Leopold seldom went out was that he was champing at the bit as he waited, with growing impatience, for the empress's response. Thanks to this first great success and the archduke's support, he was about to attain the goal he had set himself so long ago: to obtain a stable, well-paid post in Vienna for Wolfgang.

Pacing up and down like a wild animal in a cage, Leopold went several times to the archduke's palace to find out if the letter from Maria Theresa had arrived at last.

Returning, disappointed, once again, he found his son playing the clarinet. 'What use is that?' he demanded. 'We never use them in Salzburg.'

'It is going to feature in a divertimento which has been commissioned from me by a lover of the instrument.'

Given the size of the fee, Leopold was somewhat mollified. Besides, Wolfgang needed to occupy his mind during this interminable wait.

On giving this superb clarinet to the Great Magician, Thamos had emphasized its importance with a view to future works. The depth of its song would express the Mysteries of the soul, with warmth and solemnity. The universe was full of melodies, and it was opening up.

Milan, 30 November 1771

Leopold was in a terrible mood. Despite the freezing rain, he was determined to take Wolfgang to see the archduke, the better to fight his cause. While they were crossing the Domo square, they saw four bandits being hanged. Remembering the misadventure in Paris, Leopold walked faster.

The archduke's private secretary consented to receive them, but said, 'I am sorry, Herr Mozart, His Highness is not here.'

'Has he left any messages for me?'

'No, none.'

Clearly, Leopold thought, Archduke Ferdinand was avoiding the Mozarts. Since the response from Vienna had not come, and would perhaps never come, it was pointless for them to stay in Milan any longer.

'We'll go back to Salzburg,' he decided.

31

Milan, 12 December 1771

Archduke Ferdinand was glad the Mozarts had gone. He greatly admired the son's talent but could dislike the father's character and obstinacy. And it wasn't his fault if the answer from his mother was taking so long. The empress had other concerns besides the engagement of a musician.

At last, Maria Theresa's decision arrived. As he read it, the archduke sighed:

> *You ask me to take the young boy from Salzburg into my service. I do not know what as, since I do not believe I have need of a composer or useless people ... It debases service when people roam the world like beggars! Besides, Mozart has a large family.*

Evidently, while the empress was alive Wolfgang would never be employed at the Viennese court.

Ferdinand summoned his secretary. 'Inform Herr Mozart that Her Majesty is no longer recruiting musicians. She is satisfied with her current staff and has no intention of increasing it.'

Salzburg, 16 December 1771

Leopold's mood was not improving. To fail when he was so close to his goal! For he was sure by now that the empress's decision would be in the negative – assuming she even bothered to reply. And her worldly little son would not dare cross her by fighting for an insignificant musician from Salzburg.

All that effort, and for nothing! Despite the success of *Ascanio in Alba*, the balance sheet for this second stay in Italy had proved disappointing. What use was the public's applause if it did not translate into a permanent position?

Still, at least there was Salzburg. The good archbishop would surely offer Wolfgang a salaried post if he promised never to leave the city again.

As soon as he crossed the threshold of his apartment, Leopold felt the heaviness of the atmosphere.

Handkerchief in hand, her eyes red, Anna Maria did not rush to greet her husband, but remained hunched in an armchair. Beside her, Nannerl seemed equally woebegone.

'What has happened?' he asked.

'Our dear archbishop is dying, and he was due to celebrate fifty years as a priest on 10 January next, with a great festival. How cruel fate is! The whole of Salzburg is weeping.'

Leopold ran to the palace. When he got there, Sigismund von Schrattenbach had just departed this vale of tears to appear before his creator.

Distraught, Leopold saw the future darken. With that amiable and easy-going cleric, it had always been possible to come to an arrangement. What would it be like with his successor? Then there was the matter of Wolfgang's new work, *Il sogno di Scipione* ('Scipio's Dream'), specifically intended for the archbishop. The dedication would have to be altered, and perhaps even the work itself, depending on the tastes of the new master of Salzburg.

The name of Hieronymus, Count Colloredo was whispered in the corridors of the palace. Judging by their long faces and hangdog looks, the staff were already missing Schrattenbach.

Vienna, 30 December 1771

'A new lodge, The Three Sisters, has been set up in Vienna,' Geytrand informed Josef Anton.

'Who's in charge?'

'Barriochi, a silk merchant.'

'Which Rite does the lodge follow?'

'The Golden Rose-Cross. The mystics are launching an attack on Vienna, but their chances of success are slim. Many Freemasons loathe them, and they won't find recruitment easy.'

'Have we any good informants there?'

'Not yet, but it shouldn't take long. There are bound to be disappointed men with loose tongues.'

'Keep a permanent watch on the lodge. I want the names of all the Brothers involved in its work.'

Salzburg, January 1772

Outside, it was snowing. In the Mozarts' apartment, the atmosphere was one of sadness. Wolfgang was unwell with a persistent fever, and had not composed anything since finishing a little symphony in A major. Because of his fever, even his friend Anton Stadler wasn't allowed to see him.

Leopold knew that the Viennese court remained closed to Wolfgang, and the situation in Salzburg worried him enormously. Would Colloredo promote Leopold for length of service, or would he dismiss him? And what lay in store for Wolfgang? Would the new archbishop allow his musicians to travel?

To learn the answers to these questions, he would have to wait for the election, which was fixed for 14 March. The people of Salzburg disliked Colloredo, because his family were vassals of the Habsburgs and there was a risk that, under his reign, the principality would lose much of its autonomy and become more dependent on Vienna. Perhaps this obstacle would be insurmountable, but in that case who would accede to power?

Shortly after his sixteenth birthday, Wolfgang's health improved. He composed a little sonata for four hands which he played with Nannerl, then some church sonatas, *divertimenti* for string quartet, and symphonies which would be performed in Milan during their next tour. Under the watchful eye of Leopold, who was most attentive and demanded classicism and melodies that were in good taste, the boy worked on *Il sogno di Scipione*, the gift the Mozarts would make to the new archbishop.

Salzburg, 14 March 1772

'Has a decision been reached?' Leopold asked one of his colleagues.

'Not yet. There have already been five ballots, and they're still going on. Count Colloredo is hardly a unanimous choice: he's haughty, contemptuous, authoritarian, arrogant in himself but subservient to the Habsburgs – which is enough to make him hated by everyone in Salzburg. Unfortunately, he has eliminated his competitors, and nobody dares oppose him. What's more, he's proclaiming that he's in full agreement with Emperor Josef's reforms, including severe economy measures. And we musicians are directly concerned!'

144

A burning sensation tore through Leopold's stomach. He saw himself on the street, obliged to leave his apartment and struggle against poverty.

Suddenly, there was great agitation. Someone was pushing open the door of the council chamber.

The spokesman waited for complete silence before revealing the result of the vote. 'Following several ballots, Hieronymus Franz de Paula, Count Colloredo, has been elected Prince-Archbishop of Salzburg.'

32

Salzburg, 18 March 1772

Anna Maria reread the front page of the *Salzburger Intelligenzblatt*, the official newspaper that every Wednesday reported the major events at court. It was devoted to the difficult election of Colloredo, whose enthronement was to take place at the end of April.

'Will the new archbishop look favourably on us?' she asked anxiously.

Leopold scowled. 'He's an admirer of that hateful dog Voltaire and that imbecile Rousseau. We have everything to fear.'

'But if you lose your job, what will become of us?'

'We must pray to the Lord to protect us.'

Even before taking power, Colloredo proceeded to reorganize the various departments in his court, notably his body of musicians.

Leopold was summoned to the palace in order to learn his fate. Because of his local fame, his success with his violin-teaching method and his excellent service, he felt he deserved the post of Kapellmeister. Some whispered that his supporters had persuaded Colloredo to grant it to him.

All the court musicians were gathered in the palace concert hall. They waited nervously for more than an hour for the archbishop's spokesman to appear.

'His Eminence appoints as Kapellmeister Signor Fischietti, an artist with an excellent style. Leopold Mozart is confirmed in his office of deputy Kapellmeister. For reasons of economy, the Opera will be closed and the length of masses reduced by half. Nevertheless, the high quality of musical performance must be maintained. The archbishop expects thoroughness and dedication from you. Gentlemen: to work.'

Salzburg, 29 April 1772

Disappointed not to have been promoted, but relieved that he had kept his post, Leopold accepted the situation. At least Salzburg remained a firm anchor, to which Wolfgang would eventually become attached.

In accordance with his father's instructions, he had composed some conventional litanies, in which Leopold had demanded many corrections before they were presented to the archbishop.

The first work by Wolfgang to be heard by Colloredo produced neither a negative reaction nor any particular interest. A lover of the Italian style, the lord of Salzburg was planning to alter musical taste and ensure that everyone followed his lead. Since the beginning of April, several academies* had enabled notables to listen to work by Johann Christian Bach, Sammartini and other light, worldly composers.

Today, 29 April, was the date of his enthronement and his day of glory. Count Colloredo was coming to power and would put right the mistakes of his predecessors, who had been far too lax. Despite his determination to control expenditure, he accorded himself a sumptuous ceremony, at which he appeared in full regalia.

He was uninterested in *Il sogno di Scipione*, a dramatic

* The name given to concerts.

serenade in one act and twelve musical numbers by young Wolfgang Mozart, to a libretto by Metastasio. So the little work would never be performed, although the story was worthy of interest.

Scipio dreamt that two goddesses, Constance and Fortune, appeared to him and demanded that he choose one of them as his protectress. Wishing to think about it carefully, he had himself transported to the heavens, among his ancestors. And the right decision made itself clear: when he returned to earth, he would ask the more beautiful of the goddesses, Constance, to watch over him, and he would discount Fortune's inevitable anger.

Leopold was careful not to utter any protest against his august patron's decision. As for Wolfgang, like Scipio he overcame misfortune and continued to find constant inspiration. In May and June he wrote three symphonies, a brilliant *Regina coeli*, whose style was close to that of opera, and a divertimento featuring new instrumental combinations which would not shock the archbishop.

The boy often thought of his all-too-brief encounters with the man from Rücken, each of whose words counted more than hundreds of hours of sermons. Wolfgang could not yet manage to prolong them in music, but he would never give up.

Kohlo, 4 June 1772

In Kohlo, near Pfoerdten, there was to be a general assembly which would be crucial for the future of Strict Templar Observance. Baron de Hund would gladly have avoided the ordeal, but the senior officials of the Order had demanded this meeting in order to cast light on several obscure points.

The trouble emanated from an aristocrat who was very

interested in the secret sciences, Ferdinand, Duke of Brunswick, victor of the Battle of Minden.*

A serious crisis threatened to erupt and destroy the whole structure of the Order.

Between two extremely lively sessions of discussion, the baron and the duke walked in the large park, in the shade of the chestnut trees.

'Given our continuing financial difficulties,' said the duke, 'we are having to increase the fees paid by lodges and Brothers. But the main reason for discontent concerns the origin of your Masonic authority. It must be admitted, my dear Brother, that you appointed yourself leader of the Order. Because of its expansion, we ought to proceed to a properly constituted election.'

'But I'm the only Brother to have met an Unknown Superior, from Egypt.'

'That argument does not work in your favour – on the contrary, in fact. Our Knights no longer wish to be directed by mysterious men whom nobody can see. They prefer a public personality, honourably known, whose reputation will reflect well on that of the Order.'

'You are speaking of yourself, I assume?'

'I am ready to devote myself unstintingly to ensuring the development and wealth of Strict Templar Observance,' declared the Duke of Brunswick.

Baron de Hund gritted his teeth. This arrogant soldier wanted to steal away his child, the Order he had devised, created and developed.

* His Knightly name was *Eques a victoria*.

33

Vienna, July 1771

'Strict Templar Observance has taken on a new lease of life,' Geytrand told his superior. 'The Knights have just elected as their leader Ferdinand, Duke of Brunswick, an illustrious man with a spotless reputation.'

'And Baron de Hund agreed?' asked Josef Anton in astonishment.

'Well, no. He did everything he could to keep his title of Provincial Grand Master. But he's finished; nobody will listen to him any more.'

'Unless he rebels and starts plotting against the duke.'

'He wouldn't be able to, not against Ferdinand.'

Anton agreed that an aristocrat of such standing gave Strict Observance an unhoped-for status.

'Brunswick has got what he wanted,' Geytrand went on, 'but will he be able to use the instrument he has stolen from his dear Brother? According to my informants, the Templars are divided about which path to follow. The clerical branch advocates the occult sciences and mysticism, whereas the knightly branch wishes to create wealth and restore the temporal power of the Order of the Temple. They're mad!'

'All the same, we must be careful,' said Josef Anton. 'Charles de Hund was merely a dreamer; Brunswick is a man of action.

We must keep a very close watch on the development of Strict Observance in Austria and be prepared to act if necessary.'

Geytrand was delighted by the prospect.

Salzburg, 15 August 1772

After finishing three small symphonies, Wolfgang was playing skittles with Anton Stadler. Wolfgang was fast and accurate, and won the game by a clear margin.

'You've certainly recovered your health,' said Anton. 'But I'm sure you don't know about the serious event that's happened without our realizing.'

'What are you talking about? It sounds interesting.'

'Do you really want to know?'

'Don't keep me in suspense.'

Anton assumed a solemn expression. 'I'm nineteen and you're sixteen. We aren't children any more, we're well and truly young men. So it's right for us to assert ourselves and no longer behave like little boys, especially in the face of—'

Leopold burst in, shouting, 'Wonderful news! The archbishop has appointed Wolfgang Konzertmeister, with a salary of one hundred and fifty florins.'

The title was as modest as the pay that went with it, but nevertheless everyone celebrated this first salaried post over one of the delicious meals that the Mozarts' cook had the knack of producing.

Wolfgang received a strange present, three small poems entitled '*Die grossmütige Gelassenheit*' ('Generous Resignation'), '*Geheime Liebe*' ('Secret Love') and *Die Zufriedenheit* ('The Happiness of the Humble'), which he immediately set to music, while reflecting on the message his mysterious protector had sent him in this way.

To accept one's destiny; to become resigned, without

withering away and without feeling either rancour or envy; to continue to show generosity, whatever the circumstances: such a rule of life implied a detachment and liberation from the self which the young man did not yet feel capable of. To keep secret his love of the truth and the absolute, to understand that this love was the true secret, to attempt to experience it as the principal force of creation: each day Wolfgang was making progress in this direction, but with no certainty that he would attain his goal. The happiness offered through humility; true pride, which consisted of becoming aware of one's own authentic nature ... This path demanded perpetual toil, and was strewn with many failures.

In only a few words, Thamos had opened the gates of life as a man to the Great Magician.

Alt-Sedlitsch, September 1772

Because of his precarious health, Ignaz von Born could no longer work underground in the mines, so he had resigned and settled in a small town in Bohemia. Within his modest house he had set up a tiny alchemical laboratory, where he patiently continued his experiments, based on the texts Thamos had given him.

Von Born was widely recognized as an extremely gifted scientist, and had become a member of the Academies of Siena, Padua and Stockholm. However, these distinctions brought him no material benefit and, having now no regular income, he had no choice but to sell his large and treasured collection of fossils; the purchaser was an English scientist, a member of the Royal Society.

Although he bitterly regretted the loss of the collection, von Born regained – at least for a time – vital financial independence. This would enable him to finance his travels and to maintain the flame of his lodge in Prague, without neglecting the search for other Brothers who wished to experience true initiation.

Salzburg, 24 October 1772

'Come along, Wolfgang,' said Leopold. 'The carriage is waiting for us.'

The young man dragged his feet.

'Don't you want to see Italy again?'

'Oh yes, of course I do.'

'One would never guess it. Come along, hurry up.'

A few days earlier, Leopold had emerged, greatly relieved, from the new archbishop's palace. Colloredo had given permission for his two employees to leave Salzburg for a brief stay in Milan, in order to fulfil an opera commission: *Lucio Silla*, to a libretto by Giovanni de Gamerra, a poet at the Viennese court.* During his stay in Italy, young Mozart could learn the very best musical style, and then return to delight the Salzburg court with it.

As the coach drove off, a sad and withdrawn Wolfgang could not help thinking about his strange protector and his recommendations. So he set to work to compose a string quartet in D major, which he finished on 28 October during a stop at Botzen.

'Another quartet!' grumbled Leopold. 'Let us hope the Milanese like it.' This was a secondary concern compared to the commission from the Duke's Teatro Regio, which was expecting a dazzling success from the young German composer.

Fortunately, Wolfgang had already finished the recitatives for *Lucio Silla*, but there were still all the arias and ensembles – in other words, an enormous amount of work. The story had

* He later made the first Italian translation of *Die Zauberflöte*.

made an impression on Wolfgang, because of the omnipresence of death.

Lucio Silla* wants to marry the beautiful Giunia, who is in love with Cecilio, a banished senator. Despite the danger she rejects Silla – there is room for only one love in her heart – so he decides to kill his rival. Giunia and Cecilio, who has returned to Rome secretly, plot to depose Silla and free the people from tyranny, but the plot fails. Silla announces that he is to marry Giunia, who is so desperate that she publicly accuses him of having planned to murder Cecilio. Her constancy and greatness of heart overwhelm Silla, and in an abrupt change of attitude he pardons his enemies and steps down from power. Giunia and Cecilio are reunited, to live in perfect happiness.

When the Mozarts arrived in Milan, Wolfgang was horrified to find that the recitatives had been altered without anyone consulting him. All the work he had done in Salzburg had been for nothing. He must compose an entire opera before 26 December.

* The character is based on the Roman dictator Lucius Cornelius Sulla.

34

Milan, 26 December 1772

Wolfgang was so exhausted that he no longer knew what he was writing. The last notes of *Lucio Silla* had been written on 18 December, and rehearsals had begun the very next day. On this icy evening of the 26th, the premiere was being held.

He liked some parts of the libretto, among them the last aria sung by the heroine, Giunia, which he had composed in the tragic key of C minor. It expressed pain in the face of injustice, a passion for living mingled with the anguish of death, the depth of a soul which was more attached to its ideals than to its own existence.

The work's strong areas contrasted with passages of text which were too feeble to interest the composer, who used the voices as true instruments. Aware that he was exploiting only a tiny part of their possibilities, he promised himself that he would carry forward his exploration.

'My son's music is remarkable, isn't it?' Leopold said to the director of the theatre.

'There are a few pretty bravura arias, some flowery ornamentation, and some undeniably rich orchestration, Herr Mozart, but I confess that the singers, the public and I myself are all a little disconcerted. Your son has focused too much on tragedy: above all else, an opera must please and entertain people.'

The second performance of *Lucio Silla* verged on catastrophe: there were many blunders in the production, second-rate or nervous singers, and an audience which had grown restless and tired as a result of waiting too long for the performance to begin.

Although in his letters to Salzburg Leopold spoke of a huge success, in fact Wolfgang had suffered a cruel failure. His first opera would not remain in the repertoire of the duke's Teatro Regio in Milan, and would quickly sink into oblivion.

To console himself, the young man began writing a poignant adagio in E minor for string quartet, his preferred form for meditation and profundity.

Suddenly, his pen stopped in mid-air: someone had come into his room.

'Who's there?'

Wolfgang stood up and look around. There was no one there. But he sensed the presence of his mysterious friend, and seemed to hear him whispering in his ear: 'Continue as you are doing. Pay no heed to the criticism – you must build yourself.'

Milan, 17 January 1773

Leopold was wondering if the first performance of a motet by Wolfgang, *Exsultate, jubilate*, to be given at the church of San Antonio Abate,* would be received well. His last three string quartets, although pleasant, contained too many slow movements and sombre keys – not the kind of thing to charm a large audience.

The evening before, Leopold had written reassuringly to

---

* The church is sometimes called the Church of the Theatines, after the religious order with which it was associated.

his wife. In case of interference by the Austrian censors, who opened most letters, he used a private code.

In fact, everything was going badly. Milan was becoming a dead end, its court was not interested in Wolfgang, and the style of *Lucio Silla* did not incline the theatre to commission a new work from him.

Would Tuscany prove more welcoming, and would Leopold's actions bear fruit?

Exsultate, jubilate had been written for the castrato Venanzio Rauzzini, 'the *primo* who was not an *uomo*'.* It transported the audience into a climate of cheerfulness, at the heart of the angels' joyful heaven. Leopold forgot his concerns about it and felt years younger. Truly, his son had the gift of bringing peace to people's souls.

Milan, 27 February 1773

While Wolfgang was composing some acceptable new quartets, bad news arrived. There was no hope left as regards Florence and Tuscany. This time, it was pointless to deceive themselves. In Italy, Wolfgang was nobody anymore. Other fashionable composers were occupying the front of the stage.

'We must go home to Salzburg,' said Leopold. 'The opportunities here have dried up.'

'Give me two or three days.'

'Why?'

'I've received a commission from an aristocrat who wants a divertimento designed to be played in the open air.'

'Will he pay well?'

'Above all, it's a wonderful opportunity to do something completely new. I'm going to write for an orchestra of wind instruments only. Exciting, don't you think?'

* He had sung the lead in *Lucio Silla*.

'If it amuses you – but do it quickly.'

While he executed the Count of Thebes's commission, Wolfgang said his farewells to Italy in a cheerful way.

Salzburg, 13 March 1773

Happy to return to his wife, his daughter and a quiet life, Leopold nevertheless felt a profound bitterness. So many journeys, so much effort, so much work, only to end up exactly where they had begun.

His son certainly didn't lack talent, but the few successes he had scored here and there were not enough to establish him as a great composer to whom a court would have granted a permanent and well-paid post. Not Munich nor London nor Paris nor Vienna had engaged Wolfgang. There remained Salzburg; always Salzburg. After all, why not?

Without admitting final defeat, Leopold was beginning to think that destiny could not be forced. Perhaps the most important thing was simply to earn one's living, behave like a decent man and lead a life that was acceptable in the eyes of God.

The dream of glory melted away. Several times, Wolfgang had breathed in its perfume. Now, at the age of seventeen, he was becoming a man and must acquire a sense of responsibilities as he followed in his father's steps. What was dishonourable about serving an archbishop, an enlightened nobility and middle classes who liked pretty music?

Leopold worried about the attacks of solemnity that had come through in his son's latest compositions. Still, it was an understandable adolescent phase, which would disappear at the heart of a balanced family.

'How is Colloredo behaving?' Leopold asked Anna Maria.

'Like an absolute despot. He controls everything, demands that his orders are carried out on the instant, and doesn't tolerate even the smallest sign of dissent. Our new archbishop is becoming more and more unpopular, but we are his subjects. Everyone misses his predecessor – he was so humane and so charitable.'

Leopold had been right to return to Salzburg. This man Colloredo was quite capable of dismissing the deputy Kapellmeister, despite his long service, if he did not give complete and utter satisfaction. As for Wolfgang, he must avoid any manifestations of mood swings, and meet the wishes of his august patron.

35

Salzburg, late March 1773

'Your go,' said Anton Stadler. He was on tenterhooks. If Wolfgang missed his shot, he would lose the game and have to invite Anton to dinner.

Wolfgang aimed his crossbow at the target, which depicted a young woman offering a pilgrim's staff to a traveller holding a hat in his hand. The test of supreme skill was to shoot the bolt into the hat.

Wolfgang squinted at the target and fired.

'You've won again!' groaned Stadler. 'What's your secret?'

'I make up a melody, and my arm relaxes.'

'I'm going to try that.'

The attempt ended in dismal failure: Stadler's bolt missed the hat and sank into the young girl's leg.

'You're getting dangerous,' observed Wolfgang. 'Go back to your clarinet and go on practising. Then we'll have dinner together anyway.'

When he went back indoors, Wolfgang found that he had run out of manuscript paper. Putting on a thick coat, he ran to the merchant's shop.

Outside the shop doorway stood Thamos.

'Do you live near here?' asked Wolfgang.

'I travel a good deal.'

'One day, will you tell me your name?'

'That day is approaching. In the meantime, you should change the format of paper you use. Choose a smaller size, oblong in shape. Your pen will move better and your first work, thanks to this new material, will reveal a new landscape to you.'

Thamos was right. An impetuous, sombre melody with tragic resonances opened the young man's new symphony. The tension relaxed as the work progressed, but his initial momentum had a profound effect upon the musician, who was capable of clearly expressing a type of thinking very different from the graceful Italian style of his *divertimenti*, sonatas and the latest symphony composed for Salzburg's court and high society.*

Thamos had awakened within him a new musical being, whom he must learn to nourish and encourage to grow.

Paris, 7 April 1773

At last, thought Philippe, Duc de Chartres, a little order is being instilled into the jumble of French Freemasonry. He had been appointed Grand Master of a new structure, the Grand Orient de France, called upon to rule over all the lodges.

Priority was given to the administrative hierarchy, which took little interest in initiation and symbolism. In the land of Descartes and Voltaire, everything must be defined, taken in hand and controlled. French Freemasonry would now have an official voice, which respected the ruling power and the values it imposed on society.

---

* Symphony no. 26 in E flat, K184. During the Orinoco-Amazon expedition, Alain Gheerbrant played the 'savages' this symphony. Their hostility disappeared as they listened to the music, which they did not appear to find strange. See *Le Mystère Mozart*, p. 5.

Beneath the official stance other words were hidden, confined within the lodges and still in the minority. Inspired by the Encyclopedists, Rousseau, Voltaire and other less famous authors, some Brothers were talking about a necessary freedom of the individual, a brotherhood between all human beings and, above all, an equality which would put an end to the privileges of the nobility and clergy. Excluding religiosity and mysticism, the rationalists were gaining ground little by little.

One of the first measures implemented by the Grand Orient's administration was to abolish the election for life of the Venerable One, the Master of the lodge; elections would now be held annually. In their temples, the Brothers practised a democracy which did not exist outside. Could it be that they were becoming one of the elements of an essential revolution?

Salzburg, June 1773

A few weeks previously, Prince-Archbishop Colloredo had much enjoyed a pretty *concertone* for two violins, oboe and cello by Wolfgang Mozart, one of those flirtatious, swiftly forgotten productions which the prelate adored.

Today, the composer faced a sterner test. A meticulous man, Colloredo wanted to check in person that his instructions were being followed to the letter. A musician must not forget that he was a member of the household staff.

The archbishop pricked up his ears: kettledrums and trumpets, in accordance with his demands. Perfect. Then he looked at his watch several times. The solemn Mass of the Trinity, in the joyful key of C major, did not exceed the forty-five minutes now imposed on such works. This order reduced the activity of the Salzburg musicians and therefore the salaries he had to pay them. Following the example of Emperor Josef, Colloredo was concerned with economies and

162

budgetary control. Pleasant music, yes; unnecessary expenses, no. A good mass could be said in three-quarters of an hour.

Ratisbonne, June 1773

Josef Anton was pacing the floor of a salon overloaded with gilded ornamentation. For the first time, he was trying to destroy the expansion of Freemasonry in an authoritarian manner, by asking the Empire Chamber at Ratisbonne to make a decree banning Masonic gatherings, which were considered dangerous and contrary to the prevailing laws.

Although his file was very slim, he hoped that the magistrates, aware of the peril, would agree to send down this thunderbolt. His task would then be easier. The ban would be followed by the dissolution of the lodges and the imprisonment of anyone who would not cooperate. Empress Maria Theresa would be proud of him.

The president of the Empire Chamber received him coldly. 'Sit down, Count.'

The president sat down at his desk. 'The Chamber and Senate of Ratisbonne have been consulted. Their response is negative.'

'Negative? You mean . . .?'

'Ratisbonne gives permission to the Freemasons to meet. Their gatherings are no threat to security, or to the authorities, or to good morals.'

'Herr President, you are making a regrettable mistake.'

'Are you contesting our sovereign decision?'

'No, indeed not. But tell me, did the Freemasons try to influence any of the Chamber's members?'

'Yes, certainly they did. In fact, several members are themselves Freemasons. But isn't that the best guarantee? None of them wishes to lose his post and its advantages. You worry too much, my dear Count. Far from being harmful, Freemasonry contributes to the stability of our society. The Brothers drink, eat, sing, listen to music, exchange confidences, take part in a little ritual play-acting, put on rather exotic costumes and occasionally abandon themselves to mystical reveries. An excellent outlet – not unlike English clubs where one is among gentlemen.'

'Are you not worried by the plan to restore the Order of the Temple and the alchemical experiments by the Golden Rose-Cross?'

'Childish nonsense, my dear Count, laughable childish nonsense! Don't waste your time. Leave the Freemasons in peace. Believe me, they won't topple any thrones.'

Josef Anton took his leave.

This victory by Freemasonry had demonstrated the extent of its influence. The octopus had spread out rather more tentacles than he had supposed. The war promised to be long and hard. If official ways were closed to him, he would have to be even more cautious and discreet before striking. It was up to him to carry out as many investigations as possible, to build up his files and to toil away in the shadows.

36

Vienna, 1 July 1773

Leopold had decided to take his son to Vienna and spend the summer there, because of two pieces of good news. First, Colloredo would be absent during this period; when the cat was away, the mice could play. Next, one of the court musicians was seriously ill. His death – and the end could not be long – would free a post which would fit Wolfgang like a glove. So he needed to be in Vienna when the musician died and promptly obtain an audience.

Wolfgang was delighted to leave Salzburg and escape the stifling atmosphere of the principality. He, who had already travelled so much, was beginning to feel very cramped in his servant's outfit. In Vienna he could breathe more easily.

Vienna, 19 July 1773

'Dear Wolfgang, how happy I am to see you again.'

'And I to see you, Doctor Mesmer.'

'And are you well?'

'I'm a bit tired, but—'

'We'll soon cure that. Will you allow me to magnetize you?'

Franz Anton Mesmer placed his broad hands on the nape of Wolfgang's neck. Immediately, a gentle warmth diffused into the whole of the patient's body. His tension disappeared, and he felt wonderfully well.

'That's marvellous, Doctor.'

'Magnetism ought to be the prime therapy. It eliminates illnesses at their root and prevents most troubles from developing. My main preoccupation is to re-establish harmony and the circulation of energy in a disturbed organism. Unfortunately, most doctors wait for the appearance of symptoms and work things out according to them. Often, it is too late to heal the patient.'

'Do your colleagues listen to you?'

'Very few. Vienna considers me a sort of mage, and the medical authorities refuse to examine the results of my research. They will not even gather the testimonies of the patients I cure. Sometimes scientists lack curiosity and yield to conformity, especially when their careers are at stake. When a free, independent spirit emerges, and shakes up the established doctrines a little, dark forces unite to eliminate him. But we must not subside into pessimism, dear Wolfgang. Why don't you tell me a little about your adventures?'

'They end in Salzburg, in the service of Prince-Archbishop Colloredo.'

'Be wary of that petty tyrant. All he cares about is himself, and power. If he is not obeyed to the letter, he becomes ferocious.'

'So far my father and I are managing to deal with him.'

'I am going to let you hear a curiosity, my latest musical fantasy.'

In his beautiful Viennese garden, on a sweet summer's night, Mesmer played a recent invention, a glass harmonica. Although on the lookout for any new techniques, Wolfgang did not much like the shrill sounds but he accepted the fragile instrument the doctor gave him.

'Perhaps you will compose for this harmonica, whose

potential you have the talent to exploit. How long will you be staying in Vienna?'

'Until the end of the summer, probably. My father is still hoping to obtain a post for me at court.'

'You should have one by right!'

'Vienna has forgotten me, Doctor. And I am not even sure of being received by the empress. These days, I can hardly jump on to her lap and beg for her affection! And I shall never marry Princess Marie-Antoinette.'

'You shall have that audience – I still have some friends in high places. The post, though, depends on Her Majesty.'

'It is for destiny to decide. This uncertainty won't stop me working.'

'My house and my table are open to you, Wolfgang. Come whenever you wish, even without informing me beforehand. Soon, I shall introduce you to some admirers who have an interesting project to propose to you.'

Vienna, 5 August 1773

After amusing himself by writing a serenade to be played at a distant relative's wedding – in which he had ignored the conventions and introduced a miniature concerto for violin – Wolfgang had set to work on a much more arduous task.

His stay in Vienna was enabling him to become familiar with the music of the forty-one-year-old Josef Haydn, who was greatly respected by all musicians. His writing technique, his freedom of expression, and the variety of his languages fascinated Wolfgang. In order to assimilate so much new learning, he composed a series of quartets in imitation of Haydn's.* Content to follow his model's pattern, he was aware that the exercise was simply a matter of learning, and lacked originality.

* The six 'Viennese' quartets, K168–173.

But it enriched his style and gave him new means of expression.

Leopold interrupted him. 'At last!' he exclaimed. 'The empress has granted us an audience!'

Vienna, 12 August 1773

In the candlelight, Wolfgang was working on a quartet, while Leopold finished a letter to his wife. Its conclusion was under no illusions: 'Her Majesty was extremely amiable towards us. Only amiable, that was all.'

Maria Theresa had not offered Wolfgang a post. Merely receiving the Mozarts, whom she now regarded as itinerant performers with no future, seemed amply sufficient to her. Yielding to entreaties from some of her entourage, she had granted them this great honour, while giving them to understand that they had nothing to hope for. The door of the court had closed once and for all.

'Don't be so sad, father.'

'How can I not be? The empress has made fools of us. In her eyes, we don't exist.'

'At least she's freed us from our illusions.'

'A strange kind of freedom! It is in Vienna, and only in Vienna, that one can conduct a brilliant career. You deserve it, Wolfgang.'

'I'm only seventeen.'

'Seventeen! Your childhood is long finished, and your adolescence is nearly over. You are becoming a young man, and you could make a great impact in this city if you were given a stable post.'

'Well, that's impossible, so why keep on trying?'

'Impossible for the moment. But you're young and the empress is old. After her death, there will be many upheavals. The locked door might perhaps open. In the meantime, we must please the archbishop.'

'I'd like to stay in Vienna until the end of the summer, as we planned.'

'What are you hoping for?'

'To listen to some Haydn, finish my series of quartets, compose some dances for the winter in Salzburg and see Doctor Mesmer again.'

'I don't much care for that strange doctor.'

'He commissioned *Bastien und Bastienne* from me, don't forget; and he's going to offer me a new proposition before the end of August. Surely it's worth considering?'

'As long as it is not just a false promise!'

'I understand. We shall see.'

37

On a gentle summer evening, Wolfgang delighted the doctor's guests with a divertimento in D major, which accorded well with the luxuriance of the large garden in the suburbs of the Landstrasse. When the concert was over, people stayed to eat, drink and chat.

Mesmer took Wolfgang by the arm. 'I should like to introduce you to an important man, Tobias Philippe von Gebler. He is Vice-Chancellor in Vienna, but his real passion is writing. He has just finished a dramatic poem and would like to talk to you about it.'

The doctor omitted to reveal his Masonic links with Gebler, who, despite his position at court, sometimes expressed dangerous ideas regarding the abuse of power and the necessary freedom of the conscience.

Gebler was forty-seven, massively built and debonair. Wolfgang liked him, but had eyes only for the sumptuously dressed man standing beside him: the man from Rücken, the envoy from the other world, his protector. In dignity and radiance, he eclipsed von Gebler.

'My dear Mozart,' said the poet, 'allow me to present you to my friend Thamos, Count of Thebes. I'm very glad he's here, for it is thanks to him that I had the idea of writing a philosophical drama entitled *Thamos, König in Ägypten*.* It has just been published, and I would like to see it performed in Berlin. By itself, the text is not enough: appropriate music would complement it and give it more power. I consulted Gluck, but in vain. My friend advised me to come to you. Despite your young age, he considers you capable of perceiving the profound meaning of my work and translating it into notes. Does the task interest you?'

So he was called Thamos and he was King of Egypt! How pathetic the child Mozart's Rücken must have seemed to a monarch who reigned over such a vast empire! With all his being, Wolfgang perceived the importance of this moment. He was experiencing a second birth.

Rooted to the spot, he heard a weak, hesitant voice reply: 'Yes, yes . . . this project does indeed interest me.'

'Excellent!' exclaimed von Gebler. 'Let us go and sit in a quiet corner, and I'll tell you the story.'

Mesmer rejoined his other guests, and Thamos accompanied him. Wolfgang was glad of the half-light. His hands were trembling as if they were hesitant to grasp a treasure.

'The action takes place in Egypt,' explained von Gebler, 'the land of the Mysteries of initiation to supreme knowledge. The Grand Master of the initiates is called Sethos and worships the sun, the most visible expression of the creative power. His daughter, a priestess of the day-star, has been kidnapped. Prince Thamos, who is in love with her, must snatch her from the demons of the darkness who are determined to destroy the initiates. During the marriage of the prince and princess, Light will triumph. Are you won over by this swift summary, which necessarily omits many dramatic devices?'

'I am ready to start work.'

* 'Thamos, King of Egypt'.

'I'm delighted to hear it, my dear Wolfgang. I am dreaming of fine orchestration and, above all, majestic choirs. But that is your business. Of course, you will be properly remunerated. Soon we shall attend the premiere together, and it will be a triumph. Unfortunately I am obliged to leave now. Here is my poem.'

Von Gebler handed Wolfgang the text and left him alone.

After a few moments, Thamos rejoined him.

'Now I know who you are,' said Wolfgang.

'Not entirely.'

'Pharaoh of Egypt, high priest of the sun . . . Our world must seem petty and ridiculous to you.'

'Our world is in great peril, for it is turning its back on the spirit and plunging ever deeper into an all-conquering, aggressive materialism. The darkness is attempting to engulf the Light and annihilate initiation.'

'Initiation? What is that?'

'Becoming what you really are, by gaining access to the knowledge of the Mysteries. But the road to it is long and treacherous. Few people are willing to expend the necessary effort, and vanity and greed are fatal. This road demands the making of an offering and the act of creation.'

'Do you believe I am capable of following it?'

'That is for you to answer.'

'*Thamos, König in Ägypten* . . . This opera's extremely important, isn't it?'

'It will be your first step towards the accomplishment of the Great Work. Don't expect to succeed all at once. You will undergo many trials before you accomplish it. Will you have the courage and perseverance needed?'

'You don't know me very well!' Wolfgang exclaimed angrily. 'There's a fire burning inside me, and I don't know how to express it. But I shall succeed. First, though, I must assimilate all techniques and all languages in order to fashion my own.'

172

'You must learn to converse with the gods and to pass on their words without betraying them.'

'Is music capable of doing that?'

'Not music, *your* music. On condition that you consciously pass through each stage and that your heart fills with Light.'

'Will you . . . Will you help me?'

'If you wish.'

'If I try by myself, I'll fail.'

'Indeed.'

'Then you'll help me?'

'Will you accept me as both your guide and your judge?'

'And – a little bit – my friend?'

Thamos smiled. He could not speak the sacred name of Brother, but considered Wolfgang Mozart a Freemason without an apron. The Great Magician had just been born to himself.

'I have a thousand questions to ask you,' said Wolfgang eagerly.

'Begin by setting von Gebler's drama to music. This first contact with Egypt will broaden your mind and open up a realm whose immensity you have never suspected.'

'I must go back to Salzburg soon, to compose for the archbishop, and—'

'Formidable trials await you, I warned you of that. Perhaps their weight will crush you.'

'I swear to you that it won't.'

The Egyptian took the frail youth by the shoulders. 'Your destiny will demand of you a degree of courage and determination that is sometimes superhuman, for your path is not like that of other men. And yet they will need your works in order to discern the Light. You cannot yet fully grasp the meaning of my words, but you are already more than just a little musician from Salzburg. Within you, Mozart the Egyptian has been born.'

38

Vienna, 18 September 1773

Although he knew and appreciated his son's capacity for work, Leopold was stunned. Wolfgang no longer joked, no longer played with his crossbow, no longer went out, scarcely slept any more, ate at top speed and refused to enter into any discussion. He was devoting himself to the commission from von Gebler, an important person.

'Wolfgang is composing something that occupies him a great deal', he wrote to Anna Maria. Since Colloredo had confirmed Leopold in his office and Wolfgang's career was to proceed in Salzburg, they must move to larger lodgings, where everyone would be comfortable. Nannerl was not intending to marry, so he would be housing two grown-up children. Now Anna Maria had found the ideal apartment and was organizing the removal.

Leopold dared to interrupt his son. 'Will you have finished soon?'

'Soon? No. The composition of the choruses is proving difficult.'

'We must return to Salzburg.'

'I'll pay one last visit to Doctor Mesmer, then we can leave.'

The Great Magician

Rotmühle, 22 September 1773

Mesmer had taken Wolfgang to spend the day at his country house, promising that he would be back in Vienna by seven o'clock that evening. The summer was dying, and the leaves were starting to fall.

The doctor spoke at length to Wolfgang of his experiments, magnetized him to restore his energy on the threshold of the cold weather, and congratulated him on accepting von Gebler's commission.

As coffee was being served, Thamos appeared.

'Come and join us, Herr Count,' said Mesmer. 'You really must sample this plum brandy – I'm sure you won't easily forget it.'

After they had had their drinks, the doctor went off to tend his rose bushes.

'I've made progress,' said Wolfgang, 'but I'm still not satisfied. My head is teeming with new ideas, and I shall never again write the way I did before. Unfortunately, though, I have to return to Salzburg and I'm worried that I'll lose this momentum.'

'You alone would be responsible for that failure. It is up to you to transform what is imposed on you in a positive way.'

'You don't know Colloredo! We musicians are no more than servants to him, and must apply his rigid rules.'

'Accept them as trials which will enable you to progress. Enlarge your palette of sound, broaden your musical thinking.'

'And what if the archbishop condemns my work?'

'Are you afraid of adversity, Wolfgang?'

The youth's expression became fierce. 'Whatever happens, *Thamos, König in Ägypten* will be finished before the end of December.'

Salzburg, 28 September 1773

'What do you think of our new home?' asked Anna Maria brightly.

Leopold and Wolfgang explored a comfortable apartment, within a fine middle-class building on Hannibalplatz, which was known as 'the Dancing-master's House', on account of one of its owner's favourite pastimes.

Thanks to his and Wolfgang's salaries, and the money brought in by Nannerl's piano-teaching, the family could afford to pay the rent and have a reasonable standard of living, without depriving themselves.

On his arrival at the palace, Leopold learned that Colloredo had appointed a second Kapellmeister, Giuseppe Lolli, another Italian! Deputy Kapellmeister Mozart would now have to submit to two superiors instead of one, and could see his promotion getting ever further away. Never would the archbishop put a German in charge of his court musicians. Leopold swallowed his disappointment and continued to conduct himself as the perfect servant.

Berlin, 14 October 1773

On account of his title and presumed wealth, Thamos, Count of Thebes, was received into the rank of Knight in the inner order of Strict Templar Observance. Two Brothers dressed him in a purple garment, adorned with nine small knots in gold braid, over which they put a short tunic in white wool and a cape decorated on the left side with the red cross of the Temple.

Together with the other Knights and Squires gathered together from the rich middle classes, he attended the general assembly marking the triumph of the new Grand Master, the Duke of Brunswick. The duke's first balance sheet showed him in a favourable light: now established in Germany, Austria,

Switzerland and other countries, the Order benefited from high-level protection and accepted nobles, traders and influential members of civilian society. The duke was increasing its charitable activities, and in Dresden was opening a free school for orphans and poor children.

There was just one discordant note in this well-orchestrated symphony: the presence of Zinnendorf, creator of the Swedish Rite. Brunswick had hoped that the troublesome fellow would be quiet and discreet, but instead Zinnendorf drew the assembly's attention to a fundamental point.

'Do we all really belong to the same Order?' he asked. 'Allow me to doubt it. The Grand Master says he wishes to rule over all the lodges in unity, but I see no sign of that unity. The Swedish Rite is not interchangeable with Strict Templar Observance – far from it.'

'However,' said the duke, 'we are in accord over the first three degrees, Apprentice, Companion and Master, and there are only a few differences in the rituals for the fourth degree, Scottish Master.'

'I freely admit that. Our high degrees, though, are totally different.'

'That is not an insoluble problem,' said the duke. 'Do you not hope, as I do, to recall in our rituals the tragedy of the Order of the Temple and revive its symbolic and material power?'

'The Swedish Rite has no interest in idle hopes. It is concerned only with what is essential: divine magic. Our rituals, with which you are not familiar, summon up the spirits.'

'By integrating with Strict Observance and submitting to its Grand Master, you will give greater strength to the Masonic movement.'

'Do not count on it,' retorted Zinnendorf.

Thamos was most concerned. Neither of the two men would give in. Despite his authority and prestige, the Duke of

Brunswick would never succeed in getting the irascible Zinnendorf to bend to his will. Instead of working on making the rituals more profound, and learning once again how to speak the language of symbols, Freemasonry was losing itself in power struggles. The future of initiation in the Strict Observance Movement was looking less and less bright.

39

Vienna, early November 1773

For Josef Anton, the Strict Templar Observance movement's charitable foundations were a smokescreen. If he had had more powers, he would have used the taxation authorities to detect financial misdeeds, or to invent some. After the unfortunate Ratisbonne episode, he could no longer intervene directly, and he was not sure of success. But nothing would stop him. If he was patient, sooner or later he would destroy Freemasonry and its dangerous ideals.

Geytrand's smug smile promised good news. 'I've bought an informer of the highest quality,' he said. 'He's a rich merchant, an importer, publisher, printer and . . . a Knight of the inner order of the Strict Observance movement. The fellow has paid through the nose for his cape and sword.'

'How did you capture him?'

'Through a lower-ranked Brother, one of his accounting clerks. The merchant isn't what one would call scrupulously honest, and I've obtained written proof of a few of his schemes. In exchange for my silence about that, the Knight has given me all the Order's rituals and has promised to keep me informed about its development.'

'Excellent. You deserve a big bonus,' said Josef Anton.

'Thank you, Herr Count. But that's not all. The recent

assembly in Berlin saw a serious clash between Zinnendorf and the Duke of Brunswick. They parted in anger, and the breach between them is most unlikely to be healed.'

'That schism will weaken both of them.'

'Brunswick isn't discouraged. Since he sidelined Baron de Hund, he has held the reins of the Order firmly and is making it prosper. According to several Knights, there's only one serious difficulty: the lack of substance in the rituals. The Grand Master is seeking to overcome this handicap but hasn't yet found a solution, and in any case he believes that the most urgent thing is to ensure material development and, as he promised, to bring wealth to its main dignitaries.'

'We must keep a careful watch on the bankers, businessmen and others who provide money. If Brunswick succeeds, many thrones will be at risk. And there's another problem: the progress of the Golden Rose-Cross in Vienna. Those cursed alchemists are sneaking into the lodges and using secret laboratories which are difficult to detect.'

Geytrand shook his head in frustration. 'Their circles are small and are kept strictly separate, and the identities of their senior ranks are well hidden. I haven't been able to lay hands on a single useful informer.'

'So we'll use another method, and I have high hopes of it. As you know, under pressure from the governments of France, Spain and Portugal, Pope Clement has reluctantly suppressed the Order of Jesuits. Some of those good fellows want revenge, and I'm going to offer it to them. They will infiltrate the Masonic lodges, hoping to lead many of the Brothers back to the true Church, and the Golden Rose-Cross, because of its mystical tendencies, will therefore suffocate to death. Our Jesuit friends will inform us of any treasonable words or actions.'

Salzburg, December 1773

Since his return to Salzburg, Wolfgang's work had taken on a new dimension. He was no longer content to imitate his masters and copy styles, but truly sought his own language. In November he created a remarkable symphony in C major, whose four movements attained a surprising degree of opulence, marking a turning point in his very conception of this type of piece. The following month he wrote a string quintet which, although inspired by Michael Haydn, aimed precisely to disengage itself from this friendly influence, to which he had willingly submitted earlier.

Above all, he had produced his first real piano concerto.* This was not a copy of other fashionable works, but an original and charming creation. Its beginning was light-hearted and lively, followed by a slow movement imbued with poetry, and a complex finale with four themes. The complexity worried Leopold: too many technical difficulties and too much musical audacity might harm Wolfgang's reputation. Moreover, this concerto was not a commission. If the young man kept writing purely for himself, he might neglect his duties as a musician-servant.

And then, of course, there was *Thamos, König in Ägypten*. Two choruses opened the first and fifth acts of the drama, and five musical interludes punctuated the tale, the last taking the form of an orchestral storm, during the death of the traitor who had tried in vain to impose the tyranny of darkness. Wolfgang himself was thoroughly dissatisfied. The scope of the subject merited more than these few pieces of incidental music. At last a libretto had excited him from start to finish, even if the text, which was often mediocre, did not rise to the standard of the theme.

* No. 5, K175.

The very day he finished work, Wolfgang met Thamos in the street.

'I understand how you feel,' said the Egyptian. 'But remember that this is merely a first stage, designed to familiarize you with the accomplishment of the Great Work.'

'Sethos, the High Priest, Saïs, his daughter, and Thamos, the prince who will free her from the forces of darkness – all these characters should have so much to say!'

'They will, if you incorporate them into your creator's soul as you develop. At seventeen, it isn't easy to be patient.'

'When will the play be performed?'

'I shall give your score to Baron Gebler, who will send it to his friend Nicolai in Berlin. But I warn you, the project may arouse displeasure.'

'Why?'

'Naming the forces of darkness and attacking them is bound to provoke reactions, either violent or underhand.'

'But surely everyone wants to fight alongside the priests of the sun?'

'You're still naive, Wolfgang. Most people let their course be decided by events; they close their eyes and ears, and try to ignore reality.'

'Well, I certainly shan't,' declared the young man. 'If the Light didn't triumph, what meaning would our life have?'

'You are beginning a long and taxing journey,' warned the Egyptian. 'May it lead you to the Great Work you have just sketched out.' With that, he walked away.

Wolfgang forgot to eat lunch. He composed a new symphony, which for the first time was written entirely in a minor key.* The first movement, marked with a new term, *allegro con brio*, conveyed the intense emotions he felt. One day he, too, would be a priest of the sun.

---

* K183, the 'little G minor'.

40

Salzburg, 22 January 1774

'This is no good, Wolfgang, no good at all!' roared his father. 'Nobody liked your symphony in A minor – too much pathos in places, too much seriousness here and there. I know adolescence is a difficult time, but you must do your job within the rules of the art if you want to keep your post. Prince-Archbishop Colloredo dictates taste in Salzburg, and he likes music to be romantic, light, entertaining, easy to listen to during an official meal or reception. So it is this kind, and no other, that you must compose. Your own happiness and your family's depend on it. Don't bother your audience with your moods.'

Wolfgang felt like shouting, tearing up his manuscript paper and overturning his inkwell, but what good would that do? His father was right. He would forget his particularly personal projects, would not venture on to the perilous path of a new piano concerto, and would produce charming little works, well put together, which Salzburg would enjoy as though they were fancy cakes.

Fortunately, he still had *Thamos, König in Ägypten*. If it was a success, the doors of the theatres in Vienna would open to him. He decided to ask von Gebler to let him develop the musical aspects of the work into something approaching an opera describing the mysteries of Egypt. Thamos, his protector, would help him to realize the most important ideas of the sun's priests.

In the meantime, Wolfgang amused himself with Miss Pimperl, a fox-terrier bitch who was always ready to entertain him. She yapped with delight when he sat down at the piano, and listened to him attentively.

In order to calm his nerves, the musician played at crossbow-shooting and skittles, and often met his friends, though their frivolous conversations soon tired him.

'My elder brother wants to become a parish priest,' confided Anton Stadler. 'I don't – I like life too much. What about you?'

'I am in the service of the archbishop, and my conduct must be above reproach. My father will punish the smallest transgression.'

'And that's no laughing matter, I know. All the same, he married a very pretty wife. If you want, I'll introduce you to some nice girls.'

'I'm not looking for "girls", as you call them. I believe in the nobility of woman and the sanctity of marriage.'

'And great love? You'll probably be disappointed, my friend,' said Anton.

'Every day my parents show me what a truly happy marriage can be. They love and respect each other. That's what I want.'

'Isn't that a rather boring vision of ambition – especially at your age?'

Wolfgang sighed. 'Everyone tries to persuade me to flirt and have light-hearted romantic flings. But there's no chance of that.'

'So much the worse for you. You don't know what you're missing.'

184

Salzburg, 27 January 1774

Before celebrating his son's eighteenth birthday, Leopold waited impatiently for good news from Vienna. As soon as he heard of Kapellmeister Gassmann's death, he had approached all his contacts to suggest, discreetly, that Wolfgang might be a candidate for the post. He was relying a great deal upon a good friend of the family, Giuseppe Bonno, who was well known at court.

At last, a letter arrived from Vienna. As he read it, Leopold's face fell. It was not Wolfgang whom the empress had appointed as Kapellmeister, but ... Bonno. What a very good friend he was! The doors of the court would never, ever open.

Vienna, 4 April 1774

The partial performance of *Thamos, König in Ägypten* was a dismal failure. There would be no second chance. Baron von Gebler's head hung so low with disappointment that he bumped into one of the few spectators who had not left the hall.

'I beg your pardon, sir,' he said.

'Could we speak for a moment, dear Baron?' asked Josef Anton in a soft voice.

'Did you like my play?'

'Actually, it is the play's subject I'd like to discuss. It's ... dangerous.'

'Dangerous? What do you mean? But first of all, who are you?'

'Someone who knows that you are a Freemason – and I would remind you that Freemasonry is greatly disliked by Her Majesty the Empress. Don't worry, though. I mean you no harm. My name is of no importance and would mean nothing to you. On the other hand, pay attention to my advice.'

Von Gebler was alarmed. This shadowy, soft-voiced man had an air of authority. If he was acting in the empress's name, it would be wise to listen to him.

'As an author you are naturally disappointed by the play's failure, but I believe it is as well that it failed. Clearly, the priests of the sun initiated into the Mysteries stand for Freemasons fighting the powers of darkness and obscurantism upheld by the demoniacal Mirza, an incarnation of our empress.'

'You are mistaken, sir, and I cannot allow you to—'

'Your words are transparent, Baron, and the allegory's words do not conceal its subversive nature. Supporting a pernicious organization and preaching its cause, trying to convert the Viennese public, are unacceptable activities.'

'That is not my intention, I swear.'

'The play's failure will save you from some serious problems, so long as you learn the lessons of your mistake. Freemasonry will never flourish in Austria, and its followers will face many difficulties – you should distance yourself from it at once. I shall overlook your error, on condition that I never hear talk of you again.'

Gebler was silent. He did not feel he had the strength to fight back.

'One other small thing: what is the name of the talentless musician who illustrated certain passages of your play?'

'Wolfgang Mozart.'

'One of your Brother Masons?'

'Oh no! He's only a youth, a former child prodigy employed at the Salzburg court. For him, this was just one small commission among many others.'

So Mozart was not an accomplice of von Gebler. Nevertheless, Josef Anton would note down his name in the file devoted to this affair.

The Great Magician

Salzburg, 10 April 1774

Wolfgang was on the verge of tears. The Count of Thebes had met him to tell him of *Thamos*'s fate, and he felt the failure had condemned him to the prison of Salzburg and the *galant* style.

'I shan't give up, even if Gebler does,' he vowed. 'The subject of this future opera is extraordinary. I want to deepen and develop it. Will you help me?'

'Of course.'

'How shall I ever attain my goal if I don't become a priest of the sun?'

This question filled Thamos with inexpressable joy. The Great Magician was finding his way and, in the expression of the Ancients, was providing a path for his feet.

'Is that really what you want?' he asked.

'Initiation would be the key to life, wouldn't it?'

'That was indeed what was taught in Egypt.'

'Then I want that key.'

'If you are worthy, you will be granted it. But you must still prove yourself.'

'Here in Salzburg?'

'Yes, here. The place doesn't matter; what matters is the trials that will create your consciousness and your will. You are unusually gifted, so life won't spare you – quite the contrary, in fact.'

'Will I have to wait very long?'

'As long as is necessary, Wolfgang. Haste is the devil.'

41

Salzburg, May 1774

Church music, light symphonies, serenades, entertainments . . .
Wolfgang met the archbishop's requirements; though here
and there he indulged in a few musical experiments and combinations of different sounds.

The young man did not rebel, but concentrated on
improving his skills. This was an ordeal, certainly, but not a
pointless one. He would have to write thousands of notes,
explore dozens of forms before mastering a language which
was still embryonic. He, the sometime child prodigy, must
learn maturity. Colloredo and his father believed he had
submitted; they were unaware of the fire that had been lit
inside him.

Wolfgang did not deceive himself, and did not attribute any
great worth to many of the works he was obliged to produce.
They enabled him to 'get his hand in' and mould his musical
clay increasingly swiftly. They were neither a headlong pursuit
nor a superficial task, but a means of fashioning the future.

Versailles, 10 May 1774

Taxes had been increased yet again, but the baker could not
raise the price of his bread, for fear of being insulted and

attacked. If things went on like this, he would have to close down his shop.

His friend the shoemaker tapped him on the shoulder. 'He's dead!'

'The tax collector?'

'No, his boss: King Louis.'

'That's no great loss. He was a debauchee, a liar and a fool. Because of him, France is facing ruin.'

'The next one won't be much better,' grumbled the shoemaker. 'And now we've got Marie-Antoinette, an Austrian, as queen. What does she know about our problems? She'll just wallow in luxury and pleasure, like all foreign princesses.'

'The king is still the king, though,' the baker reminded him. 'He'll make her behave properly.'

'I don't believe that. Everything must be changed.'

'How?'

'By changing everything,' insisted the shoemaker.

Prague, 2 June 1774

Despite his precarious financial situation, Ignaz von Born was continuing his initiation quest. While searching through the documents at his disposal, reassembling the scattered elements of the Tradition, he contacted as many Freemasons as possible, but most of them did not want to depart from their routine and their intellectual comfort. Von Born was undismayed. He did not envisage a mass movement, preferring to form firm links with a small number of Brothers.

On this fine spring day, two happy events occurred. The first was his election as a Fellow of the Royal Society in London – in other words, international recognition of his scientific achievements. The second was a visit from Thamos.

'Forgive me for asking,' said von Born, 'but how do you bear your exile?'

'When I left Egypt on the orders of Abbot Hermes,' said Thamos, 'I knew I would never see my monastery again. The barbarians burnt it, murdered my Brothers and tried to destroy all the treasures built up over the centuries.'

'Didn't the Abbot foresee this disaster?'

'As successor to the Great Seer, the superior of the initiates in Heliopolis, Hermes looked reality in the face. The secret of hieroglyphs, the words of the gods, has never been lost, but passed on from the mouth of the master to the disciple's ear. In these cruel times, it was essential to preserve fundamental texts, some of which go back to the golden age when the pyramids were built. The sands of the desert will be their shrine, until the eyes of a searcher brings them back to life. The West is hurtling towards disaster, on the path to spiritual extinction. That is why I was given the task of passing on *The Book of Thoth*.'

'I shall try to prove worthy of your trust,' declared von Born, in a voice full of emotion. 'You can rely on my determination and perseverance.'

Despite his meagre material means, his fragile health and his isolation, the mineralogist seemed to Thamos the Freemason best suited to creating the current of initiation the Great Magician would need. So he gave him new extracts from *The Book of Thoth*, over which he had spent long hours poring before appearing before Abbot Hermes, who verified his grasp of its sacred content.

Fully aware of the burden now resting on his shoulders, Ignaz von Born explored the alchemical manual from the Egyptian town of Hermontis, *The Book of the Night*, retracing the stages of the sun's resurrection through the immense body of the sky-goddess, and texts on the eye of the sun, the creative principle.

'Modern Freemasonry seems incapable of gaining access to such great and profound Mysteries,' he said.

190

'Prepare it and transform it, my Brother. That is your vital duty. Otherwise, the Great Magician will not shine forth.'

Salzburg, June 1774

Wolfgang allowed himself a moment's complete relaxation by composing his first concerto for a wind instrument, the bassoon, with an orchestra reduced to its most simple expression. It was a small, unpretentious work, rustic and juvenile, which gave him a few hours' relaxation before executing a couple of commissions from the archbishop, who was very fond of his 'brief masses'. Miss Pimperl loved the sound of the bassoon and the countrified nature of the concerto.

As he was taking her for her daily walk, Wolfgang met Thamos.

'Have you any news of von Gebler?' he asked eagerly.

'Don't trust him any more. He isn't the man to run even the smallest risk. His work displeased the authorities, so in future he will restrict himself to less daring poetry.'

'Do you mean the authorities would take the side of darkness against the Light?'

'The main preoccupation of whoever holds political power is retaining it, whatever the methods and the compromises. But that is no reason to abandon *Thamos*, the foundation stone of your future works.'

'I'm doing nothing interesting at the moment. *Galant* music has become my daily bread, and I'm stuffed full of it!'

'Have you given up working to improve your knowledge of the instruments and techniques of composition?'

'Oh no! That's my only way of not suffocating.'

'There is another way.'

'What is it?'

'Reading. First, you should buy some language dictionaries. Given your memories of travelling and your aptitudes, you must speak Italian and French fluently, and have reached a good standard in English. Use the dictionaries to refresh your command of these languages. Then you can escape by means of Apulaeus' *The Golden Ass* and Heliodorus' *Ethiopics*, novels of initiation in which these classical authors deal with the theme of the trials and the necessary transformations of one's being before one can enter the realm of Isis. I shall add a few plays by an English dramatist, William Shakespeare, which will contribute to your training as a composer of opera.'

'Opera? You really believe I'm capable of it?'

'Read and read again, Wolfgang.'

42

Berlin, 16 July 1774

Ferdinand, Duke of Brunswick rubbed his hands. In recent months, several French lodges – in Strasbourg, Lyon, Bordeaux and Montpellier – had rallied to Strict Observance. And on this fine summer's day, King Friedrich had authorized the existence of Freemasonry in the states he controlled.

The duke had come to Berlin to contact influential men who had decided to support his cause. Through functions like receptions and dinners, he created a large network of relationships and asserted himself as a true leader, relegating Baron de Hund to the shadows.

Ferdinand was not interested only in power and honours, though. He believed in his mission and continued to rue the weakness of the rituals. Dissension among Brothers, their lack of initiation culture, and the inadequacy of research were preventing the Order from strengthening its foundations. Fully aware of these problems, the Grand Master was determined to find a remedy for them.

Vienna, 20 July 1774

Geytrand was in a bad mood. 'Bad news from Berlin, Herr Count,' he said. 'King Friedrich has granted his protection to Freemasonry.'

'It isn't bad news at all,' countered Josef Anton. 'On the contrary, it's very good news.'

'I don't understand, sir.'

'Friedrich wants to control everything and know everything. The best way to make the Freemasons emerge into the full light of day, and thus be able to identify them, was to pretend to trust them. Those naive fools now think they have the king's ear. They don't know of his deep loyalty to the Jesuits, whose infiltration into the lodges is already a real success. Not only are they procuring valuable information for us, but they are also bringing many lost sheep back into the bosom of the Church. Those brilliant vermin are even infiltrating the Golden Rose-Cross.'

Geytrand could not hide his astonishment. 'What? The Golden Rose-Cross itself? Have you really penetrated into their compartmentalized structure?'

'Yes, by taking my inspiration from the lessons given by the Jesuits.'

'So the worm is in the fruit!'

Josef Anton's half-smile expressed extreme satisfaction.

Salzburg, 30 September 1774

On the feast day of Saint Jerome, Prince-Archbishop Colloredo was being feted.

After relaxing by composing some charming piano variations, Wolfgang felt nervous once again. The court orchestra was to play his Serenade in D major written in honour of Colloredo, and the work did not altogether respect the rules.

More developed than usual, it included an andante marked, for the first time, with the term *cantabile*, 'singing'. Shut away in Salzburg, a prisoner of his post as servant-musician, Wolfgang escaped through the song of the instruments and the variety of keys. Would Colloredo notice and rebuke his servant?

Fortunately, a serenade was only an amusement, which was merely half listened to. With other cares on his mind, and pleased by the obedience of his faithful subjects and their marks of esteem, the archbishop remained in a good temper and had an excellent day.

Salzburg, Autumn 1774

Five new piano sonatas: in composing them, Wolfgang went back to a genre he had practised in 1766 and since abandoned. He had hoped to trace a new path, but emerged from the experiment extremely discontented. Virtuosity, a light-hearted style inspired by Josef Haydn, a lack of depth ... He wouldn't play these sonatas in public and wouldn't publish them. He seemed to be moving ever further away from *Thamos, König in Ägypten*.

When he took Miss Pimperl for walks, there was no sign of the Egyptian. He was probably travelling again; would he ever come back to Salzburg?

'I may have some good news,' announced Leopold. 'The Elector of Bavaria has commissioned you to produce an *opera buffa* for the carnival in Munich.'

'Why only "may have"?'

'Because we need permission from Colloredo.'

Wolfgang's face fell. 'The Grand Mufti won't let us leave.'

'I shall try to persuade him.'

The archbishop agreed to receive his deputy Kapellmeister, but his manner was haughty and distant. 'Is there a problem, Herr Mozart?'

'Oh no, Excellency. It is merely that I am planning a visit to Munich, and—'

'My people work in Salzburg, not in Munich.'

'It is so that my son may fulfil an opera commission, Your Grace.'

'From whom?'

'From Maximilian III, Elector of Bavaria.'

'Ah.' Colloredo was keen to maintain cordial relations with all crowned heads and heads of principalities, big or small. 'In that case,' he said curtly, 'the matter is worthy of consideration. It will be an opera in the Italian style, I trust?'

'Of course, Your Grace. It will be called *La finta giardiniera* – "The Counterfeit Gardener". The author of the libretto is Raniero de' Calzabigi, a disciple of Gluck.'

'That is an indication of quality. See that your son brings honour to the reputation of the musicians of my court. I give you both permission to travel to Munich.'

Munich, 8 December 1774

What a joy it was to leave Salzburg! On the journey Wolfgang had read Goethe's *Werther*; he did not care much for the profusion of exaggerated sentiments.

As for Leopold, he digested the news of Gluck's appointment as composer to the royal court in Vienna, with a salary of 2,000 florins a year. For his son, the road to the Austrian capital seemed cut off for ever.

On their arrival in Munich, the Mozarts were welcomed by Canon Pernat and Count Seeau, *Intendant* of musical events at the Bavarian court. 'A perfect hypocrite,' Wolfgang thought immediately.

'Is the opera finished?' asked the count.

'It is at an advanced stage,' replied Leopold. 'Wolfgang will soon complete it.'

'That is fortunate, for the elector is expecting a great deal from this opera. Entertaining the dear citizens of Munich seems of the utmost importance to him.'

'That man Seeau is going to cause us trouble,' predicted Wolfgang when he and his father were alone.

'Whatever happens, we mustn't lose our tempers with him. If the opera's a success, other commissions will follow.'

Despite toothache which required urgent treatment, on 16 December Wolfgang finished the three acts of *La finta giardiniera*. He found its libretto of little interest, apart from the character of the heroine, Violante, who was beautiful, loving and faithful. He found it exciting to translate into music the feelings of a woman with a pure heart and a noble soul.

When Count Seeau informed the Mozarts that the premiere had been postponed, Wolfgang was not surprised. That two-faced schemer had the look of a born liar.

The arrival of Nannerl, on 5 January 1775, was an opportunity to sample a few local entertainments. Although she was staying with an extremely pious old lady, the three Mozarts attended balls in Munich while they waited for the authorities to make up their minds.

43

Munich, 13 January 1775

The Salvatortheater was full for the first performance of
La finta giardiniera. Would young Mozart's *opera buffa* be
entertaining?

There was certainly nothing cheerful about the beginning.
Count Belfiore, who was in love with the Marquise Violante,
was mad with unfounded jealousy. So jealous that he killed her
rather than see her give herself to a rival. Returning home, the
murderer became betrothed to the charming Arminda. Neither
his all-consuming love nor his mourning had lasted very long.

But Violante was in fact not dead. As soon as she was
well again, she set out with her servant Roberto to find the
would-be murderer. Once she reached Belfiore's lands, she concealed her identity by pretending to be a gardener, Sandrina,
who was in service to Don Anchise, uncle of Arminda,
Belfiore's wife. Roberto became the don's servant.

At this stage, the audience at last relaxed. Through disguises
and false names, the evil doer was bound to be punished in a
riot of open gaiety.

While Don Anchise coveted the noble and honourable
Sandrina, Roberto made advances to the don's pretty maid-
servant, Serpetta, but she rejected him. Eventually, Sandrina
revealed her true identity to Belfiore, who threw himself at her

feet and implored forgiveness. Alas, this was really nothing to laugh about, for the young woman, instead of taking her revenge or forgiving him, persuaded the ruffian that she really had deceived him.

Completely disorientated by this, the Munich audience was relieved and reassured by a happy ending featuring three weddings: that of Violante to Belfiore; that of his abandoned wife, Arminda, to a new lover; and that of the two servants, Roberto and Serpetta.

Just one person was left over: Don Anchise, who failed to win favour of any beautiful lady. Everyone was hoping for an openly comic scene, but the unfortunate man could love no one but the gardener Sandrina, and sank into a sort of dementia.

'It's an odd sort of *opera buffa*,' concluded one listener. 'That young Mozart fellow knows how to tell a story in music, but there are too many tragic notes and passages in minor keys. How did the elector react?'

'He applauded,' noted his neighbour.

'And Count Seeau?'

'He didn't seem very enthusiastic. In my opinion, the author wavers constantly between tragic and comic. And that over-complicated libretto – what a bore!'

Not everyone agreed. The influential critic C. F. D. Schubart wrote in the *Deutsche Chronik*: 'If Mozart is not a delicate flower, he will become one of the greatest composers who have ever lived.'

Munich, February 1775

Wolfgang wrote to his anxious mother, telling her that the elector and the Munich nobility had liked his opera. He ended his letter by saying, 'We shall be coming home soon enough.'

'Don't be annoyed,' his father warned him. 'I've just received a commission from the archbishop. He wants a short, pleasant mass.'

Although irritated, the young man quickly complied and produced a short mass in which the violins imitated the twittering of sparrows. It was almost stupid, but entertaining. In the Credo he accentuated the word '*descendit*'; only he knew that it signified 'How I wish Colloredo would collapse and leave me in peace!' He could think of nothing better for his nineteenth year.

It was carnival time, and Leopold and his two children joined the revellers. Forgetting their cares, they attended balls and delighted in watching the pagan rites announcing the end of winter and the return of the light.

Leopold awaited the commission for a new opera which would launch his son's career in Munich. When would Count Seeau finally give him the good news? In the end he lost patience and forced a meeting with the *Intendant*.

'What is it, Herr Mozart?'

'*La finta giardiniera* was a great success, wasn't it?'

'Opinions differ.'

'And what is yours, Herr Count?'

'Your son certainly has talent. However, to my mind some passages seemed a little too serious for an *opera buffa*. It is carnival time, and the people of Munich want to enjoy themselves. So these stories about mad people, in which one is not quite sure who is who . . .'

'Wolfgang is not responsible for the libretto.'

'I quite understand that, Herr Mozart. Now, on a different subject: Prince Maximilian desires a motet designed for the offertory of a mass. Could your son compose one quickly?'

'You may rely on him.'

In total opposition to the light music played in Salzburg, Wolfgang created a very austere piece, *Misericordias Domini*, in D minor, in an archaic style. Proud of this homage to the old masters, he sent the score to Padre Martini and was cruelly disappointed by his response: 'A success in the ... modern taste.'

He could not dwell on his disappointment, for he was obliged to earn his living. He wrote a charming piano sonata, rich in virtuosity, to a commission from the wealthy Baron von Dürnitz. Then he fought a duel, on harpsichords, with the virtuoso Ignaz van Beecke before an audience of sensation-seekers. Although as good technically as Wolfgang, van Beecke lacked poetic feeling. The victors of the joust were wine and beer, in honour of the valiant musicians.

Munich, March 1775

At the beginning of March Leopold went to see Count Seeau again.

'I am extremely busy, Herr Mozart, and I have scarcely any time to speak with you.'

'Was Elector Maximilian pleased with the motet?'

'He has not expressed any criticism.'

'No compliments, either?'

'No.'

'Do you envisage commissioning a new opera?'

'I must think about it.'

'If he is given enough time, my son will compose a work much more attractive than *La finta giardiniera*.'

'The thing is, that opera lacked gaiety. I suspect your son's abilities are limited. But he gives the Prince-Archbishop of Salzburg satisfaction, so why is he seeking his fortune elsewhere? Stay at home, Herr Mozart, and enjoy your privileged position there.'

The visit to Munich had been a failure. Leopold told Wolfgang only that Count Seeau was undecided, handicapped as he was by his uncertain artistic tastes.

The realization was cruel. There would be no commission for a new opera for next Lent, no varied scores for the Bavarian court, no religious music.

On 6 March 1775, the Mozarts left Munich for Salzburg.

44

Seated beside Archduke Maximilian Franz, fourth and last son of Empress Maria Theresa, Prince-Archbishop Colloredo was proud to offer his illustrious guest, who was passing through the city, a little *dramma per musica* in two acts and fourteen musical items, *Il rè pastore* ('The Shepherd King'), from the lively pen of young Mozart, to a libretto by Metastasio. Wolfgang had had to work quickly, and this work was nothing like the grand opera he longed to write.

Alexander the Great at first wanted to grant the throne of Sidon to an unsuitable candidate. Realizing his error, he chose better candidates, including a shepherd, who, however, wanted to stay with his flock. Eventually, everything ended for the best, thanks to the clear-sightedness of Alexander – which clearly equalled that of Colloredo.

Colloredo was delighted. Clearly pleased with the warm welcome he had been given, the archduke was bound to praise the archbishop to the court in Vienna, where the future of the region was decided. If Josef II succeeded in imposing the reforms he sought, Colloredo would be able to maintain Salzburg's prosperity.

Brunswick, 26 May 1775

The inhabitants of the good city of Brunswick observed a strange spectacle. Guided by Provincial Grand Master Charles de Hund, the Knights of Strict Templar Observance strode down the main streets to the House of the Order, where the Grand Master, Duke Ferdinand, was waiting for them.

Planned to last until 6 July, the Masonic general assembly brought together all the dignitaries and promised some lively debates. Three committees would ensure the Order's development: the first would deal with finances, the second with politics and the third with ceremonies. Their work would lead to reports, whose content would enable the Grand Master to take decisions.

This first great official display in the duke's domain met with considerable popular success. At once intrigued and admiring, passers-by much enjoyed the march of the superbly dressed Knights.

While his assistants were solving the problems of stewardship, the Grand Master had a private meeting with Baron de Hund, who looked thin and ill.

'Sit down, my dear Brother,' said the duke. 'Would you like some water, herb tea or indeed a stronger drink?'

'A little water, please.'

The duke himself served his guest. 'Your health worries me.'

'I am very ill,' admitted the baron, 'and my days are numbered.'

'I am extremely sorry to hear it. The best doctors in Brunswick will try to cure you.'

'It's too late.'

'Don't be so pessimistic.'

'If Strict Observance survives me, I shall have succeeded, shan't I?'

The Duke was embarrassed. 'My dear Brother, unfortunately you have many enemies. Small minds reproach you for a lack of precision on the origins of the Order and the legitimacy of your spiritual power.'

'I have already said everything there is to say on that subject.'

'Your explanations lack consistency. In all sincerity, you defend yourself very badly. And I fear that even your most loyal supporters may desert you.'

'To die alone and discredited . . .'

'Given my responsibilities, I have a duty to speak clearly, even if I deplore the necessary cruelty.'

The baron felt incapable of fighting any more. 'What do you want from me?'

'First, that you approve my decision to transfer the Order's seat of government from Dresden to Brunswick. Second, that you approve the appointment of Brothers close to me to posts of responsibility. Last, that you withdraw to allow me to exercise total power. In exchange for your support, I shall protect you. Whatever your errors and inadequacies, I shall take responsibility for them. You will thus be able to take care of yourself in complete peace.'

Charles de Hund slumped in his chair and closed his eyes, utterly overwhelmed by exhaustion.

Vienna, July 1775

Emperor Josef had demonstrated his firmness by subduing a peasants' revolt in Bohemia; he was determined to maintain the grandeur of the empire by affirming its authority. However, he knew also how and when to take popular measures, such as opening the Augarten gardens to the public.

Josef Anton was concerned that the emperor might introduce too much liberalism, which would weaken the police and harm the empire's security. Many Freemasons encouraged this tendency, at least in words.

On his return from Brunswick, Geytrand immediately reported to his superior.

'Masonic assemblies are veritable mines of information,' he said delightedly. 'Some participants are so happy to be invited that they talk willingly. I found one so vain that he told me everything. Baron de Hund is very ill and, even though he founded the Order, has been sent home to Dresden, where he will die, abandoned and scorned. The Duke of Brunswick, on the other hand, is hale and hearty . . .'

'In other words, the duke has taken full power.'

'With Hund out of the way, he has filled all the key posts with men loyal to him, which means he can control the Order's finances and direct its politics according to his own vision.'

'What exactly does he want?'

'To restore the Order of the Temple and give it back the splendour of yesteryear. And this Grand Master is of much greater stature than Baron de Hund. Not to take him seriously would be a mistake.'

'What about the content of the rituals?'

'In this respect the assembly was a failure. The duke had hoped to persuade the monks and priests to offer their esoteric knowledge to the Knights, but it was a waste of effort. The scholars refuse to give up their secrets – not very brotherly! The Grand Master will have to ease tensions among the factions and impose better discipline. It remains to be seen whether he can maintain peaceful coexistence between the various branches of the Order.'

'He's a dangerous man,' said Josef Anton. 'Dangerous, but not untouchable.'

45

Salzburg, August 1775

The heat was too much for Miss Pimperl, and she spent the day sleeping in the Mozart family's large apartment. Wolfgang took her for walks early in the morning and late in the evening, always taking along a rag-ball which the dog usually ended up stealing from him.

His friend Anton Stadler was playing the field, but he, Wolfgang, had to keep on and on composing. A second violin concerto, which came into existence on 14 June, was written in the French style, and so was superficial and refined. Then came a church sonata, a serenade, and a divertimento intended to add gaiety to one of the archbishop's meals, organized at the castle of Mirabell, his own little Versailles. In other words, nothing profound.

Depressed, the young man went back to his funeral cantata of 1767 and added a final chorus. This dialogue between the Soul and the Angel, this evocation of death and the world beyond, enabled him to escape for a few hours from the light-hearted trifles imposed on him by Colloredo.

And then one evening Thamos reappeared during Miss Pimperl's evening walk – she was overjoyed to see him.

Wolfgang was equally delighted. 'I thought you'd abandoned me!' he exclaimed.

'You were abandoning yourself.'

'I am given a specific task to perform, and I perform it. The archbishop likes only one type of music, and none of his servant musicians can escape from it.'

'Not even you?'

'The prison bars are too strong.'

'Have you given up composing for yourself, outside the framework of your commissions?'

'Almost, although I recently completed an old half-finished funeral cantata which has nothing light about it.'

'So we meet again. Why should I take an interest in a mediocre person who is unable to fight against adversity?'

'Mediocre? Me? I think I've proved I'm rather more than that!'

'Are you sure you have?'

Wolfgang hesitated, but held out. 'I've given the best of myself, I've—'

'Not yet. And you aren't following the right path: you're allowing yourself to be caught out by your own fluency.'

'The archbishop requires—'

'And you compose. Take care you don't fall asleep.'

'If *Thamos* had succeeded, I wouldn't be in this position.'

'Forget the ifs. Create your own will and your own art. Only they will open the door of knowledge to you.'

Salzburg, 12 September 1775

When he read the score of his son's third violin concerto, Leopold was surprised and worried. True, it more or less respected the *galant* style, the final rondo in the French style was bound to please Colloredo, and the slow movement, an adagio, had a rather melancholy feel but would not bore the audience. On the other hand, the initial allegro was out of place: it was forceful, it developed themes in a minor mode, and it offered some surprising exchanges between soloist and orchestra.

'This opening,' said Leopold. 'Perhaps you should moderate—'

'The movement progresses in a natural way, doesn't it?'

'Colloredo's ears aren't used to so much complexity. It's almost like a sort of . . . explosion.'

'Perhaps it will wake up the Grand Mufti's soul.'

Leopold's fears were unfounded: the concerto didn't shock Colloredo at all, because he barely listened to it. He cared only about his new programme of economies.

Would the household musicians have to bear the brunt of them?

Lyon, September 1775

Jean-Baptiste Willermoz was a forty-five-year-old trader in fabrics. He had the face of a man who enjoyed good living, with thick eyebrows, sensual lips and large, rather innocent eyes. Cordial, friendly and generous, he undertook charitable works and seemed to lead the quiet life of an upper-middle-class Lyonais.

However, his true ideal was not to amass an immense fortune. A Freemason from the age of twenty, Willermoz was the spiritual heir of Martines de Pasqually, an enthusiast of Gnosticism, the Kabbalah and magic, who had died in 1774 in San Domingo. In 1758, Willermoz had founded the Lodge of True Friends, and in 1760 the Lodge of the Regular Masters of Lyon. Now he was Venerable Master for life of the Lodge of the Perfect Friendship, which he had also created, and he continued in his energetic attempts to spread the Masonic ideal.

Willermoz had become one of the leaders of the French branch of Strict Templar Observance. He believed it could represent the future of Freemasonry, so long as it developed an authentic spirituality, which most lodges sadly lacked. Not content with presiding over and organizing the lodges in Lyon, he engaged in voluminous correspondence with numerous mystics and Freemasons in order to propagate his ideas. Strict Observance would, he hoped, enable him to mould the movement and conquer the whole of France.

He must exercise the utmost caution, however, and must not reveal his true intentions too soon, for he did not know the new Grand Master, Ferdinand of Brunswick. Would the duke be unyielding and closed, or open to mystic visions? Another thing worried him: the fact that the Templar Order was based in Germany displeased some patriotic French Bothers. Willermoz would have to proceed in small steps and wait for favourable circumstances before asserting himself as an incontestable leader, at first in the manner of an *éminence grise*, then in the full light of day.

Salzburg, 15 November 1775

Leopold was furious. On 30 September, Colloredo had closed the court theatre in order to save money. This was very bad news for the court musicians, who were deprived of a precious source of work.

Faced with more or less veiled pressure from many sources, the archbishop consented to open a new theatre in the Mirabell park, near his palace, but an impresario would present strolling troupes there; no privileges would be granted to the musicians of Salzburg. Their scope for creating music had therefore shrunk markedly. Fortunately, the two Mozarts were spared further loss, and retained their court posts.

In the final rondo of his fourth violin concerto, which was inspired by Boccherini, Wolfgang had amused himself by including a folk tune from Alsace, which earned the work – which was acceptable to the Grand Mufti's ears – the nickname of the 'Strasbourg Concerto'. Leopold was pleased to see that his son had returned to reason, but less pleased by the fifth concerto, in A major, because its slow movement had worrying depths and the finale had excessive rhythmic intensity.

'It's too weighty and too dense,' he concluded. 'You should replace this adagio.'

'As you wish, father. I have decided not to write any more concertos for violin and orchestra. I have reached the limits of a suffocating genre.'

That evening, while out walking Miss Pimperl, who loved playing in the snow, Wolfgang met Thamos.

'I was pleased by your reaction, Wolfgang.'

'My father isn't! He bans anything excessive, so as not to displease Colloredo.'

'Perhaps the archbishop will like the forthcoming opera to be performed in his new theatre.'

'It's in the Italian style, I hope? If not, its failure is guaranteed.'

'It's in the style of Mozart in training.'

'What do you mean?'

'Can't you guess? With the help of a few influential contacts, I have managed to arrange a performance of *Thamos, König in Ägypten*'.

46

Salzburg, 3 January 1776

Despite the bad weather, the performance of *Thamos* was a ray of sunshine for Wolfgang.

Prince-Archbishop Colloredo's verdict hit him like a thunderbolt. He did not dislike von Gebler's play, for he interpreted it according to the philosophy of Light and saw in it no political allusions to the Austrian government; on the other hand, he thought young Mozart's choruses were pointless. At the end of the day, it was a minor work and would soon be forgotten.

As they emerged from the theatre, the Egyptian consoled Wolfgang. 'Forget the criticism and continue to work on this theme, even if you don't write a note. Slowly, very slowly, the Mysteries will nourish your thoughts.'

'But the Grand Mufti hates my music.'

'Not the sort that enables you to earn your living and deepen your knowledge of styles and instruments. This performance has provided us with a piece of valuable information: Colloredo was neither shocked nor angry, because all he saw was a sort of innocent fairytale, evoking distant antiquity. Little by little, you will learn how to create forms which, without betraying the message, will please all audiences, from the most learned to the most uneducated. Some people will appreciate the magic, others the style, the majority will allow themselves to be charmed, and a very small number will perceive the vital truth.'

'This vital truth, is it the teachings of the priests of the sun?'

'Go on charming Salzburg and prove to me that you can do so without losing your soul.'

Salzburg, 27 January 1776

Wolfgang was treated to a tremendous feast to celebrate his twentieth birthday. Overcome with a creative fever, he had just composed a delicious piano concerto, an amusing 'nocturnal serenade' a divertimento* whose solemn trio in G minor made one forget that the work was intended to cheer one of Colloredo's meals, a church sonata and a concerto for three pianos adapted to the technical abilities of a young virtuoso, Countess Josefa.

'The archbishop, the court and the aristocracy appreciate the quality and quantity of your work,' Leopold told him. 'In church and in the salons, you are recognized as a true professional. And I have good news for you: several wealthy ladies want you to give them piano lessons.'

'I'm not interested in teaching.'

'It's important, Wolfgang. For one thing, one cannot refuse persons of high rank; for another, the financial rewards will be far from negligible. Are you ashamed to follow in your father's footsteps and become a good teacher?'

'No, of course not.'

'Then let us put an end to this bickering. Your future is all mapped out: serenades and entertainments for the court and wealthy music-lovers, litanies and masses for the Church, and

---

* K240. The theme of the finale of the 'Jupiter' Symphony is sketched out in it.

teaching for persons of quality. Quite an achievement at the age of twenty.'

'Yes, it's excellent,' agreed Anna Maria. 'And who wouldn't want to live out their days happily in Salzburg?'

Berlin, April 1776

Former pastor Wöllner, a member of the Strict Templar Observance movement since 1768, had at last obtained the post he had so coveted: Venerable Master of the celebrated Three Globes Lodge. With his Brother and friend Bischoffswerder, an army officer, he also controlled the Frederick with the Golden Lion Lodge.

Through these lodges, the two accomplices, encouraged by power, intended to introduce into Berlin the old system of the Golden Rose-Cross, whose secret missionaries they were. Missionaries, yes, but also double agents, since they were launching their campaign with the agreement and support of the Jesuits.

Neither Brother realized that the Jesuits were acting under the influence of Josef Anton, whose undermining work was beginning to produce results. Since he could not attack Freemasonry head-on, he would continually inject poison into it in order to eat away at it from the inside.

Josef Anton was not content merely to observe and to add to his dossiers. Now he was taking active steps.

Salzburg, April 1776

'Delightful, delicious, marvellous! This piano concerto is so distinguished. I am enchanted by it. Herr Mozart, you are a magician.'

Wolfgang bowed.

Antonia, Countess Lützow was visibly fascinated by the fluid music produced by the young composer who was so well liked among high society in Salzburg. The fact that he had dedicated his C major concerto to her would make many other ladies jealous.

'I'd like to take more lessons,' said the countess, 'so that I can play it without making mistakes.'

'My days are very full, and—'

'I beg you, Herr Mozart.'

'Take a seat at the piano.'

Wolfgang corrected a few of his pupil's many mistakes and promised her another lesson soon. Then he went to Anton Stadler's home to challenge him to a shooting competition and so get rid of his tension. God, how teaching exasperated him!

Pleasing his parents by proving his abilities to them was not enough to make him happy. If the future consisted of slowly growing old while wearing the uniform of a musician-servant, subject to the demands of a petty tyrant, what point was there in building it? But, thanks to Thamos, Wolfgang continued to hope. And he would not disappoint his friend from another world.

Ingolstadt, 1 May 1776

Adam Weishaupt was twenty-eight, a law professor and soon to be a senior figure at the university in the little town of Ingolstadt in Bavaria. He was living through exceptional times. Born in this ancient stronghold of the Jesuits, whose Order, although dissolved, continued to operate secretly, he had decided to fight against the Church, Catholicism and its followers. Weishaupt was an atheist, who believed that their influence on education and higher learning was appalling. This stupid religion herded people together and prevented individuals from thinking freely.

How could he fight obscurantism, except by gathering

together strong-minded men determined to strike decisive blows against it? In creating the secret society of the Illuminati, in Bavaria on 1 May, Weishaupt was providing himself with the necessary instrument to realize his dream.

His faithful followers as yet numbered only a few, but they acted as scouts and propagators of the Light. Most of them wanted to establish a compromise between reason and a less sectarian religion, without subscribing to the revolutionary ideas of certain French philosophers, though they criticized the privileges of kings and princes, especially when those kings and princes exercised their powers undiscriminatingly and incompetently. Moreover, this was not a particularly unusual position: it was widespread throughout the theatre and literature.

But it had still to be taken from theory into practice, while avoiding violence. Firmly believing that Catholicism had distorted spirituality, the Illuminati had great respect for the teachings of the Ancients, notably the Egyptians.

When the founders met, several decisions were taken: absolute secrecy, partitioning of groups, intensive intellectual work, strict discipline, secular education, the publication of brochures, and the close scrutiny of all applications – a detailed summary of life and career from every applicant. Moreover, the names of members and their meeting places would be coded.*

Success would involve the conquest of Freemasonry, the ideal basis for spreading a new philosophy.

---

* 'Athens' denoted Munich, 'Eleusis' Ingolstadt, 'Heliopolis' Weimar and 'Egypt' Austria. Weishaupt was called 'Spartacus' and Sonnenfels, a Freemason and professor of political science in Vienna, was known as 'Fabius'.

47

Salzburg, May 1776

Not a single person in the audience was bored by Wolfgang Mozart's new Mass in C major, for the music was scintillating. Rather distanced from the usual religious framework, it was scarcely conducive to quiet meditation. No longer able to bow to Colloredo's demands, the young man had finally composed a *missa longa*, a 'long mass', which because of its length could not be performed in the cathedral. The church of St Peter had provided a venue for it, much to the delight of the faithful.

'I had a wonderful time,' said Anton Stadler. 'But aren't you in danger of annoying the Church?'

'If they're sad and depressed, I'll give them back their energy.'

'Our dear religious folk don't have a very well-developed sense of humour.'

'I had to free myself from a straitjacket. Producing each mass exactly according to Colloredo's specifications was becoming unbearable.'

Vienna, 20 May 1776

'There's been a top-level meeting,' Geytrand told Josef Anton. 'One of the Duke of Brunswick's manservants informed me that the Grand Master of the Templar Order has just played host to the Grand Master of the Swedish Rite, the Duke of Saxe-Gotha. A delicious lunch, apparently, accompanied by wines of the highest quality.'

'Was there anything important, apart from this diplomatic feast?'

'The two dukes tried to put an end to the hostilities between their Masonic movements. Each has the conquest of Europe in his sights, and the discussion was a thorny one.'

'Is there to be a sacred union or a major confrontation?'

'Neither, it seems. Saxe-Gotha doesn't want trouble, but refuses to dissolve his brotherhood into Strict Observance. As for Brunswick, he won't set limits on his ambitions. It appears that only two concessions were made: the Templars won't move into Sweden, and the Swedish Rite will silence those of its members who are too virulently anti-Templar. But this false peace has already been broken.'

'How?'

'Zinnendorf's in Vienna, hoping to rally four lodges to the Swedish Rite.'

'Naturally he is being followed at all times?'

'Naturally, Herr Count, as is his official emissary, von Sudthausen.'

'He has requested an audience with Emperor Josef,' revealed Josef Anton.

Geytrand was appalled. 'Is the Swedish Rite hoping to gain official recognition?'

'Probably.'

'That would be a disaster!'

'Don't worry. I have supplied His Majesty with a most instructive dossier.'

Vienna, 26 May 1776

Von Sudthausen was extremely disappointed. The plan to fuse the Templar Order and the Swedish Rite had failed miserably. The dreams of his friend Zinnendorf had been shattered, unless the audience with Josef led to a positive result.

The emperor's demeanour was extremely cold.

'Majesty, I beg you to be the protector of the Masonic lodges belonging to the Swedish Rite. The Brothers are wholly respectful of your supreme authority and of the laws you promulgate. Only men of quality are admitted into our assemblies, where no subversive talk would ever be tolerated. You may count on the absolute and sincere loyalty of the Freemasons.'

'Very good, but you already have one lodge adhering to the Swedish Rite, which seems amply sufficient to me. I will authorize its existence, so long as there is strict respect for our laws.'

'You have our thanks, Majesty. Your high patronage would—'

'Do not depend upon it. A liberal spirit must be neither weak nor partisan. To favour Freemasonry would mean conflict with many highly placed persons, beginning with Her Majesty the Empress.'

'I am aware of that, Majesty, but—'

'This audience is at an end.'

Von Sudthausen withdrew. The Swedish Rite would never establish itself in Vienna.

Salzburg, 10 June 1776

On the feast day of St Anthony of Padua, Countess Lodron organized a great celebration in the saint's honour. The revels were to be accompanied by light, sophisticated music, including a divertimento by young Mozart. After all, the archbishop was extremely fond of listening to melodies during meals taken in society.

Among the guests was the Count of Thebes, a foreign aristocrat who was as wealthy as he was discreet. A great traveller, he gave large sums of money to homes and schools for orphans and children who had been disinherited. Wolfgang could not help wondering why the Egyptian took part in events like this.

Thamos sat impassively through the divertimento, not allowing himself to display even a glimmer of emotion when, at the start of the finale, which was unexpectedly solemn, he perceived the first indications of the Great Work.*

As soon as the work ended, the audience began to chat. Taking advantage of the noise and fuss, Thamos disappeared. Wolfgang felt a stab of deep distress: did this mean that Thamos was seriously displeased?

* The piece was the Divertimento in F, K247, parts of which were incorporated into the priests' chorus in *Die Zauberflöte*.

48

Vienna, 20 July 1776

Forty-three-year-old Joseph von Sonnenfels, professor of political science at the University of Vienna, had been the first Austrian lawyer to defend the ideas of the philosophy of Light in his periodical, *Man without Prejudices*. Well liked by Emperor Josef, he had just achieved a great victory: the abolition of torture. The emperor knew Sonnenfels belonged to the Masonic lodge called True Concord, but did not know he was also one of Bavaria's Illuminati, full of enthusiasm for Weishaupt's great plans.

An excellent piece of news encouraged Sonnenfels as he pursued his aims. The first president of the newly created United States of America, was to be a Freemason, George Washington, one of whose major concerns was freedom of conscience.

When he was summoned to the palace, Sonnenfels resolved not to draw back. If the expected criticism from the emperor materialized, he would try to explain that his positions were well founded. Josef seemed less closed-minded than Maria Theresa, and believed in the need to adopt liberal reforms, but up to what point?

'Herr Professor,' declared the emperor, 'I have an urgent task for you. Some might consider it minor, but I regard it as important. You are not indifferent to cultural policies, I assume?'

'On the contrary, Majesty.'

'I want a national theatre in Vienna, administered by the court. Which should it be, and how do you suggest it be organized?'

Fortunately, Sonnenfels had a gift for thinking fast. 'The Burgtheater. I would get rid of the deplorable farces which are numbing the minds of the general public, and set up a fine institution to produce German musical works, alternating with Italian ones.'

'You have my agreement. Set to work.'

Salzburg, summer 1776

On 20 July, a large orchestra played Wolfgang's long and joyful serenade written for the wedding of Elisabeth Haffner, daughter of a rich trader and Salzburg *burgmeister*. The same gaiety was present in the D major divertimento, incorporating French dances, that was played on Nannerl's twenty-fifth birthday. But then this slightly forced cheerfulness was shattered by another divertimento, for piano, violin and cello, whose slow movement expressed a troubling sadness.

Wolfgang was afraid that, if he continued to compose romantic, superficial music, it would lead him into an impasse. And then there was Thamos's disappearance, which he took to be tantamount to disapproval. It was impossible to confide in his father, his mother or his sister. The only one who understood was Miss Pimperl, who was always ready to play and drive away the dark shadows.

'There is nothing shameful about your work,' declared the voice he had been longing to hear.

'Thamos! Do you mean you don't despise me?'

'Far from it, Wolfgang. You prove your serious commitment

every day by carrying out your duties conscientiously. Here and there, your true future is beginning to pierce through. But you will still have to blacken a lot more manuscript paper.'

'I'm only twenty, and I'm already an insignificant official in the service of a petty tyrant who wants to dictate every aspect of musical taste.'

'You are learning your trade and fashioning yourself weapons with a view to future battles. One facet of intelligence is the ability to adapt, is it not?'

'Sometimes, I just want to smash the instruments and throw the pieces in the archbishop's face, to find out if he has a grain of sensitivity!'

'Don't stifle that wish.'

'Are you . . . Do you mean I should rebel?'

'That would be premature. Doing the right thing at the right moment is the principal skill of a good magician. You will need to progress through many stages before you can exercise it. Having been a child prodigy does not make your task any easier.'

'I'm not a child any more.'

'So much the better, Wolfgang. Now, to work.'

Wiesbaden, 15 August 1776

The Masonic assembly brought together delegates from many lodges and several important visitors. Thamos was seated beside Johann Joachim Christoph Bode, and found his neighbour extremely turbulent: the fiery, impatient Brother constantly inveighed against the speakers, whom he considered lukewarm and boring.

'You haven't heard the worst yet,' he confided to Thamos. 'Now they're going to announce the Messiah, the saviour of Freemasonry.'

'What is he called?'

'Gottlieb, Baron von Gugomos, a counsellor in Rastatt's government. Ah, here he is.'

The new prophet began to speak and immediately got to the heart of the subject. 'I was initiated in Rome and I know the great secrets. Totally filled with the higher spirit, I have come to drag you out of the darkness and teach you the truth. If the lodges obey me and renounce the errors of their ways, they will leave the way of the Devil and advance along the way of God.'

'We don't want anything to do with your God!' exploded Bode. 'A Freemason must escape from the Church's clutches and think freely.'

Gugomos gazed at him sadly. 'Calm yourself, my Brother, and don't become a persecutor of the truth I embody. Or else—'

'Or else what?'

'I have a mastery of poisons, notably *aqua toffana*, which leaves few traces and strikes down perjurers and traitors like a thunderbolt. At the cemetery, my faithful will sing mourning psalms beside the tomb of the Brother they have justly slain.'

'This charlatan is completely mad!' roared Bode. 'Expel him from the assembly!'

The president of the session put an end to the meeting. It was clear that Gugomos was not entirely in his right mind.

'Freemasonry dishonours itself by accepting those who are mentally ill, like him,' Bode said to Thamos.

'What do you propose, Brother?'

'A radical change of direction. First, eradicate the Jesuits and their spies, who are hiding behind Masonic aprons. Then incline our perverted society towards justice and equality.'

'Don't you think that might bring a fierce reaction from the authorities?'

'In the lodges we can speak freely. These ideas will be more powerful than a vast army. I give you my word as Bode the unbeliever: thrones will come crashing down and new values will assert themselves.'

As he left Wiesbaden on 4 September, at the end of a futile general assembly, Thamos thought of Abbot Hermes and prayed to him for help. He needed all his master's wisdom, derived from the eternal East, to persuade himself that Freemasonry would be the framework within which the Great Magician would blossom forth.

Vienna, 7 September 1776

'The Wiesbaden assembly ended in confusion,' Geytrand reported to Josef Anton. 'A raving madman who called himself Baron Gugomos even threatened to poison Brothers who refused to obey him unquestioningly.'

'Was that just a show, or was the threat real?'

'The "baron" was expelled, but he claimed to be expert in the use of a fearsome poison called *aqua toffana*. I've checked, and it does indeed exist. Administered in small doses over a long period, it leaves scarcely a trace.'

'Interesting,' commented Anton, noting down the details. 'Try to obtain some – using the utmost discretion.'

'That goes without saying, Herr Count.'

49

Wolfgang had greatly enjoyed himself writing '*Clarice cara*', a comic aria for tenor in which the singer played the part of a ridiculous prattler demanding all sorts of qualities from his future wife. It followed the composition of '*Ombra felice . . . Io ti lascio*' for alto, the heart-rending farewells of Aeneas and the beautiful Dido, whose love's only outcome was death.

The young man swung between sadness and gaiety, no longer knowing how to express what he felt deep within him. Thamos could help him, true, but Wolfgang never knew when they would meet. And Leopold understood nothing of the seriousness of his moods. Only one man could tell him what path to follow: Padre Martini.

It was important that Wolfgang did not talk to the Padre about his romantic little pieces designed to entertain Colloredo and Salzburg's high society. Padre Martini liked only serious compositions and religious music. If the young man sent him a cry for help, the response was bound to be favourable. The Padre would invite him to Bologna and procure work for him.

So Wolfgang took up his finest quill pen and weighed each of the words upon which his destiny depended:

The Great Magician

Very Reverend Father and Master, My very esteemed Master, the veneration, esteem and respect that I bear towards you incline me to dare importune you by way of this letter, and to send hereby enclosed a feeble sample of my music, submitting it to your sovereign judgement. Last year, I wrote an opera buffa, La finta giardiniera, *at Munich, in Bavaria. A few days after I left that city, His Highness the Elector wished also to hear something of my counterpoint music. I was therefore obliged to write this motet in great haste, so that there was time to copy out the score for His Highness, and to transcribe the parts so that the piece could be performed the following Sunday, during the offertory at the Great Mass.*

My very dear and esteemed Father and Master, I ask you earnestly to give me your opinion, with total frankness and without reservation. We are in this world in order to learn permanently, and in order to enlighten each other by exchanging our thoughts, and to attempt to make progress in the science and the arts. How many times – oh, how many times! – I have felt the desire to live closer to you and to converse with you!

My father occupies the post of Kapellmeister at the cathedral, which gives me the chance to write for it as much as I wish. Unfortunately, the prince-archbishop is not fond of the old styles. Our religious music is very different from what is played in Italy, particularly since a Mass must not last longer than three-quarters of an hour. So this genre of composition requires a particular way of working, not to mention the fact that the mass, despite its brevity, must include all the instruments, including military trumpets! Ah yes, my very dear Father, that is how it is.

How good it would be to be able to tell you many other things. I humbly beg all the members of the Accademia to grant me their favour, and constantly regret being so far

227

away from the man whom I venerate most in the world, and whose humble and very devoted servant I remain.

Paris, October 1776

'Your request interested me, Monsieur Mauvillon, said the Comte de Mirabeau in his authoritative voice.* 'Why did you contact me in such great secrecy?'

'Because I am the envoy of a young brotherhood, the Illuminati of Bavaria, whose ideas should appeal to you.'

'What are they?'

'Here is a paper I produced following long working sessions with the Illuminati. In it, we advocate the abolition of serfdom, of compulsory labour on state projects, of lettres de cachet and corporate bodies. In our view, it is urgent that we fight against despotism and intolerance.'

'A laudable programme, Mauvillon, but very dangerous.'

'That is why secrecy is necessary.'

'The Illuminati of Bavaria, you say ... Have you been identified by the police?'

'Not yet. There are only a few of us, but we bring together renowned intellectuals. Their thoughts will soon be unleashed upon Europe. France seems to us to be the country most open to a profound change in ways of thinking.'

'Grave crises are in the offing,' warned Mirabeau.

'And you, my lord, will play a determining part in them.'

'I intend to do so, but entirely legally. One must not go too far or too quickly.'

'That is also our view. Would you be willing to join our coterie?'

'I shall think about it.'

* Born in 1749, Mirabeau was to become president of the National Assembly in 1791, shortly before his death.

Mauvillon had no doubt: he had just recruited a new Illuminatus, whose influence would be considerable.

Meinigen, 28 October 1776

Baron de Hund was not strong enough to go to the Masonic gathering that some Brothers had organized in his honour, delighted as they were that he was visiting their city. Depressed, worn out, feeling his work slipping away from him, he had stopped fighting.

The baron took to his bed and summoned a Templar Knight in whom he had complete trust.

'I am about to sleep my last sleep,' he informed him. 'I want to be buried in the chapel on my Lipse estate, at the foot of the altar. Dress me in the clothing of a Provincial Grand Master of Strict Templar Observance, and have my titles, my arms and those of the Order engraved on my tombstone.'

Clasping to his heart a small red book bound in Cordoba leather, containing the Templar rituals, Charles de Hund closed his eyes.

50

Vienna, November 1776

'The founder of Strict Templar Observance, Charles de Hund, has died and been buried,' Geytrand told Josef Anton. 'The Grand Master won't shed many tears over it – now he has complete freedom of action.'

'He must still find a successor to lead the very important seventh province of the Templar Order. The baron had hardly any influence left, but he still had some prestige as the Order's founder.'

'Brunswick will choose a man of straw, whom he can manipulate as he wishes.'

'I'm not so sure,' disagreed Josef Anton. 'The seventh province is the Order's sword-point, and there will be no shortage of strong candidates. The baron was broken and ill, and had accepted the supremacy of the Grand Master. It may not be the same with his successors.'

'In that case, there will be some fierce fights and Freemasonry will be weakened.'

'We mustn't rejoice too soon. Let us wait for the appointment of the new leader of this famous province – to which Austria belongs, don't forget.'

'My network of spies will keep us well informed,' promised Geytrand.

Salzburg, December 1776

'You don't look at all happy,' said Anton Stadler to Wolfgang, who was stroking Miss Pimperl's belly as she lay on her back with her paws in the air. 'At twenty, you should be thinking about other things besides writing masses.'

Tired of superficial little works, disappointed not to have received a swift response from Padre Martini, to his father's great astonishment Wolfgang had composed nothing in October. Introverted and solitary, he was consolidating his decision to become a serious writer and to devote himself henceforth to church music.

This time, Thamos would have no reason to reproach him for getting lost in the twists and turns of frivolity. In November, his Mass in C major, highlighting in particular the Credo, had been performed in Salzburg Cathedral. Although it lasted less than three-quarters of an hour, it displayed real fervour. Could the God of the Christians offer the young man peace and the answer to his countless questions about himself, his art and his future?

A *missa brevis* for the ordination of Count von Spaur, future head of chapter at the cathedral, another *missa brevis* which included an organ solo, a *missa longa* punctuated with intense accents, a church sonata ... Wolfgang was making his mark, but Thamos did not reappear.

'This evening,' said Anton, 'I'm giving a little party with some nice girls I know, who'd very much like to meet you. Such a pious, serious boy ... they're curious about you. Don't miss it.'

'Sorry, I have to work.'

Vienna, December 1776

As he set down his modest luggage in his modest official lodgings at the University of Vienna, Ignaz von Born at last admitted that this was not a waking dream. Aware of his international reputation and concerned not to sideline a scholar of such standing, the empress had granted him a post as a mineralogist.

She, the fierce opponent of Freemasonry, must be completely unaware of von Born's involvement and ideals. But she would discover them sooner or later, for he planned to attend the Viennese lodges and there identify Brothers who wished to experience true initiation. He must be extremely cautious and pass for one of those inoffensive Freemasons who spent their meetings eating and drinking.

Someone knocked on the door. His first visitor: probably an administrator or a colleague.

'Thamos!'

'I am happy to see you living in Vienna, my Brother. Thanks to your new post, which will free you from material cares, you will be able to devote yourself to the construction of a type of Freemasonry based on initiation.'

'I owe the post to you, don't I?'

'Let us not exaggerate. I merely passed on information about you to influential people at court. Nobody was ensuring that your skills received the reward they deserve, and I felt that someone should. A mere helping hand, for it is your hard work and its recognition by several scientific institutions which have forced the empire to stop ignoring you.'

'I don't know how to—'

'To celebrate your installation, I've brought a bottle of vintage wine.'

The two Brothers toasted each other.

'Do you regret the death of Baron de Hund?' asked von Born.

'The death of a founder is always a grave matter. For all his faults, he believed in the resurgence of an Order capable of preventing materialism from being unleashed upon Europe. But he did not understand that too many administrative structures would shatter the spiritual dynamism and that the weakness of the rituals would cause blindness.'

'What about the Duke of Brunswick? Will he understand?'

'Let us hope so, but he must first keep control of the seventh province. If one of his opponents seizes it, Strict Observance is at risk of falling apart.'

'The consequences for the future of Freemasonry would be serious,' said von Born. 'But I have no intention of taking part in that battle.'

'You have better things to do, indeed. Unfortunately, Vienna is not the ideal setting.'

'I shall maintain close and secret links with Prague, a fall-back position in the event of danger. Nobody can predict the authorities' fluctuations and their attitude to the lodges.'

'Even more serious,' said Thamos, 'is the lodges' current state: a great deal of talk, conventional ceremonies, and very little research into initiation. They are navigating between various rites without heading towards the East. Here is a new chapter of *The Book of Thoth*, which will help you to see through some of the dark shadows.'

The Tradition, which everyone thought had been silenced for ever, was offering itself to the alchemist. Despite the magnitude of the task, he vowed that he would explore the tiniest aspect of this treasure and make it live again, with the help of the Egyptian.

'Be wary of tale-bearers and false Brothers,' warned Thamos. 'It is among them that the imperial police recruit informers. Freemasonry is tolerated only so long as the authorities know very precisely what is happening.'

Von Born nodded. 'Respect for secrecy will be one of the first values to be won back. Achieving it won't be easy, I fear, because first of all we will have to gather together men of their word, men who seek knowledge and initiation.'

'The great temples of ancient Egypt contained only a small number of initiates,' said Thamos. 'Around them, hundreds of people lived on their Light. It is not necessary to hope in order to attempt, my Brother, nor to succeed in order to persevere.'

51

Salzburg, 18 December 1776

At first Wolfgang didn't dare read the letter from Padre Martini. At last it had come: the answer he had waited for for so long, the invitation to return to Italy to be with the illustrious master, to compose church music and rigorous works.

The young man shut himself in his bedroom and read the words that were going to free him from Salzburg.

My young friend, at the same time as your kind letter, I received the motets. I examined them with pleasure, from one end to the other, and I must tell you in all honesty that they pleased me a great deal, for in them I found everything that distinguishes modern music – that is to say, good harmony, mature modulations, excellently handled movement of the violins, natural flow of the voices, and remarkable elaboration. I rejoice particularly to see that, since the day when I had the pleasure, in Bologna, of hearing you on the harpsichord, you have made such great progress in composition. But you must continue to exert yourself tirelessly. Indeed, the nature of music demands deep study and exercise, as long as one lives.*

* The rest of Padre Martini's letter has not survived.

It was a crushing disappointment. No invitation, no offer of a post, no commission for a religious work, followed these platitudinous words. Padre Martini cared nothing for Wolfgang's future and was interested only in his own erudite works, not wishing to be importuned by anybody.

Wolfgang did not acknowledge receipt of the letter and would never write to the Padre again. Abandoned, betrayed, he would not humiliate himself.

When he eventually emerged from his room, his mother was worried. 'You're so pale! Are you ill?'

'On the contrary, you see me freed from a useless burden. Losing one's illusions lightens one.'

'Did Padre Martini invite you to Bologna?' asked Leopold.

'He is far too busy.'

Salzburg, 31 December 1776

The archbishop and his subjects all celebrated the New Year gaily with the pleasures of the table. Gathered around their festive board, the Mozart family and their friends were not in the least expecting the surprise Wolfgang had in store for them. Since he no longer composed anything but masses, they thought he would end up steeped in piety, spending his time celebrating the Lord's praises.

'To this worthy company,' he announced, 'I offer a *notturno* to gladden hearts on the threshold of the New Year.'

Four small ensembles, each comprising a string quartet and two horns, began an entertaining score, a witty parody of the *galant* style so prized by the aristocracy and Salzburg's middle classes. When one of the little orchestras enunciated a phrase, the three others echoed it. The humour delighted the revellers.

At the end of this musical joke, which coincided with the last second of the dying year and the first of 1777, everyone embraced and wished each other excellent health.

Wolfgang slipped away and went for a walk in the snow. He needed to be alone.

'Laughing at oneself gives strength,' said Thamos's deep voice. 'After so much religious fervour, a little relaxation was indeed necessary.'

'Did you hear my *missae*?'

'I was in the congregation.'

'What did you think of them?'

'An obligatory stage, a few fine soaring moments, an honourable attempt to converse with God.'

'Only honourable . . . So I failed?'

'You were right to explore that path and to correct the tendency that was leading you towards an excess of lightness, but you will never be a good believer, sheeplike and submissive.'

'But I do believe in all-powerful God. I—' Wolfgang broke off. Reciting a litany bored him. 'What is there beyond belief?'

'Knowledge,' replied Thamos.

'How can I acquire it?'

'Continue to build yourself through music. Happy New Year, Wolfgang.'

Brunswick, 5 January 1777

Ferdinand of Brunswick was not enjoying the start of the new year. The death of Charles de Hund had brought him more problems than advantages. And the worst was yet to come, for the chance of governing the seventh province was already arousing greed and ambition in many people.

This would soon be snuffed out, because of the sudden appearance in the foreground of a great lord against whom none dared measure himself: Prince Carl of Sudermania, younger brother of King Gustav III of Sweden. Some were

promising the throne to this lover of occultism and mysticism.*
He was the successor to the Duke of Saxe-Gotha at the head of
the Swedish Rite, but also a Brother of the Strict Observance
movement and an honorary member of the Concord Lodge,
in Brunswick, on Ferdinand's privileged territory.

Contemptuous of the first three degrees of Freemasonry,
Prince Carl was interested only in the high ranks. And he
would not be content with just the seventh province. He would
try to seize control of the Templar Order, then of all German
Freemasonry, before perhaps conquering Europe.

The Grand Master of Strict Observance must prevent this
dangerous rival from gaining a foothold, and would strew his
way with obstacles – if he encountered too many, the prince
would surely beat a retreat.

'The Count of Thebes has arrived,' declared the duke's
private secretary.

The duke waited feverishly for the Unknown Superior,
who would certainly help him to preserve the Order from outside attacks and internal quarrels. No Brother knew of this
privileged contact, because any talk risked breaking these
tenuous links for ever.

Once again, Thamos impressed him. The light in his eyes
seemed not of this world, and his innate, lordly elegance
asserted itself in an almost supernatural way.

The Egyptian instantly raised the central issue: 'Is Baron de
Hund's death causing you serious concerns?'

'I shall defend the Order to my last breath and will not allow
any schemer to steal it from me.'

'The aims of the Swedish Rite are by no means negligible,'
said Thamos, 'but there is another danger threatening you.'

So the Unknown Superior was fully aware of Prince Carl's
plans. The Grand Master was eager to hear his revelations.

---

* He was to reign from 1809 to 1818, as Charles XIII.

'Berlin has changed camps. Although they are Brothers of Strict Observance, former pastor Wöllner and his friend Bischoffswerder, a soldier, have got their hands on two influential lodges, the Three Globes and Frederick with the Golden Lion. With the king's tacit consent, they are imposing the rituals of the Golden Rose-Cross, to the detriment of the Templar Order. The Rosicrucians are emerging from the shadows where they have been lurking, and are trying to gain the adherence of as many Freemasons as possible, and even of outsiders. Texts are circulating already, both inside and outside the lodges.'

'Those adventurers have no claim to legitimacy!' exclaimed the duke.

'Their tradition has links with yours,' Thamos reminded him. 'Initiation comes from Egypt, where it was granted to Moses. Solomon, the prophets, the Essenes, the followers of Eleusis and the Pythagoreans formed an uninterrupted chain, designed to preserve the original wisdom. Thanks to an Egyptian priest in Alexandria, the first Christians were initiated there. And this secret knowledge, gathered by mages and alchemists, continues to be taught.'

'No initiate must be unaware of the vital role of the Order of the Temple,' declared Ferdinand.

'Demonstrate it.'

The Grand Master was almost speechless with astonishment. 'What . . . How?'

'By becoming a Rosicrucian yourself. You will thus avoid a split or conflict between two Masonic movements. Moreover, what you learn will enable you to enrich your own rituals. The future of Strict Templar Observance depends on this course of action.'

52

Salzburg, 27 January 1777

On the occasion of Wolfgang's twenty-first birthday, Miss Pimperl was allowed a second piece of tart and some Spanish tobacco, which she sniffed with delight.

After the meal, Leopold drew his son aside, to stand by a window in the large apartment. Snow was falling in fat flakes; Salzburg was shivering.

'Eastern Europe is becoming more and more dangerous. Your mother and sister don't understand politics and are content to manage our family life well. We must tackle this subject, man to man. Even if you give complete satisfaction to Prince-Archbishop Colloredo, we must look to the future. Our city won't always enjoy its current prosperity, especially if war breaks out.'

'Are you planning another tour?'

'I'm thinking of Paris. The French won't involve themselves in a new war, and you had great success there. Versailles, a dazzling and wealthy court, the support of our friend Grimm, refined salons, famous concerts . . . I'm preparing for our visit by writing to our friends there.'

'But will Colloredo allow us to leave?'

'That's a delicate problem. It's up to me to persuade him.'

'When will we be packing our bags?'

'I don't know, Wolfgang. Everything depends on what I hear from the people I write to.'

This prospect delighted the young man. Into the final theme of his Divertimento in B flat major, intended to entertain the Grand Mufti during an official meal, he slipped a theme which was both graceful and profound.* It opened up a horizon which he knew, from the moment he fashioned it, would light up hitherto unsuspected landscapes. Then he hurried to finish another official piece, the last in a series of six divertimentos, a conventional collection, quickly expedited, whose main virtue consisted of aiding the archbishop's digestion.

'What about stopping work and meeting a charming young lady?' suggested Anton Stadler.

'Each to his own life,' retorted Wolfgang irritably.

'Let me be more precise: she's a pianist from Paris.'

Mademoiselle Jeunehomme was neither beautiful nor ugly, but had a great deal of conversation. 'Are you really the child prodigy?'

'I've grown up.'

'Usually the little monsters lose their talent as they get older, but you're still a composer, aren't you?'

'Perhaps because I've always been one.'

'I'm enjoying exploring a little principality like Salzburg – there's no shortage of musical activities.'

'It can't compare with Paris, I assume?'

'The most beautiful city in the world is still the centre of arts and letters. No one who doesn't shine there can aspire to universal fame.'

'Does Baron Grimm still rule Parisian culture?' asked Wolfgang.

'Yes. If his opinion isn't favourble, it's impossible to build

---

* It prefigures the duet '*Sull' aria*' between the Countess and Susanna in *Le nozze di Figaro*; the divertimento is K270.

a career. He sorts the wheat from the chaff and arbitrates in disputes.'

'One can be nobody's slave, not thinking about any audience or envisaging any success, and yet express the freedom to create.'

'I don't understand.'

Feverishly, Wolfgang composed a remarkable piano concerto.* Salzburg had never heard anything like it: a dramatic dialogue between the soloist and the orchestra, a profusion of themes, a slow movement in which solitude rejected despair and an allegro overflowing with joy, declaring a will to break free of one's chains and set off on an adventure.

Mlle Jeunehomme's visit was not the result of pure chance, but a sign of destiny, offering the composer the chance to deploy a degree of energy he had not realized he possessed.

'This is your first true piano concerto,' said Thamos, stroking Miss Pimperl, who was enjoying her walk in the snow.

'While I was writing it, I forgot about the demands of *galanterie* and Salzburg taste. Another kind of music is beginning to speak to me; it's still far away and yet it's so close . . .'

'When are you leaving for Paris?'

'My father is still corresponding, in coded messages, with his various contacts, in order to arrange it. The Grand Mufti must agree to it, and it isn't certain that he will. Still, my father's very determined, so perhaps he'll persuade him by wearing him down. It really is time to leave Salzburg. If I stay here I'm in danger of spoiling everything.'

'Would you give up the idea if formidable trials were predicted all along your way?'

'No. They're necessary and inevitable. Given a choice between a slow death in Salzburg and the risks of adventure,

---

* No. 9 in E flat minor, K271, known as the 'Young Man'.

I choose the second. And I shall prove to you that I deserve your respect.'

Vienna, 20 March 1777

Josef Anton finished reading a dozen or so reports from reliable informers. All arrived at the same conclusion: the struggle between Duke Ferdinand and Prince Carl was likely to be fierce. It was impossible to predict, at this stage in a confrontation which was still muted, which would overcome the other and control Freemasonry, particularly since their respective manoeuvres were proving to be somewhat tortuous.

While heading his own Rite, the Swedish duke also belonged to Strict Templar Observance, whose German Grand Master was threatened by the sudden determination to expand on the part of the very secret Golden Rose-Cross, which he had just joined, no doubt the better to destroy it.

Berlin worried Josef Anton. A former monk who had become an alchemist, Dom Pernety, was also allied with the Golden Rose-Cross, which pleased the authorities very much, unaware as they were of the danger hidden beneath the occult trappings and mystical appearances. Fortunately, Jesuit spies were keeping Josef Anton informed, and continuing their fine work of undermining the movement by inclining the leaders towards an innocuous Christianity.

If Freemasonry was reduced to a more or less discreet association of revellers who respected power, and if the outcome of the Golden Rose-Cross's manipulations was traditional belief in Jesus Christ, Josef Anton could sleep peacefully again.

But he did not believe in miracles. Not all Freemasons would allow themselves to be circumvented so easily, and some would continue to hatch plots against the established order. Flushing them out would be difficult and would take a long time.

53

Salzburg, 20 March 1777

Prince-Archbishop Colloredo's steward bowed deferentially before his august employer.

'May I be permitted to inform your lordship of a slightly . . . scandalous situation?'

'I am listening.'

'A musician close to the Mozart family overheard a conversation between father and son, during a pause between the two halves of a concert. They are planning to go abroad.'

'Have they a particular destination in mind?'

'Paris.'

Colloredo dismissed the steward, who would receive a small reward. So the Mozarts wanted to travel again, did they? The new master of Salzburg would not have his predecessor's weaknesses. His servant musicians owed total obedience to him.

Salzburg, 30 March 1777

Although Countess Lodron had greatly enjoyed the delightful divertimento Wolfgang had composed for her, which conjured up the fun and masques of the carnival, the young man himself did not feel his heart was in the work. An attempt at a trio for

244

two violins and a cello had been laid aside, owing to a lack of inspiration.

One single question obsessed Wolfgang: when would Colloredo answer his father's request for several months' leave of absence? Leopold had weighed each word, and displayed the most humble submissiveness, in the hope that his all-powerful employer would prove understanding. After all, Wolfgang's success abroad would reflect well on the Salzburg court.

One morning, while out shooting with Anton Stadler, Wolfgang aimed at the head of an man wearing a big hat; his profile vaguely resembled Colloredo's.

'You're very accurate today,' said Anton.

'Anger is sometimes a good counsellor.'

'Not when it comes to meeting our dear archbishop. Beside his, an iron fist would seem a bit weak. Whatever you do, don't attack him: he'd break you. We musicians are mere servants and must learn to keep our mouths shut.'

'You may, but I won't. I'm in service to music, not to a tyrant.'

'He's the one who enables you to keep composing and having your music played.'

Irritated, Wolfgang missed the target.

Vienna, 25 June 1777

Geytrand was jubilant. 'The Freemasons of the Swedish Rite are furious,' he told Josef Anton. 'The official deliberations that were supposed to end in the triumphal election of their patron, Prince Carl of Sudermania, ended inconclusively.'

'Will the Duke of Brunswick dare reject the candidature of such an important man?'

'Not out of hand, no. He talks of the need to consult all the leading Freemason officials and persuade them without hurting anyone, and that will take a great deal of time. In reality, both

Germans and Danes detest the Swedish duke and will never accept him as Provincial Grand Master.'

'In other words, Brunswick is playing a double game.'

'In my opinion,' said Geytrand, 'he suspects the prince of wanting to take his place and conquer the whole of Freemasonry.'

This news made Josef Anton so happy that he gave one of his rare smiles. 'So we're on the eve of a major confrontation between two important warriors, each determined to destroy the other. At the end of this fratricidal duel, Freemasonry may have been bled dry, the Brothers discouraged and their ideals forgotten.'

'It's a wonderful prospect, Herr Count.'

'We mustn't sit idle, though. Tell your spies to spread as many rumours as possible, in order to stoke up the quarrel and increase mutual suspicions. It would be good to reach a point of no return, where all possibility of compromise has been destroyed.'

'I shall enjoy blackening both dukes' intentions,' promised Geytrand.

What a splendid opportunity to destroy the Masonic structure that was being created. Playing on the two opponents' vanity and will for power would produce excellent results. There was only one worry: the emergence of a victor. It would be better if both were mortally wounded and Freemasonry discredited.

54

Prince-Archbishop Colloredo sneered, and looked at Leopold with apparent surprise.

'You wished to see me, Herr Mozart?'

'It is about my request, Your Eminence. The demands upon your time have prevented you from responding, but my son and I would dearly like to obtain your agreement.'

'Remind me of this request.'

'We would like to leave Salzburg for a few months in order to give concerts abroad and—'

'Impossible,' cut in Colloredo. 'Emperor Josef is soon to visit our fair city, and I shall need all my musicians to offer him a few fine pieces in the Italian style.'

'Would our departure be possible after then?'

Colloredo toyed with his goose-quill pen. 'Your son may leave. But not you.'

After writing two church sonatas, divertimenti and quadrilles to earn his salary, Wolfgang composed an oboe concerto for Giuseppe Ferlendis, a soloist at the chapel in Salzburg. As he listened to the slow movement, the archbishop's expression darkened. He did not like this music.

As soon as the last notes had faded away, he sent for Leopold. 'I have changed my mind. Neither you nor your son may leave Salzburg. You are my servants and must therefore remain constantly at my disposal.'

'Your Eminence—'

'My decision is final.'

Dinner at the Mozart home was gloomy. Neither Leopold nor Mozart had any appetite for the cook's delicious hare. Even Miss Pimperl, sensing her master's depression, only picked at her food.

'Don't dwell on it,' advised Anna Maria. 'Our family's happy, we're all in good health, we live in a comfortable apartment and we have everything we need. The Lord is protecting us, so why ask for more?'

'The Grand Mufti's tyranny is becoming unbearable,' declared Wolfgang.

'Don't be a malcontent, my son. The archbishop pays you and your father fair salaries, and you're free to compose the music you love, aren't you?'

'No, that's precisely what I'm not.'

The cheerful arrival of Anton Stadler, who always managed to make even Nannerl smile, lightened the atmosphere.

'Forgive me, but I'm going to take Wolfgang away from you. A young singer with a most beautiful voice, Josefa Dušek, has arrived from Prague and wants to meet him.'

Leopold gave his assent. A little enjoyment would soothe his son.

Salzburg, late July 1777

It was the third time Wolfgang had seen the pretty twenty-four-year-old Josefa, who would soon be returning to her native city.

'I'll leave you two alone,' said Anton Stadler, and he closed the door of the music room behind him.

Although he was shy, Wolfgang managed to express himself

directly. 'You have the most beautiful voice I have ever heard, and even the most taxing technical difficulties are as nothing to you.'

'That's a big compliment,' smiled Josefa, who was sensitive to the young musician's peculiar charm.

'Would you sing an aria I've written for you?'*

'For me? Just for me?'

'Just for you. It's a dramatic aria, a complete story, based on a poem by Vittorio Cigna-Santi.'

'What is the story?' asked Josepha, intrigued by the prospect.

'The lover of beautiful Andromeda, who is passionately in love with him, is mortally wounded. At first, she cries out her rebellion, and expresses her unbearable pain; then she resigns herself, accepting fate; lastly she achieves serenity, promising herself that she'll rejoin her lover beyond death.'

The singer was impressed by Wolfgang's score. When she had finished reading through it, she said, 'It's a complete opera in only a few bars – but very difficult to sing!'

'I ask you to become Andromeda, Josefa, to live her terrible ordeal, to plunge into despair, to find a kind of hope, and to see beyond the visible world.'

The young woman shivered. 'You ask a great deal.'

'You can do it, I'm sure you can. Will you try?'

She could not refuse.

After several rehearsals punctuated by helpful interruptions from the composer, Josefa Dušek had become Andromeda.

Anton Stadler broke the spell. 'It's late, lovebirds, and all our friends are starving to death. Hurry up. To the table!'

* *'Ah, lo previdi ... Ah, t'invola agl'occhi miei'*, K272.

Salzburg, 1 August 1777

'Don't go that far,' Leopold advised his son.

'Colloredo leaves me no choice.'

'I'll try to persuade him to be less intransigent. Perhaps he'll allow us a few weeks.'

'That wouldn't be enough, as you well know. Such a long journey will take several months, and the date of return may vary according to the circumstances. So today I am going to tender my resignation to the archbishop.'

Leopold bit his lip. Colloredo's reaction was liable to be explosive.

'Have you really thought about this, Wolfgang?'

'So much that I'm finding it almost impossible to compose. My resignation will set me free.'

'Shouldn't you wait a little?'

'I must leave Salzburg before the bad weather. If I wait too long, the roads will be impassable.'

Unable to think of any more arguments, Leopold gave in. His son would either destroy his own career or take flight in a new direction.

Salzburg, 28 August 1777

Nervously, Leopold opened the letter from the archbishop and read out the crucial sentence: 'Father and son are authorized, according to the Gospel, to seek their fortunes elsewhere.'

'That's wonderful!' exclaimed Wolfgang. 'Dearest father, we're leaving together.'

Leopold looked glum. 'You and I have been thrown out,' he said, 'and neither of us will be earning a salary. Nannerl's piano-teaching won't bring in enough to keep the household going. I shall be fifty-eight in November, Wolfgang, and I can't accept being dismissed like this after so many years of good and loyal service. You're young and can take risks, but I can't.'

Leopold laid siege to Colloredo's office and assumed his most malleable attitude. A few days later, a new decree was promulgated: Leopold kept his post and remained in the archbishop's service. As for Wolfgang, his dismissal stood, and he could do what he pleased.

Delighted with his freedom, Wolfgang thought to thank Heaven for it through the intermediary of the Virgin Mary, for whom he composed a *missa brevis* and an offertory; both were given at St Peter's rather than in the cathedral, Colloredo's domain. He adopted a popular style, sometimes close to *opera buffa* and far from stuffy religiosity. In a gradual dedicated to 'St Mary, Mother of God', he concentrated on the prayer 'Protect me through life, defend me at the final moment of death.'

As he set these words to music, the young man had a premonition that his journey to Paris would overturn his peaceful life and entail extreme difficulties. But he had sworn not to retract.

55

Berlin, September 1777

Although disappointed by the laziness and apathy of most of the Brothers of the Order of African Architects, Friedrich von Köppen had, with von Hymnen's help, put both Thamos's revelations and his own research to good use and published a book entitled *Crata Repoa, or Initiation into the Ancient Mysteries of the Egyptian Priests.*

It was a thunderbolt which would awaken the slumbering Lodges and remind them of the true origins of initiation, which must henceforth inspire them. It was *Crata Repoa*, the secret clergy of initiates founded by Menes, who had built the first temple from which all Masonic temples derived.

When Thamos entered his office, Köppen at once stood up and asked, 'Did you like my book?'

'It marks a new stage on the path of the Tradition, but there are still many more to go through.'

'All the Brothers will be overwhelmed, won't they?'

'Perhaps not.'

'But the reference to Egypt is vital!'

'At the moment,' said Thamos, 'the great lords are in dispute over Masonic power, and they will take little heed of symbolism.'

Köppen sat down again, suddenly aged by several years.

252

'My own Brothers scarcely ever visit the library,' he confessed. 'The alchemical laboratory is visited only by amateurs, and the natural-history room might as well be closed. And there's so much research to do. We're on the threshold of great discoveries which could transform Freemasonry, but most Brothers prefer routine and ready-made doctrines.'

'Don't be downhearted. As always, just a few men will change the course of events.'

Salzburg, 23 September 1777

'Is this really sensible, dear husband?' asked Anna Maria.

'It's the only solution I can think of. Although he's twenty-one, Wolfgang still often behaves like a child, so he must be watched over and prevented from making disastrous mistakes. I'm not allowed to leave Salzburg, so you'll have to go with him.'

'I don't like travelling.'

'I know, my dear, and I'm aware of the trials I'm imposing upon you. But leaving Wolfgang to his own devices would be a grave mistake.'

As usual Anna Maria gave in, though leaving Salzburg and her contented life there almost broke her heart.

'Get to Paris as soon as possible,' advised Leopold. 'Wolfgang will be a great success there as both pianist and composer. Once he's made his fortune, you can return.'

'Will it take long?' asked Anna Maria unhappily.

'I'm sure it won't. With the help of Baron Grimm and his influential contacts, our son will make his mark without difficulty. As for Colloredo, he'll be obliged to recognize his talent and will be glad of his fame, which will reflect well on Salzburg. But you must take care not to let Wolfgang spend too much money or get involved in silly scrapes.'

Thanks to the war-chest accumulated by Leopold and some

borrowing, the costs of travel were covered. After their arrival, receipts from the concerts would take over. Glory and wealth were sure to crown this new adventure.

When Wolfgang and his mother climbed into the carriage, Nannerl vomited and Miss Pimperl whined so loudly that the young man was obliged to console her by letting her smell her favourite treat, Spanish tobacco. Leopold wiped away a tear. Never had a departure been so sad.

That evening, Wolfgang wrote to his father:

We have all we need, except Papa. Mother and I beg him to be cheerful and always joyful, thinking that HC, the Grand Mufti, is nothing but an imbecile. Moreover, God is compassionate, sympathetic and charitable.'

Munich, 30 September 1777

The long journey began rather well, with good weather, a pleasant city and a welcoming inn owned by a music lover, Albert (nicknamed 'the Scholar'), who was delighted to receive the Mozarts.

'Salzburg isn't the place for me, that's for sure,' Wolfgang confided to his mother.

'Why don't you love our beautiful city?'

'The atmosphere is suffocating, there is a narrow-minded tyrant, the musicians are second-rate . . . How can one blossom in such a narrow setting?'

'Don't be so critical, my dear. Above all, remember your father's advice and heed his warnings.'

Wolfgang reread a vital passage from the first of Leopold's letters to reach Munich: '*Don't write any more wicked things about the Mufti. Remember that I'm here and that a letter like that might get lost or fall into the wrong hands.'*

Anna Maria said worriedly, 'Don't you realize that your father might be arrested and imprisoned?'

'Don't fret so much.'

'Calling the archbishop an imbecile is a serious offence. In future, moderate your language.'

In a playful mood, the young man broke into a song whose improvised words were not about Colloredo's glory.

'I'm starving,' he said when the song was done. 'After lunch, I shall go and see Count Seeau. Perhaps he'll give me some interesting work.'

Wolfgang wondered when Thamos would reappear. But, alas, he did not feature among the innkeeper's customers.

Vienna, 30 September 1777

At the age of thirty-five, Ignaz von Born had – without wishing it – become one of the leading scientific figures in the city. Empress Maria Theresa was extremely pleased with the diligent and professional way in which he was reorganizing the mineralogical section of the Imperial Museum. Thanks to this job, which he loved, von Born no longer had any financial worries and could discreetly spend time with Viennese Freemasons.

He was delighted to learn that Thamos was in Vienna again, and received him in his office, which was full of samples of rare stones.

'I've brought you a book,' said Thamos, 'the results of the work of the Order of African Architects. It's a study of the Mysteries celebrated by the priests of ancient Egypt.'

'I shall gulp it down!'

'Don't expect any tremendous revelations, for you already know a great many things. Here are some more.' He handed von Born another chapter of *The Book of Thoth*.

255

Worried that the Egyptian might disappear for ever, the mineralogist did not enquire how many more chapters this crucial work contained. Instead, he asked, 'Does the African Order have a future?'

'Its founder, Friedrich von Köppen, seems rather pessimistic, but he is persevering. Have you met any Brothers of worth?'

'My first explorations have been rather disappointing, and I have to go carefully because the lodges are being watched by the police.'

'Is there a senior officer who coordinates all the information?'

'I don't know.'

'Continue to be very careful,' advised Thamos. 'Until we identify the enemy and measure his power, he can strike at any moment.'

56

Munich, 30 September 1777

Wolfgang received quite a friendly welcome from Munich's music *Intendant,* Count Seeau, who arranged an audience with Elector Maximilian.

He greeted the composer with a broad smile. 'From what one hears, you have left Salzburg once and for all.'

'Once and for all, Highness.'

'Why have you taken such a serious decision? Did you come into conflict with Prince-Archbishop Colloredo?'

'I asked permission to travel but he refused, so I was obliged to hand him my resignation. Salzburg is no place for me, and I will do honour to Munich.'

'I do not doubt it, Mozart, but that will not further your career, for there are no vacant posts at court. See if Count Seeau can organize a concert for you. I am happy to have seen you again, and wish you good fortune.'

Maximilian was not going to annoy Colloredo by taking on a rebellious musician he had dismissed. Between the great of the world, certain rules were respected. Besides, the elector's political ambitions obliged him to remain on good terms with the rulers of neighbouring principalities. This young fellow Mozart might become an embarrassment. Fortunately, Count Seeau would have the skill to dismiss him gently.

Munich, 10 October 1777

As he wrote to his father, Wolfgang was never really happy except when composing, which was his passion and his sole joy. Now he was facing the hard reality of an outside world whose laws he knew nothing about.

Should he set off again for Italy, to create a new opera there? But without influential contacts, and perhaps being already forgotten there, it might be a waste of time. Should he stay in Munich, give concerts at Albert's inn and get by on his modest earnings? Hardly an exciting prospect! A much better idea: write four German operas each year, some *buffa*, the rest *seria*, and join the court.

But Maximilian had firmly rejected him, and Count Seeau was avoiding answering his questions. And his father's letters urged him to leave Munich as soon as possible and continue his journey to Paris.

Furious at such a dismal failure, Wolfgang sought one more interview with Count Seeau. 'The people of Munich will like my German operas, I'm sure of it.'

The count's manner was suave and distant. 'The programme for the next few years has already been drawn up. Besides, the German style of opera has many opponents, and it might displease listeners who are accustomed to the Italian taste. I am very sorry, but Munich can do nothing for you.'

Wolfgang hurried out of the palace. His appetite was gone, and he did not enjoy the food served by the innkeeper.

'Nobles always believe what they're told and never examine anything for themselves,' he said to his mother. 'We're setting off again.'

The Great Magician

Augsburg, 11 October 1777

Leaving Munich early in the morning, Wolfgang and his mother arrived in Augsburg that evening and settled in at the Lamb Inn. Next day, the young man went to see Johann Andreas Stein, a piano-maker.

It was because of him that the Mozarts had stopped in Augsburg, where the arts held little sway. Here lived his nineteen-year-old cousin Maria Anna Thekla, whom Wolfgang called his 'Bäsle',* an amusing, bright and saucy young girl with whom he joked about everything and nothing, inventing absurd words and phrases that were sometimes scatological. Even his pious mother laughed at this nonsense, sometimes using it herself.

When he entered Stein's workshop, Wolfgang immediately spotted a superb piano which made his mouth water.

Suspiciously, the maker barred his way. 'What do you want?'

'I should like to try that piano.'

'Are you amateur or professional?'

'Professional.'

'What's your name?'

'Trazom.'†

Stein frowned: he didn't know the name. 'I've only just finished that piano, which cost me many hours' work. Unless you're a real musician, you won't appreciate its sound quality.'

'Please, Herr Stein, please let me play just a few notes.'

Impressed by the intensity of this ordinary-looking young man, the piano-maker agreed.

Wolfgang improvised: first a very simple melody, then a few ornaments and then a flourish of such virtuosity that Stein stood open-mouthed. He could have listened for hours to this

---

* An affectionate diminutive of *Base*, 'cousin'.

† Mozart backwards – he sometimes introduced himself thus.

genius of a pianist, who brought unimagined resources out of the instrument.

By the time the young man's hands ceased running over the keyboard, the craftsman had been moved almost to tears.

'What name did you say?'

'Trazom.'

'I've heard of a child prodigy who became a musician at the Salzburg court, Wolfgang Mozart, who some music-lovers claim has retained his gifts ... That's you, isn't it? I have the honour of having Herr Mozart before me, isn't that so?'

'When I strike hard, I can leave my finger on the key or lift it off: the sound stops at the very moment when I wish it to – I can attack the keys as I wish. The sound is always equal. It doesn't sound disagreeable, it's neither too loud nor too soft, and it doesn't blur the notes: in a word, it is perfectly balanced. Your piano is a marvel, Herr Stein.'

'You won't find one that's more strongly built. Its sounding-board will never break, and do you know why? Because I exposed it to the sun, to the rain, to the snow and to all the devils. Previous ones came apart, but this one passed all its many tests. I was sure of its strength, but I stuck on little pieces of wood to make it even more better, and this is the result: one gets unequalled clarity, notably in the low octaves. But even so it isn't perfect yet. I'm planning to add a sort of pedal which one presses with the knee. Would you like to try the prototype?'

Wolfgang didn't hesitate for a second. Stein was a sort of mage who created incomparable instruments in the service of music. What quality of expression, what potential for nuances, compared to the old harpsichord or to ordinary pianos! Wolfgang's ear perceived an infinity of melodies which would make these keys sing.

'How much do you charge for one of these wonderful instruments?'

260

'At least three hundred florins.'

Wolfgang's face fell. 'Unfortunately, I can't afford that much. But perhaps one day . . .'

'In the meantime, Herr Mozart, I shall place one at your disposal this very evening, if you will agree to give a concert.'

57

Augsburg, 12 October 1777

Wolfgang sensed that the notables of the little town were only half listening to him, so in annoyance he cut short his performance.

The moment he left the piano, the burgomaster's son hailed him. 'You wear an interesting decoration, Herr Mozart. What is it, and who gave it to you?'

'His Holiness the Pope gave it to me – it's the cross of a Knight of the Golden Spur. I don't usually wear it in public.'

'How much does it cost?'

'I've no idea.'

'Could you lend it to me so I can have a copy made?'

'Certainly not.'

'You are very ungracious,' complained an over-powdered old townswoman. 'Our burgomaster's son would look much better in that cross than you do.'

'Come on,' demanded the son rudely, 'lend me your jewel. Don't worry, I'll give it back to you.'

The audience was starting to laugh at Mozart.

'It's strange,' he said. 'It's easier for me to acquire decorations than it would be for you to become what I am, even if you died twice and were reborn. Now, kindly stop bothering me.'

Turning his back on the sneering old lady and the lad puffed-up with vanity, he angrily left the hall.

Augsburg, 22 October 1777

Despite his initial disappointment, Wolfgang gave other concerts at Stein's premises, but the takings there were only meagre. Between his public appearances, he took pleasure in playing the organ in local churches and relaxing in the company of his cousin Maria Anna, who poked fun at the worthies of Augsburg with biting sarcasm.

'I've had enough of them – more than I can say,' Wolfgang confided to her. 'I'd be very happy to find myself again in a place with a proper court. This evening's performance will be my last one here. I couldn't bear to stay any longer – your damned town is as suffocating as Salzburg.'

The performance attracted only a small audience and brought in only ninety florins.

'So you're leaving us now,' said Stein sadly.

'Yes. I'm going to Paris.'

'A great Paris critic was in town this evening.'

'Do you know his name?'

'Grimm, I think.'

Grimm, the Mozarts' protector, had passed through Augsburg without coming to see Wolfgang? No, Stein must have got the name wrong. The baron would never have behaved so unkindly.

That night the young man could not get to sleep. He was haunted by one of Leopold's warnings: 'You know me: I am neither a pedant nor a bigot, and still less am I pompously pious. But you will not reject a prayer by your father: look to the salvation of your soul.'

Nettled, Wolfgang thought resolutely: 'Papa must not worry. I have God constantly before my eyes. I recognize His omnipotence and fear His anger; but I also recognize His love, compassion and pity for His creatures: He will never abandon those who serve him. If everything goes according to His will, so will it go according to mine. And therefore I cannot fail to be happy and contented.'

And contented Wolfgang assuredly was as he left inhospitable Augsburg and its painful memories behind him.

Vienna, October 1777

Among the landmarks of the Austrian capital, the Imperial and Royal Library compelled the admiration of all those who had the good fortune to use it. It contained thousands of volumes, forming veritable walls which were interspersed by porphyry columns. The reflective, almost solemn atmosphere was conducive to study, and researchers came from all over Europe to garner many aspects of learning. The post of director at the illustrious library was one of the most coveted in Vienna, so the court waited impatiently to learn who the new incumbent was.

The appointment of Baron Gottfried van Swieten, a distinguished and cultivated forty-four-year-old diplomat, son of the empress's personal physician, met with unanimous approval. The baron had spent seven years in Berlin, but would now be based in Vienna.

One of the benefits of the post was a large official apartment, right inside the library itself, on a level with the main gallery and looking out on to Josefplatz. It was there that he received Thamos, one of his first visitors.

The Egyptian admired the aesthetics of the office, decorated with arabesques on a green background, but noted that van Swieten had put on weight and seemed careworn.

'Congratulations on your appointment, Baron.'

'I could not dream of a better one. It's an ideal observation post and sufficiently out of the public eye to enable me to pursue all my activities.'

'Will you keep in contact with the lodges in Berlin?'

'With those and others. At present our main concern is the future of Strict Templar Observance. A few Viennese Freemasons are working on this Rite, whose progress is in danger of being halted, both because of internal dissent and because of attacks from outside. Not a very favourable climate for the birth of a lodge capable of welcoming the Great Magician.'

'Despite these very real difficulties,' said Thamos, 'there is good news. A Brother of exceptional gifts has recently settled in Vienna. He will try to bring together Freemasons who wish to create a true initiation, based on Egyptian tradition.'

'What is his name?'

Thamos's eyes became even more piercing than usual. 'If I tell you, we are bound together by secrecy for ever.'

'Are we not already bound, Count of Thebes?'

'He is Ignaz von Born.'

'The great mineralogist summoned to Vienna by the empress herself! He will have to act with great discretion. We will meet at difficult meetings, but you alone will know our true bonds.'

'A hostile force could reduce them to nothing.'

'What are you thinking of?'

'The secret police. Freemasons are followed and spied upon, aren't they?'

'Followed? Probably. Spied upon? I think not. The empress's suspicions don't go that far.'

'I fear you may be being over-optimistic.'

'Have you any firm evidence?'

'I think there may be a mastermind behind it all, someone hiding in the shadows and determined to destroy Freemasonry.'

Van Swieten did not hide his scepticism. 'An *éminence grise* at the head of a secret service? It would be impossible without the empress's agreement.'

'Which she would give, wouldn't she?'

'It seems unlikely that any offences have been committed, but I'm far from having learnt all the court's secrets, so I don't discount your theory. Checking it will probably take a long time because I'll have to tread warily. Assuming that you're right, this secret service will have a network of spies whose extent will have to be assessed. A threat like that . . . Will we be strong enough to ward it off?'

'Let us begin by identifying it properly. Then we can try to find the right weapons with which to fight it.'

'Whatever the danger, my Brother, you may depend on me.'

58

Mannheim, 4 November 1777

After his unhappy stay in Augsburg, Mozart was coming back to life. Mannheim, the city of the palatinate's elector, Karl Theodor, an authoritative and influential man, boasted an exceptional orchestra, composed of outstanding musicians. The day after his arrival, 30 October, the young man met most of them, firmly determined to convince them of his talent. *'They think that because I am small and young nothing large and mature can exist inside me!'* he wrote to his father. *'Well, they will soon know better.'*

The *Konzertmeister*, Christian Cannabich, a cheerful man of forty-six, took Wolfgang under his wing and made his task easier. Professional relations turned into friendship, and the composer had a wonderful time playing with the best players in Germany and perhaps in all Europe.

At the height of happiness, he wrote die Bäsle a letter full of salacious and scatological jokes, using a sort of code which the mischievous Maria Anna could decipher, the better to outdo each other in outrageousness. To be far from Salzburg, laughing and freely making music: what joy!

Cannabich brought him down to earth. 'Put on your best clothes. You are expected at court.'

He was received by two men: Count Savioli, the *Intendant* of court music, and the elector's official confessor, Father Vogler, a Jesuit and deputy Kapellmeister; each was as unpleasant as the other. They greeted him coldly.

'Salzburg is a magnificent city,' said Count Savioli. 'Why did you leave?'

'Travelling teaches me an enormous amount. And Mannheim's orchestra is incomparable, isn't it?'

'So it is said, so it is said ... But all music posts are filled. Even if one became available, only a performer of the highest quality would be engaged.'

'My colleagues will answer for my skills, Herr Count. I am also a composer and I would love to present to the Mannheim court some of my works – I'm sure they would find them enchanting.'

'Beware of enchantment,' warned Father Vogler. 'It is a ruse employed by the Devil to lure souls away from the path of righteousness. Have you written any religious music?'

'Yes indeed, for St Stephen's Cathedral and St Peter's Church in Salzburg.'

'I hope you do not imitate licentious and worldly light composers like Johann Christian Bach?'

'I am sorry to disappoint you, father, but I respect and admire him. He helped me a great deal when I was in London.'

The Jesuit's expression became openly hostile.

'What exactly is it you want?' asked Count Savioli sharply.

'To play the day after tomorrow in the presence of Elector Karl Theodor, whom I had the honour and pleasure of meeting fifteen years ago.'

'His Highness is very busy – as are we: you may withdraw.'

From the very first second, Count Savioli and Father Vogler had disliked the young man. They watched him leave with relief.

'The most important thing is that he does not become established in Mannheim,' said the Jesuit.

'I agree. But he has talent, and the musicians of the orchestra are singing his praises, which have reached the elector's ears – given his love of the arts, he will undoubtedly attend the concert.'

'This fellow Mozart is a circus performer! Why was he banished from Colloredo's court?'

'He wanted to travel, it seems, and the archbishop was unwilling to pay wages to an absent musician.'

'What if there were more serious reasons? An adventurer who likes that man Bach's music can't be a good Christian. You and I must put the elector on his guard. Under no circumstances must he allow himself to be enchanted.'

Vienna, 4 November 1777

The Templar Brothers of the Three Eagles Lodge were extremely worried. Aware that their premises were being watched by the police, they met at the house of one of their leaders, in the presence of a visiting Brother, Ignaz von Born, whose seriousness and natural authority impressed them.

'Are we safe here?' asked the Master.

'An External Coverer will alert us in the event of danger,' replied the senior Brother.*

'Are we really in danger?' asked a Brother anxiously.

'Not in danger, no, but we are completely discredited. A bogus Templar stole our rituals and is selling copies secretly. Outsiders will learn all about them – and so will the police.'

'What do they contain that is compromising?' asked the senior Brother. 'We don't attack the ruling powers, or undermine morality.'

---

* In the old lodges, two Master Masons held the offices of Internal Coverer and External Coverer, whose task was to protect the lodge from all forms of attack.

'Many aspects could be misinterpreted,' said the Master. 'For example, the authorities may well see the Templars' necessary vengeance as a call to rebel against the Church and against kings. I consider these revelations extremely serious. And I regret to say that the scandal does not stop there. The impostor also stole several Brothers' subscriptions, and they have brought complaints against the Order alleging malpractice and incompetence.'

The discussion went on for a long time. Some Brothers tried to play down the probable effects of these events; others said that disaster was inevitable.

Ignaz von Born listened to them in silence. He realized that this lodge would not be a suitable setting for the initiation of the Great Magician. His quest must continue.

Vienna, 5 November 1777

'Well done,' said Josef Anton to Geytrand.

'Thank you, Herr Count. I must confess I'm rather pleased with this modest scheme, whose results have surpassed my hopes. In Austria, Strict Observance has suffered some very severe blows, from which it will have difficulty recovering.'

'While our files grow ever fuller. Some passages in the Templar Order's rituals clearly show its dangerous nature and its determination to undermine our way of life. Unfortunately, though, we haven't found a manifesto or a properly constituted declaration of war. I shall need more in order to get authorization for police raids and the final closure of all the lodges.'

'We're on the right track,' said Geytrand.

'How did your spy manage to infiltrate the lodges and steal the rituals and fees?'

'It wasn't too difficult – the Freemasons are much more naive than we thought. Many of them talk too much and no longer take any notice of the law of secrecy.'

'Give him a good bonus, and tell him to disappear.'

'Don't worry, Herr Count. He's already on his way back to Paris, and you won't hear any more of him. As for the Strict Observance lodges in Vienna, they'll soon fall apart.'

59

Mannheim, 6 November 1777

At the end of a highly successful concert, in which the audience had been dazzled by Mozart's talent, Karl Theodor greeted him warmly.

The elector was particularly proud of having created a little Versailles, where academies of science and the fine arts flourished, not to mention the superb library. A protector of artists, he was a warm-hearted man.

'Fifteen years have passed, Mozart. You are no longer a child prodigy but an accomplished musician.'

'Your orchestra is an absolute marvel, Your Highness. It's a joy to play with such artists.'

'Are you planning on staying long in Mannheim?'

'May I confide in Your Highness?'

'By all means.'

'I should like to compose a German opera and see it performed here.'

'That would be a fine project, but a difficult one to bring to fruition. In the meantime, will you be taking part in any other concerts?'

'It would be a great pleasure to do so.'

'I shall introduce you to some of my close friends who may be in need of a good teacher. Will you agree to play that role?'

'It would be an honour, Highness.'

'Splendid, splendid! Make the most of Mannheim, enjoy yourself and delight us with your talent. We shall meet again soon.'

Wolfgang loathed teaching: giving lessons to amateurs of differing abilities was a waste of time which could have been spent composing. But since he must do it . . .

Pleased with this encouraging contact, he wrote a brilliant piano sonata incorporating the technical advances made possible by Stein's new pianoforte, and a romantic little song in the French style, '*Oiseaux, si tous les ans*', which he was sure Father Vogler would absolutely detest.

Mannheim, 10 November 1777

'Have you been paid properly for your concerts?' asked Anna Maria.

'I've received nothing but five watches – as if I spend my whole life looking at the time. People listen to me and applaud, but they don't pay me. It seems that the little fellow from Salzburg must be content with little gifts.'

'How are we to survive?' said Anna Maria anxiously.

'I have many friends in Mannheim. They'll help us.'

'And then they'll have to be repaid. Shouldn't we obey your father and go straight to Paris?

'Don't worry, we will go. First, though, I want to make use of all Mannheim's resources. Can you imagine it, a German opera? The elector likes me, and with his help I'll succeed.'

So far from home, Anna Maria was in low spirits. She had not the heart to argue with her son.

He relaxed by writing a letter to his Bäsle: '*The Romans, on whom I rest my backside, are always, have always been, and will always remain, penniless.*' It didn't mean anything, but he said it anyway.

While on his way to see Christian Cannabich, Wolfgang fell in with his guide and mentor.

'Thamos! I thought you'd forgotten about me!'

'Mannheim suits you: you're composing brilliant, joyful pieces.'

'The orchestra's wonderful. It enables me to hear sounds I thought were impossible to achieve. There are so many unknown lands to discover. I can't write lyrical words, because I'm not a poet. I can't handle shapes artistically enough to create an interplay of light and shade: I'm not a painter. Nor can I express my feelings and thoughts through actions or pantomime, because I'm not a dancer. But I can do it through sound, because I am a musician.'

'What are you hoping to gain from Mannheim?'

'A post as a composer at court.'

'You have enemies here '

'I know, Count Savioli and the Jesuit; they'd like to see me leave post-haste. But Elector Karl Theodor likes me. In return for his protection, I'm to give piano lessons to his 'close friends' – that is, his mistresses and illegitimate children. He's a cheerful rogue who's come to an arrangement with Christian morality. Personally, I don't care for it much, but each to his own way of life. All I want is to have enough to live on and to compose with as few constraints as possible. *Thamos, König in Ägypten* ... I haven't forgotten it. If Mannheim welcomes a German opera, will that please you?'

'I pray that this city will understand you.'

Mannheim, 11 November 1777

To entertain himself, Wolfgang played the organ in the court chapel, beginning with the Kyrie, which he finished in an entirely classical manner. After the priest had sung the Gloria, he launched into a chord so surprising that the faithful all turn to stare at him.

Since they were at least emerging from their devotional

torpor, the organist made the notes really ring out, much to the congregation's surprise. Without waiting for Father Vogler's reaction, Wolfgang left the keyboard and went for lunch at the Cannabichs' house.

When he returned, very late, his mother was waiting for him, looking grim.

'Your father asked me to supervise you, Wolfgang, and I fear that your behaviour is not that of a good and pious boy.'

'Don't worry, mother. I make up doggerel and joke with the young lads and girls, and we dream up all sorts of silly pranks, some less respectable than others, but only in our thoughts, not in actual fact.'

'But aren't you straying dangerously close to sin?'

'That isn't a game for which I have much enthusiasm.'

'All the same . . .'

Wolfgang embraced his mother. 'I'm still a pious, decent boy who worships God and his parents.'

Mannheim, 22 November 1777

The musical celebrations in honour of the elector's birthday were drawing to an end, and Wolfgang had played no part in them. The Jesuit and his accomplice, Count Savioli, were more dangerous than he had thought. He was sure they had persuaded their patron to exclude him from the festivities.

Although reduced to giving piano lessons, Wolfgang did not despair of achieving his goals, particularly since Cannabich had heard persistent rumours that Karl Theodor was thinking of appointing Mozart private tutor to his natural children, which would mean both a firm footing at court and time to compose.

With a little luck, his journey would end in Mannheim. He longed to hear its marvellous orchestra interpreting his symphonies, his concertos, and the opera that would develop the message of *Thamos*.

60

Mannheim, 29 November 1777

> *You still do not realize that one must have other things in one's head besides idiotic jokes,* Leopold wrote. *Otherwise, one falls into the mire, destitute. And without money, one has no friends. The goal of the journey, the necessary goal, was, is and must be to find a position of employment, or at least to bring in some money.*

Stung by this unjust criticism, Wolfgang dared to answer his father in words that came straight from the heart:

> *I am not carefree. I am merely prepared for every eventuality, which enables me to wait and to bear everything with patience, provided that my honour and my unblemished name of Mozart do not suffer thereby. I beg you not to rejoice too soon, nor to cause yourself pain, either: let what will be, be; all is well. For happiness consists solely in the idea one has of it.*

Anna Maria was not only sad and lonely but desperately bored. She hardly ever went out, and her son often left her on her own, preferring to dine and joke with his friends. The late-autumn weather was so cold that when she wrote to her husband she could hardly use her pen, for it was almost frozen solid. While allowing a few worries to come across, she tried to reassure him. Since Wolfgang was serious about his course of action, they must await the elector's response.

Mannheim, 9 December 1777

Although invited to the concert at court, Wolfgang took no interest in the music and stared fixedly at Count Savioli. As soon as the interminable evening came to an end, he tackled the count, who had not condescended to greet the visitor from Salzburg.

'May I speak to you, Herr Count?'

'I am tired. My secretaries will give you an appointment.'

'They told me that you would not be free for several weeks, and I can wait no longer.'

'Wait for what, Mozart?'

'For the elector's answer. Is he going to engage me in his court, in some way or another?'

Count Savioli's answer came as a stinging shock. 'I very much regret it, but he is not.'

Leaving the hapless musician, he rejoined Father Vogler, who had witnessed the scene with a smile on his lips. Both were obeying the orders of their lord, who did not want a dispute with Prince-Archbishop Colloredo.

Wolfgang Mozart had no future in Mannheim.

Mannheim, 10 December 1777

'He refused you a job?' gasped Christian Cannabich. 'He wouldn't even give you the job of tutoring his bastards?'

'Not even that,' replied Mozart, emptying his wine glass. 'I've waited so long, and for such a disappointing result . . .'

'Don't let yourself be beaten down. Your musician friends

will help you. You can eat at one or other of our houses, and your lessons will pay for your accommodation. It would be extremely unwise to continue your journey in the depths of winter.'

Despite his failure, Wolfgang was determined not to lose heart. He could still make music in the company of Mannheim's fine musicians, and that would be an enduring delight.

'Let us allow things to proceed as they will and must!' he exclaimed. 'What use is vain speculation? We don't know what's going to happen, do we? And yet ... yes, we do know: it is whatever God wants! Come, a cheerful allegro!'

Reassured, Cannabich refilled his friend's glass. Together, they broke into a joyful canon mocking stupidity and injustice.

Munich, December 1777

Despite the progress their ideas were making among intellectuals, the Illuminati of Bavaria still had too few members to undertake a profound reform of society. According to the movement's leader, Adam Weishaupt, there was only one solution: to use the channel of Freemasonry, particularly Strict Templar Observance, whose all-conquering aspect he found highly attractive.

At the age of twenty-nine, this brilliant lawyer from the University of Ingoldstadt had rare energy and strength of conviction. His renown opened the doors of a Templar lodge in Munich to him; it was delighted to welcome such an eminent mind.

Weishaupt had barely been initiated into the Order when he began the task of undermining it. Many Freemasons, if not all, believed in God, but very few liked the Jesuits. And their faith was perhaps not as firm as they thought.

Since a man received the Light when he became a Freemason, said Weishaupt, he ought to shine that Light in the world outside, by fighting against the obscurantism of a depraved religion whose sole aim was to cloud people's minds. Freemasonry could become the spearhead of a new philosophy stressing the primacy of reason, the necessity for progress, and access to education for all.

His words shocked only a few Brothers who were too reactionary to envisage the smallest change. Most lent a ready ear and began fruitful discussions.

As for Weishaupt, he was not indifferent to the ritual. Despite its naiveties and its glaring imperfections, it emitted a certain magic which logic could not dissect. The Illuminati needed Freemasonry, and Freemasonry needed the Illuminati. By intermingling, the two organizations would both grow stronger, until the moment when Weishaupt's ideas imposed themselves.

Mannheim, 25 December 1777

Wolfgang grumbled angrily about the Dutchman Ferdinand Dejean, who was taking a very long time to pay a very meagre sum for a quartet for flute, violin, viola and cello. But he soon forgot such unpleasant matters when he went to a reception given by one of Mannheim's leading figures, Theobald Marchand.

To his astonishment he found the Count of Thebes there, deep in discussion with a young man of twenty-two with an unusually solemn face.

Marchand belonged to the college of founders of the main lodge in Mannheim. He invited Mozart to try some excellent white wine and to sample some of the delicacies set out on the tables. Then he took care of the other guests while Thamos talked to Wolfgang.

'Herr Mozart, I should like to introduce a distinguished diplomat, Otto, Baron von Gemmingen, with whom I have spoken at length about your *Thamos, König in Ägypten*. Like you and me, he is interested in the esotericism of the Pharaonic civilization and in ancient initiations, and he is carrying out extensive studies into these very complex matters.'

Such a recommendation from the Egyptian was worth its weight in gold. Wolfgang felt immediate respect for Otto von Gemmingen, whose solemn bearing impressed him.

'I am working on a symbolic drama which will be entitled *Semiramis*,' said the young baron. 'Would you be willing to set it to music?'

'I am most eager to read your text and I shall do my very best.' A new, grand, exciting project! Mannheim would yet be a distinct success.

'Will you be staying here long?' asked von Gemmingen.

'My father wishes me to become successful in Paris, but I am enjoying myself very much here and have no wish to leave.'

The baron was a Freemason, and Thamos considered him a suitable Brother to construct the temple. By the time Mozart eventually arrived in Paris, von Gemmingen would have alerted a Brother there.

61

Mannheim, 30 December 1777

Christian Cannabich woke Wolfgang. 'Karl Theodor has gone!'

The musician rubbed his eyes. 'Gone? Gone where?'

'Maximilian III is dead. As heir presumptive to the throne of Bavaria, Karl Theodor is hoping to conquer Munich. There are serious problems ahead.'

'What problems?'

'There is a risk that Austria and Prussia will tear each other apart over the succession. If our elector fails, but persists in his claim, it will lead to war.'

Wolfgang would not miss Maximilian, who had been an ally of Colloredo.

'For Mannheim,' Cannabich went on, 'the elector's departure is something of a catastrophe. Artistic life will come to a halt, and the city will turn in on itself. No more concerts, no more festivities – the immediate future looks positively dismal.'

Kirchheim-Boland, 23 January 1778

Wolfgang was on his way to see the Princess of Orange in order to give a concert, but he was not travelling alone. A pretty eighteen-year-old singer, Aloysia Weber, and her father, Franz Fridolin, were accompanying him.

After losing his post as a court administrator, Herr Fridolin had settled in Mannheim, where he worked as a copyist for the court theatre, a prompter and sometimes a singer, making the best possible use of his small bass voice. At the age of forty-five, he seemed worn-out but was bravely raising his three daughters.

'In the old days, my family was a noble one,' said Fridolin. 'Now, because of many misfortunes, my dear wife, my children and myself are just poor people struggling against adversity. But we are still good, decent Germans.'

'You should be proud of yourself, Herr Weber,' said Wolfgang.

'How old are you, young man?'

'I shall be twenty-two on the twenty-seventh.'

'Marvellous! You have your whole life before you. With your talent, you will go far.'

'Your daughter Aloysia's talent will be an invaluable help. Her voice is so pure and expressive that she is sure to inspire me to write some fine arias for my new opera.'

'When will it be finished?'

'I don't know yet. If I can avoid going to Paris, I'll compose it in Vienna and it will bring me at least a thousand florins.'

'A thousand florins! That's a fine sum.'

'Aloysia will become the most famous and best-paid singer in Vienna.'

Shy and reserved, the young girl merely smiled at Wolfgang, who devoured her with his eyes.

Vienna, opera, wealth ... he wanted so much to believe in the dream. He had fallen madly in love with Aloysia the moment he heard her sing, but without fame and money how could he ever win her heart?

Overcome by new feelings, which he could not control, Wolfgang thought constantly about her. Her father's sternness and moral rigour pleased him: Aloysia was not allowed to go out alone, and Fridolin watched over her all the time.

The concert on 24 January brought in only a modest sum. Wolfgang gave the major part of it to Fridolin Weber. There would be other, more lucrative engagements, and he would continue to show his generosity.

Forgetting all about his mother, who had remained alone in Mannheim, Wolfgang spent delicious hours in the company of Aloysia and her father. Just once, Fridolin granted the young folk permission to go for a walk in the snowy countryside while he smoked a pipe at the inn.

Wolfgang spoke of his plans, Aloysia of her hopes, and they laughed together as they talked about the peccadilloes and manias of certain musicians. High in a clear blue sky, a soft winter sun was shining.

'Aloysia . . .'

'Let's go back to the inn, Herr Mozart. My father and I must get back to Mannheim.'

'May I see you again?'

'I should very much like to sing one of your compositions.'

'You do me too much honour! As for me, I never tire of hearing you. A voice as expressive as yours is a true miracle.'

'You flatter me. I still have a great deal of work to do before I can appear on stage.'

'Well, we can work together.'

Mannheim, 4 February 1778

Wolfgang found his mother at the home of the royal counsellor, Herr Serrarius, who had granted them hospitality in exchange for piano lessons for his stepdaughter Therese, nicknamed 'the Nymph'.

'You haven't written to your father since 17 January,' Anna Maria said reproachfully. 'This is the first time you've left him so long without sending him your news.'

'You've done it for me, mother.'

'Where have you been these last few days?'

'I gave a concert at the home of a noble lady.'

'Alone?'

'No, with a female singer.'

'Is she young?'

'Quite young.'

'My son, I—'

'Don't worry, mother. I'll never travel in the company of licentious or debauched people whose conduct and opinions I don't approve of.'

'What is her name?'

'Aloysia. She's the eldest daughter of a very good man, Fridolin Weber, a copyist at the theatre in Mannheim. Their family has suffered reversals of fortune but has behaved with exemplary dignity. It's such good luck to have met them. I'll tell father straight away, because we've devised a splendid plan: a concert tour in Italy. Aloysia will become a *prima donna*, and I shall regain my reputation.'

'Aren't you getting excited rather too soon?'

'If you heard Aloysia sing, you wouldn't doubt for a second that she'll score a triumph. I've never heard such a wonderful voice.'

Transported to heights of exaltation, Wolfgang poured out his dreams in music.

But Anna Maria was upset and anxious, and secretly added a postscript to her letter to her husband before handing the letter to the postal service: '*He would do anything for these people.*' And 'these people', her intuition told her, might not be as decent as they claimed to be.

62

Schleswig, February 1778

The Duke of Brunswick was no longer alone in leading the Templar Order. At his side now stood Prince Karl of Hesse, governor of Schleswig-Holstein. The prince had been initiated in 1775, and his Knight's name was *Carolus a Leone Resurgente*. He prided himself on having studied several Rites before rallying to the Templar cause, the only one that could give Freemasonry the status it deserved.

Hesse was an expert in the occult sciences, and in one of his castles he had assembled a host of alchemists, in the hope of being present at the realization of the Great Work. Not at all discouraged by the failure of these second-rate scientists, he continued to research the secret of all secrets and frequented the most extravagant people, wondering if a real sage might be hiding among the charlatans.

Between Ferdinand of Brunswick and Karl of Hesse, an unshakeable bond of friendship had rapidly been forged. Hesse did not covet Brunswick's place, which he considered his friend more than worthy of occupying, while Brunswick listened to the advice of Hesse, who was a man of tireless curiosity.

'We shall govern the Order together,' promised the duke. 'But we must be aware that above us reign Unknown Superiors.'

'Have you met one?' asked the prince curiously.

'I have indeed had that good fortune. Thanks to his help, Strict Observance is continuing on its path without fear of being destroyed by external attacks. But we have still to strengthen the Order proper.'

'We are living in the last days of history,' declared Karl. 'Only Christ can save us from nothingness. I have the grace to receive radiant signs from the Lord, and all that I accomplish is dictated by Him or the spirits He directs. Let us set off together in search of the true Masonic secret, my Brother. Let us forget vainglory and nostalgia for the past. Yes, the Unknown Superiors will open the way for us and will enable us to build a spiritual Order in the service of God.'

Duke Ferdinand was won over by his friend's enthusiasm. Assisted by such a committed man, whose beliefs mirrored his own, he was sure to succeed.

There was just one small matter which might be awkward: the Templar origins of Strict Observance, and its declared determination to restore the temporal power of the old chivalric Order. Did many initiates still believe in such a future?

Mannheim, 7 February 1778

Leopold was certain that his son loved him not only as a father but also as his best and most dependable friend. In a letter, Wolfgang tried to explain his nascent love to him, without betraying the depth of his feelings.

We are not nobles, nor well-born rich gentlemen, but of low extraction, humble and poor, and consequently I have no need of a rich wife. Our wealth dies with us, for we have it in our heads. And no one can take it from us, unless someone cuts our heads off, after which we don't need anything any more! I want to make a wife happy, not create my own happiness at her expense.

For Wolfgang, love must be real and reasonable, free from frivolity and excess, which prevented serene happiness. He regarded a wife as the equal of her husband, who swore respect and fidelity to her; and a vow once made could not be taken back.

Many of his friends in Salzburg, who were revellers and cynics, did not share his convictions, and their attitude as young cocks of the walk displeased him enormously. He would never cheapen himself and regard a woman as an object to be conquered.

Mannheim, 19 February 1778

The Dutchman Dejean eventually paid up after a little more pressure was put on him. Wolfgang had provided him with some short, light works: such as four quartets for flute, violin, viola and cello, and a flute concerto in G major comprising a notably tender adagio which he hoped Aloysia would like. A Kyrie in E flat major was the only part completed so far of a mass he was writing for Karl Theodor in the hope of obtaining a post in the court chapel. But the elector was staying on in Munich, trying to disentangle the webs of political intrigue that opposed the extension of his powers.

Leopold's reply to his letter hit him like a blow from a club.

If you continue to build castles in Spain, and if you have nothing in your head but future plans, you will neglect all current, vital matters. Your head is full of things which make you unfit at present. In all things, you have proved hot-tempered and impetuous; your good heart means that you no longer see the defects of those who heap praise upon you. It will depend upon your wisdom whether you are a vulgar musician forgotten by the world or a celebrated Kapellmeister whose name will be written in the book of

posterity. Your plan almost made me go mad! Go to Paris,
and seek the support of the great. Either be Caesar, or be
nothing!

Overwhelmed, Wolfgang replied that same day. Of course, he
recognized the magnitude of the sacrifices his father had made
in order to aid his career – for instance by running heavily into
debt in order to enable his son to go to Paris and score a
resounding success there.

Paris, not Italy. Paris with his mother, not Italy with
Aloysia. Wolfgang surrendered to Leopold's arguments and
gave up his plans for a tour.

After he had finished his letter, he developed a high fever and
went to bed without dinner.

Vienna, 21 February 1778

'I have spoken about your role to Baron van Swieten,' Thamos
told von Born. 'His own mission is to protect the Masonic
lodges while leading people to believe that he is hostile to them.
By gaining the authorities' trust, he may eventually learn the
names of our most dangerous and most determined enemies.
Now you know his secret.'

'My lips are sealed,' promised von Born, moved by the
Egyptian's trust.

'Van Swieten can never meet you at an official lodge, because
of police surveillance.'

'I will arrange research sessions here and there with Brothers
who genuinely wish to experience the Mysteries glossed over
in the rituals, and we shall build with the aid of *The Book of*
Thoth.'

'Tobias von Gebler will not be among the builders,' said
the Egyptian. 'After the failure of *Thamos, König in Ägypten*
he lost his faith, and he now confines himself to a superficial

life in Berlin, asking no more of Freemasonry than a vague philosophy.'

'There are a lot of Brothers like him,' said von Born sadly. 'Where is the Great Magician?'

"In Mannheim. He is in love and would like to marry the singer he has fallen for. But his father is insisting that he at last goes to Paris.'

'What advice have you given him?'

'None,' replied Thamos. 'It is up to him to forge his own destiny during this probationary period. Otherwise, later on he would be unable to face the ordeals of initiation.'

63

Mannheim, 23 February 1778

Leopold's latest letter drove the nail home:

> *Thousands of people have no great gift such as yours from God. What a responsibility! Would it not be infinitely unfortunate for such a great genius to lose its way? You run more risks than the millions of people who do not have your talent, for you are far more exposed to attacks, on the one hand, and to flattery, on the other. You have a little too much pride and self-love, and also you are too familiar with people: you open your heart to everyone. I did not expect anything from Colloredo. From you I was expecting everything.*

Now recovered from his fever, Wolfgang refused to believe his father's suspicions. He respected good Fridolin Weber and loved Aloysia passionately, although he could not confess it to her.

'*Among my many defects,*' he replied to Leopold, '*I have this one: always believing that friends who know me, know me. In which case there is no need for words. Ah! If they do not know me, where could I find the right words to enlighten them?*'

Refusing to yield to sadness, Wolfgang strove to forget his

impending departure. He composed four sonatas for piano and violin full of amusing, joyful and popular dialogues, an aria, '*Se al labbro*', for the amiable but elderly tenor Anton Raaff, whose vocal abilities were by now somewhat limited; an *arietta*, '*Dans un bois solitaire*', for the soprano Augusta Wendling (it deplored the conduct of a young woman 'In a lonely wood'); and, most importantly, a recitative and aria, '*Non sò d'onde viene*', which was intended for Aloysia and whose words expressed his feelings: 'I do not know from whence this tender inclination comes to me, this emotion which fills my heart unawares, this shiver which courses through my blood.'

Wolfgang presented the aria to her and predicted, 'With this piece, you'll triumph in Italy.'

'What about you?'

'I must go to Paris. My father demands it.'

'But you promised me . . .'

'I must obey him, Aloysia. As soon as I've achieved the success he requires of me, I'll come back. Will you think of me a little?'

'How can you doubt it?'

Vienna, 1 March 1778

Baron van Swieten was treading on eggshells. As director of the Imperial and Royal Library he should be concerned with science and culture, not with state security and the police. So, during his conversations with leading court figures, he proceeded by means of allusions. At the slightest sign of reticence, he beat a hasty retreat and returned to the subject of the great authors, or rare books to be acquired.

His work and his management fully satisfied Empress Maria Theresa and Emperor Josef. At a reception, van Swieten had an opportunity to meet the head of the Viennese police, who was falsely jovial.

'My congratulations, Herr Prefect. Under your management, our famous library is becoming even richer and increasing the cultural prestige of our beautiful capital. Fortunately, we are hunting down those harmful ideas which will never have any place in our society.'

'Are you thinking of French philosophy?'

'Exactly. It's a virulent plague whose pustules must be burnt away, like a certain Freemasonry.'

'A dangerous sect, in my opinion.'

'And in mine, Baron.'

'I hope that you are taking all the necessary measures?'

'Have no fear.'

'I'm very reassured to know there's a skilled man like you in charge.'

The policeman lowered his voice. 'I am not in charge of this case. Her Majesty the Empress deals with it personally. What better guarantee could there be?'

Van Swieten nodded his agreement. He could not ask for details without arousing the man's suspicions, but his mind was busy.

Clearly, Maria Theresa had set up a parallel department charged with watching the Freemasons. Who ran this department, what means did he have at his disposal, and how far was he planning to go? Answering these crucial questions would not be easy. If van Swieten made even the smallest mistake, he would be utterly disgraced and would be dismissed from his offices.

Mannheim, 13 March 1778

Wolfgang faced a busy day, as exciting as it was heart-rending. In the morning, he gave his last lesson to 'the Nymph', step-daughter of the court counsellor, Serrarius, who had granted him hospitality. As a final act of gratitude, he presented the counsellor with a sonata for piano and violin.

Anna Maria was happy to see her son at last obeying his father. While she was finishing the packing, Wolfgang went to see Otto von Gemmingen. The previous day, the young Freemason had taken part in a Masonic gathering along with Thamos.

'Baron, I have begun to set your drama, *Semiramis*, to music.'

'That's excellent news, Herr Mozart.'

'Unfortunately, I must leave Mannheim for Paris. I do not know what obligations await me there, so I regret it is impossible for me to give you the exact date when I will finish the work.'

'I quite understand, and I thank you for your openness. When one has the good fortune to work with a creator like you, how can one not be patient? I have a good friend in Paris, the minister delegated to the Palatinate. I shall ask him to help you as much as he can with his modest means.'

'You do me great honour, Baron.'

'You deserve it, Herr Mozart, for you are no ordinary man. However . . .' He hesitated. 'I don't wish to discourage you, but do you think you might be harbouring too many illusions regarding the French? As a people they are both fickle and pretentious; they believe they are right about everything and consider themselves superior to the entire world. Parisian musicians do not generally give a warm welcome to foreigners, whom they regard as incapable of adapting to their genius and entering one of their inner circles.'

Wolfgang went to see the Webers. He found Aloysia and her father rehearsing the aria he had written for her; she was interpreting it perfectly, with controlled emotion and without intemperate excess.

'I must leave,' he told them sadly.

'When will you return to Mannheim?' asked Fridolin.

'As soon as possible. The trip is going to bore me.'

'But won't it enable you to achieve well-deserved success and fame?'

'My father hopes so.'

'Obeying him proves that you are a good boy. My daughter and I place great hope in you. Come back to us rich and famous, Wolfgang.'

'I promise you I shall do my best.'

'The French will throw themselves at your feet, I'm certain of it.'

'Permit me to be a little less optimistic.'

'Certainly not, Wolfgang, no! Have confidence in yourself and all will be well. Here is a gift to entertain you during the journey.' Fridolin handed him the German edition of Molière's *Comédies*.

As Wolfgang leafed through it, he stopped at a play entitled *Don Juan*, whose theme had circulated all round Europe.

'Thank you, Herr Weber. I hope to find the idea for a future opera in these pages.'

64

Paris, 23 March 1778

'I have never been so bored in my whole life,' Wolfgang confessed to his mother as they arrived in Paris after a nine-day journey.

Anna Maria had not, it is true, been lively company. She took little interest in her son's works, criticized his conduct with the Webers, whom she did not like, and voiced her distress at being kept away from her beloved Salzburg.

Their accommodation, a small, very dark room with not enough space for a piano, did not bring back their smiles.

'I cannot possibly work here,' declared Wolfgang.

'If you go out all the time, I'll have nobody to talk to. I can't understand a word of the language, and the Parisians are very unfriendly.'

'I must contact several people as quickly as possible, and find work. Settle yourself in as best you can.'

Thanks to the letters sent by his father to pave the way, Wolfgang was received by Baron Grimm and Madame d'Epinay the very next day, 24 March.

'I am delighted to meet a brilliant Austrian composer,' said the latter, gazing at him with interest. She saw a shy young man of medium height, pale-complexioned, with fine fair hair, a long, strong nose and bright eyes.

'I am not Austrian, Madame,' Wolfgang corrected her. 'I am German.'

'Your father has great hopes of you,' cut in Grimm, 'but Paris doesn't know the works you wrote in Salzburg, and it wants something new.'

'Can you help me?'

'My friends Jean Le Gros, director of the Concert Spirituel,* and Jean-Georges Noverre, ballet master at the Opéra, will present you with a variety of proposals. I warn you, the competition is fierce and it will not be easy to make your mark. The best way to earn your living is to give lessons to enlightened amateurs. Madame d'Epinay and the Duc de Guisnes will find pupils for you.'

When Mozart had left, Grimm frowned disdainfully. 'When he was a child prodigy, he interested me. But now . . . There are hundreds of musicians like him.'

'With his awkward shyness and nervous disposition, I found him rather appealing,' said Madame d'Epinay.

'Amuse yourself if it pleases you, dear friend, but don't waste your time. Trust my judgement, which everyone knows is infallible: that little German has no future.'

Paris, 25 March 1778

Count von Sickingen was the elector palatine's minister in Paris. He greeted Mozart warmly. Passionate about music, and a committed Freemason, he had read and reread the letter from his Brother, Otto von Gemmingen, recommending the composer to him.

'First, let us discuss accommodation. Are you comfortable where you are?'

---

* The organization, founded in 1725, which presented most public concerts in Paris.

'Not in the least,' said Wolfgang, 'but my mother and I have very limited means.'

'You shall stay at the Hôtel des Quatre Fils Aymon, in rue du Gros-Chenet. Have you any useful contacts among your French colleagues?'

'I've met Baron Grimm. He referred me to Le Gros and Noverre.'

Von Sickingen did not hide his feelings. 'I detest that man Grimm. He's pretentious, boastful, treacherous, self-interested – and his friends aren't much better. But they control musical life in Paris, and nothing can be done without them. They consider themselves the best in the world, and foreigners are unwelcome. Forgive my frankness, but it would be wrong of me to comfort you with mere illusions.'

'My father comforted himself more than he did me,' replied Wolfgang.

'My door will always be open,' promised the count. 'If you have any difficulties, don't hesitate to tell me. I shall plead your cause to the musicians I know, but your success will inevitably have to be won through Le Gros.'

Halfway between hope and despair, but glad to have at least one friend in Paris, Wolfgang left to rejoin his unhappy mother.

As soon as he had gone, Count von Sickingen opened the door of the small salon where Thamos has been waiting, and asked, 'Did you hear our conversation, Brother?'

'I didn't miss a word.'

'I fear your protégé is poorly armed for a fight with this pitiless city.'

'They are all pitiless,' said the Egyptian, 'and the formation of his character demands the fearsome tests he is to undergo.'

'What if he cannot bear them?'

'Then I shall know I was mistaken.'

Paris, 5 April 1778

Leopold would be satisfied: Wolfgang's Parisian stay had started rather well. Overwhelmed with work, he wrote a concerto for flute and harp, a *sinfonia concertante* and an opera about the love of Alexander and Roxane, scribbled down some choruses to insert into a *Miserere* by old Holzbauer in order to adapt it to Parisian taste, and, most of all, he taught.

'Are you happy?' Anna Maria asked. She herself was still lonely and felt very isolated.

'I hate giving lessons. My talent as a composer was given me by God, and I must not and cannot bury it like this. And I loathe this vile Parisian *galanterie* – it's simply a veneer for hypocrites who want to hide their immorality.'

'Your father has never been wrong, Wolfgang. We are here solely for your benefit.'

The young man put on his coat.

'Are you going out again?'

'I must try to make my mark with Le Gros, one of the key men in Parisian music.'

'No doubt you'd rather be enjoying yourself with the Webers . . .'

Wolfgang did not reply.

Le Gros, head of the Concert Spirituel, invited him to demonstrate his talents as a pianist before a chosen audience. With gusto, Wolfgang improvised a pastiche of a fashionable Italian 'master', Giovanni Cambini, whose music he considered thoroughly mediocre. He highlighted Cambini's peculiarities, and smiles appeared on his listeners' faces.

At the end of this ironic and successful stylistic exercise, applause rang out. Only one listener was clearly unenthusiastic: Cambini himself, of whose presence Wolfgang had been unaware.

The furious Italian drew Le Gros aside. 'That amateurish

German ridiculed me! You are my friend and must bring him to heel. A talentless unknown cannot mock a composer of my importance like this, a composer who is loved by all Paris.'

'Calm yourself, my friend. The fellow will pay dearly for his impertinence.'

65

Paris, 6 April 1778

The composer François-Joseph Gossec was forty-four years old and beginning to be talked about. In 1770 he had founded the Concert des Amateurs to give performances of music too 'progressive' for the Concert Sprituel. He was a committed Freemason and was deeply disappointed by the lukewarm politics of the lodges, which would not commit themselves to a profound reform of society. The Concert des Amateurs brought together many Brothers and, beyond music, it enabled them to express their ideals.

When he met Wolfgang Mozart, he tried to recruit him. 'You come from Salzburg, I believe.'

'Indeed.'

'What is it like there?'

'Prince-Archbishop Colloredo governs, and his musicians have to bow to all his demands.'

'That must be unbearable, dear colleague.'

'It is why I'm in Paris.'

'An excellent idea! Soon France will become the homeland of liberty and equality, for it will shake off all oppressive yokes.'

'I don't ask as much as that,' said Wolfgang. 'I'd like to find a brilliant court and an intelligent prince who wouldn't prevent me from expressing my art.'

'Don't be content with so little. You must follow Rousseau, Voltaire and Diderot. and "strangle the last priest with the entrails of the last king".'

The mere idea thoroughly alarmed Wolfgang. 'But violence is the worst of all solutions.'

'The end justifies the means. We must shatter the Church's stranglehold and overthrow the tyrants' thrones. Sooner or later, the whole of Europe will understand.'

'Well, Monsieur, I shall be an exception.'

Wolfgang would not try to meet either Voltaire or Rousseau, nor their disciples. The thoughts of those revolutionaries did not interest him.

Gossec shrugged. He would not help this reactionary young German to conquer Paris.

Paris, 20 April 1778

Thamos derived little satisfaction from his visits to the Parisian lodges. People ate and drank a great deal there, and they talked a lot. Only rarely did anyone ponder the significance of the rituals. Sometimes criticized, sometimes praised, the ideas of the Encyclopedists and the rationalists were gaining ground, even among members of the nobility.

The Egyptian took part in the work of an original lodge, that of the Philalethes, Les Amis de la Vérité (Friends of Truth).* They had accumulated a rich collection of works devoted to Freemasonry and did not disdain the study of alchemy and magic. However, the whole body of work suffered from a singular lack of coherence, and answered more to curiosity than to a true spiritual search. Proceeding in small steps and

---

* The lodge aimed to become an independent Order comprising a 'small Freemasonry' made up of six degrees and a 'high Freemasonry' with six other degrees from various systems.

without much hope, Thamos tried to direct them, knowing that this setting would not be suitable for the Great Magician, who himself had just rejected the revolutionary tendency embodied by Gossec.

Paris, late April 1778

By thinking about Aloysia and spending time with a few German musicians who were passing through Paris, Wolfgang became a little more cheerful, despite the burden of his lessons. His concerto for flute and harp had pleased the Duc de Guisnes and his daughter. It was remarkably elegant and refined, and proved to Parisians that German music was by no means lacking in poetry.

But it was another work, composed for his friends in Mannheim, which enabled Wolfgang to express the richness of his thought. This piece, a sinfonia concertante for clarinet, oboe, cor anglais and bassoon, had unusual scope, expressing both a desire for optimism and a seriousness sometimes so intense that one could easily have attributed it to a composer of great maturity. As he wrote it, Wolfgang had felt himself changing register.

Now here he was in an antechamber, pacing up and down as he waited for the feebly talented Le Gros to deign to receive him.

At last, the office door opened. 'Come in, Mozart. I have heard good things of your concerto for flute and harp. That style pleases my audience.'

'Will my sinfonia concertante be played at the Concert Spirituel?'

'Slow down! I must draw up the programme with great care, for fear of displeasing the audience and lowering the Concert's prestige. Baron Grimm oversees it with extreme rigour, and you know how important his judgement is. Any negative criticism would ruin me.'

'Don't you like my Sinfonia?'

'First, it is too long; second, it's a little too modern and in a genre which is too new for Parisian good taste.'

'You mean you won't have it played?'

'I shall study it in detail before making my final decision. But do continue to give your piano lessons. According to Madame d'Epinay, your pupils are delighted.'

At that moment, Wolfgang knew that Paris would never accept him. Behind Le Gros stood another man of the same ilk, and another, and so on to infinity. This land was not his, this sky rejected him, the mentality of this vain, enclosed world sickened him.

Although his mother was growing more bored and lonely by the day in a city to which she simply could not become accustomed, Wolfgang did not intend to go home. He knew her reproaches and recriminations would drag him down into depression; only his friends from Mannheim would prevent him from going under. Tonight, the only French product worthy of praise, wine, would flow in torrents.

66

Hermannsstadt, 1 May 1778

Watched intently by Hungarian Freemasons from the Lodge of the Three Water-lilies, Prince Alexander Murusi unfolded the map of the medieval Order of the Temple's possessions in Hungary, Transylvania and Slavonia.

'My Brothers, see the extraordinary success of the predecessors upon whom we model ourselves. They were exceedingly wealthy, and they reigned over Europe and dictated how monarchs behaved. Strict Observance cannot be reduced to an intellectual theory. It declares loud and long that we are worthy of such an example.'

'What do you suggest?' asked an elderly Brother, who looked rather worried.

'We must not remain inert and submissive under the dictatorship of mediocrity. I propose gathering together the funds needed to raise a Templar army which will set off to reconquer its lost territory. Talk achieves nothing; we must act. We must alert all Strict Observance Lodges, rouse them from their torpor, put on our capes and our armour, and become warriors of God again.'

White-faced, Grand Master Ferdinand of Brunswick began to speak. His informants had not lied to him; serious diversions from the proper course were in danger of occurring.

'I understand Prince Alexander's enthusiasm, but I must remind him that the essential core of our rites is allegorical. Of course we think with longing of the great past of the Order of the Temple, but each era develops its own spirit. The time of the Crusades is past.'

The prince protested, 'Respected Grand Master, you promised the resurrection of the Templars.'

'Only in spirit, my Brother, not in a warlike and violent manner. Let us spread the spiritual message of the old Templars, not the clash of weapons.'

Murusi was disappointed, but most of the Brothers were greatly relieved. The Duke of Brunswick knew he had narrowly averted a disaster.

Paris, 1 May 1778

On his way to see the Duchesse de Chabot, Wolfgang's thoughts were sombre. The stupid French seemed to think he was still seven years old and treated him as though he had no future. Write an opera? No point even thinking about it. Even in the event of success, he would earn precious little from it, because in this country everything was taxed to the hilt, which made artistic creation profitless.

The constant round of visits in order to sell himself was exhausting him. Because of the exorbitant cost of travelling by carriage, he had to walk through dirty, muddy streets. Three words summed Paris up: an indescribable cesspit.

When Wolfgang gave a concert for aristocrats in need of entertainment, he heard words like 'prodigious', 'inconceivable' and 'astonishing'. The following day, nobody remembered his name. The French constantly flirted with vulgarity by practising hypocrisy to a unique degree.

As for Baron Grimm, who was busy hiring geniuses who would soon be forgotten, he no longer took any interest in

Mozart, a little German lost in a big city whose arcane secrets he would never decipher.

Spring was wintry, the day dark and threatening. When he reached his destination, a manservant showed him into an ice-cold salon, with an unlit fire. Interminable minutes elapsed. Wolfgang grew cold.

At last the stylish but haughty Duchesse de Chabot deigned to make an appearance.

'Try my piano, young man. My friends will be delighted to hear you. I understand that the agility of your fingers is remarkable.'

'At the moment, Madame, they are frozen solid. Is the concert room heated?'

'Of course. Follow me.' She was lying.

Quaffing piping-hot drinks, her friends ignored the arrival of this servant charged with producing some pleasant background noise.

Although he was shivering, his hands stiff with cold, Wolfgang tried to live up to his reputation. But the pianoforte deserved to be thrown out with the rubbish. As for the audience, they joked, exchanged useless chatter and paid no attention whatever to the variations he played.

In fury, he stopped. Sparse applause greeted his per-formance.

The Duc de Chabot made his entrance. 'Why do you not continue?'

'Even if I were given the best piano in Europe, I would have no pleasure whatsoever in playing it for people who understand nothing and wish to understand nothing, and who do not feel the music with me as I play it.'

'Monsieur, I shall listen to you. Pray recommence.'

Wolfgang agreed to sit down again at the loathsome piano, but cut short the concert. That evening, with his feet resting on a hot-water bottle, he wrote to his father:

If there was a place here where people had ears, a heart to feeling with, if they even understood something about music, if they had taste, I would laugh pleasantly at all these things. But I am surrounded only by brutes and beasts in the matter of music. How, moreover, could it be otherwise? They are no different in their other actions, motives and passions. The French are and will remain donkeys.

Paris, 13 May 1778

Sad, almost grating, the sonata for violin and piano in E minor expressed Wolfgang's disappointment. However, the forthcoming publication of his variations on the air '*Je suis Lindor*' would be his first serious appearance at the heart of the Parisian universe. Varying its rhythms and melodies, the composer had chosen the air composed by a man called Dezede on words spoken by Count Almaviva in *Le Barbier de Séville*, at the moment when he is passing himself off as a young commoner in the eyes of Rosine. One day, perhaps, Wolfgang would use this story in another way.

His true goal was still to have his Sinfonia concertante performed at last, so he laid siege to the office of Le Gros.

'What do you want, Monsieur Mozart?'

'Your decision regarding the work I entrusted to you.'

'Which work?'

'My Sinfonia concertante.'

'I don't recall . . .'

'You said you thought it too long, too modern, too—'

'Ah, yes, I do vaguely remember. Let us forget it, if you will. It is quite unsuitable for the Concert Spirituel, but you will assuredly do better work. Continue to give lessons and perfect your skills.'

Back at his lodgings and looking grim, Wolfgang came under attack from his mother.

'I don't see my son all day, I stay alone in the room as though I were under arrest, I don't even know what the weather is like, I talk to no one – I'm afraid I shall lose the ability to speak! Besides, your father's getting impatient. See Baron Grimm again and ask him to find you a good situation.'

Wolfgang refused to argue. Fortunately, soon afterward he received a visit from a kindly horn-player who liked his work and recognized his talents as a player.

'It seems,' said the visitor, 'that a post as an organist at Versailles is becoming vacant. You should apply.'

Versailles, the theatre of his childhood glory!

'Is it paid well?'

'No, very badly.'

'And is it a first step, or the end of the road?'

'To be honest, little progress is possible. Nevertheless—'

'I'm afraid the court no longer interests me. People would talk to me constantly about my exploits as an over-talented youth, and I have no desire to compose pompous, boring church music. In order to create, one must remain inspired. The court of Versailles is not for me.'

67

Paris, 5 June 1778

After a difficult day in which a feverish Anna Maria had complained once again of her isolation, she fell asleep, dreaming of her dear Salzburg.

Wolfgang wrote a piano sonata in A minor expressing his rebellion against failure, his moments of despair when faced with a situation which amounted to an impasse, but also his wish to go forward nevertheless.*

'*Often I find neither rhyme nor reason in things,*' he wrote to Leopold. '*Is it cold? Is it hot? I have no real joy in anything.*'

Only his friendship with Count von Sickingen enabled Wolfgang to keep his head above water. He found a degree of peace in finishing a sonata for piano and violin which he had begun in Mannheim. Then he accepted a commission for some ballet music, hoping that it might lead to music for an opera.

'The musical world is talking of nothing but the quarrel between Gluck's admirers and Piccinni's,' the Count told him. 'Have you chosen a side?'

'That kind of debate doesn't interest me,' replied Wolfgang. 'Why get locked into such sterile arguments?'

'Not declaring your position will draw fire from both camps.'

---

* K310. Some musicologists date it to after the death of his mother.

'There are imbeciles everywhere.'

'The whole of Paris is weeping over the death of Voltaire, on 30 May. Did you know that he was not content with the Académie and the Comédie-Française? At the age of eighty-four, he had just joined the Masonic Lodge of the Nine Sisters, a very exclusive circle. God, how that old fellow loved honours!'

'He died like a dog, the blackguard; he got what he deserved.'

The harshness of this judgement astonished the Count. 'You have little liking for the philosophy of Light, it seems.'

'To me it seems just as dark as this new German literary tendency, *Sturm und Drang*, or 'Storm and Stress', which consists of yearning for storms and inner turmoil, the better to weep over oneself. All that matters is the quest for serenity, with its procession of ordeals which one must try to overcome stoically.'

Paris, 11 June 1778

On the poster announcing the performance of the ballet *Les Petits Riens*, 'Little Nothings', the name of the composer – Mozart – had not even been mentioned. When Wolfgang, very proud of his new success, had the honour to be received by the Opéra's ballet master, Jean-Georges Noverre, he dared complain about it.

'The public aren't interested in the music, my dear Mozart, they're interested in the dancers. It is the physical performance that they come to see. Your work was not unpleasing. You should continue in the same manner.'

'I would prefer to compose an opera.'

'In the tradition of Gluck or of Piccinni?'

'Neither.'

'You must pick one or the other.'

'Are there no other choices?'

'Not at the moment. Paris knows what it wants. Give up your project: you aren't made for such an arduous genre.'

Wolfgang decided not to tell his father about the affair of *Les Petits Riens*, in which his name had failed to break out obscurity. Better not to sadden Leopold any further; he must be beginning to realize what a fiasco this Parisian exile was.

Mattisholm Castle, Sweden, 12 June 1778

Ferdinand of Brunswick, Grand Master of Strict Templar Observance, was launching a new campaign against Prince Carl's candidacy for the leadership of the Order's seventh province.

The Danes, members of that province, would never accept being led by a Swedish prince in line for the highest offices. And the Brothers in Saxony and Lower Germany would want one of their own countrymen. Faced with such opposition, surely the prince would eventually give up?

As he was preparing to leave Denmark, Duke Ferdinand received a surprising communication: his formidable rival invited him to Sweden, to Mattisholm Castle, for a Brotherly discussion. It was impossible to refuse on pain of gravely offending the prince and unleashing open warfare whose first victim would be Strict Observance.

The Swede greeted his guest with great courtesy. After an excellent dinner, they withdrew to a private chamber, away from indiscreet ears.

'We do not know each other well, my dear Brunswick. Above all, you do not know the Swedish Rite. Does a Freemason not always wish to learn and push back the frontiers of ignorance?'

'You are preaching to the converted. But your Rite seems to me somewhat inaccessible.'

'What if I were to give you the key?'

311

'How?'

'By initiating you to the rank of Swedish Grand Officer. In that way, we would understand each other better and our Brotherly relations would improve accordingly.'

Ferdinand put on a show of satisfaction, although he was suspicious that his opponent might be plotting something.

As it turned out, Prince Carl's manoeuvre backfired on him, for Ferdinand was bitterly disappointed by the paucity of the Swedish Rite, which taught him absolutely nothing. Hiding his feelings, he congratulated himself on this fine Brotherly relationship, which allowed his enemy to believe that he had persuaded him not to oppose him any more.

If the Swedish Rite gains control of Strict Observance, thought Duke Ferdinand, before long Freemasonry will vanish without a trace.

Paris, 18 June 1778

Through the intervention of the tenor Anton Raaff, who much admired the composer, Le Gros eventually allowed himself to be persuaded to present Mozart's new symphony at the Concert Spirituel – although he demanded several changes to it.* Using strong contrasts, Wolfgang had calculated the moments when the Parisian audience would applaud. He was right every time. These people loved only effects.

Happy to have been at last heard, if not listened to, the musician went to the Palais Royal, where he first offered his thanks to God and then ate an ice. However, he did not deceive himself: this was but a small success, and might lead no further. Still as cold and distant as before, Le Gros hardly seemed determined to welcome him into the circle of recognized composers.

* No. 31 in D, K297, known as the 'Parisian'.

To his father, Wolfgang wrote about a sort of triumph. The pious lie would comfort Leopold.

Back at his lodgings, he found his mother unwell. She said she was suffering from an intestinal infection which her medicine was not easing. On 20 June, she fell prey to a high fever but refused to see any French doctor. Through his friends, Wolfgang found a doctor who spoke German, and he examined the patient on the 24th, when she lost her hearing. On the 29th, he judged her case hopeless. On the 30th her son summoned another doctor, who confirmed the diagnosis.

After confessing and receiving the last rites, Anna Maria sank into delirium. On 3 July 1778, at twenty-one minutes past ten in the evening, she died.

68

Paris, 3 July 1778

Overwhelmed, Wolfgang gazed at Anna Maria's peaceful face. This was his first direct encounter with death ... the death of his mother at the age of fifty-eight.

He had experienced every moment of her dying hours with a strange serenity. It was not he but Anna Maria who was suffering; tears and lamentations could be of no help to her. On the contrary, by showing her his affection and his trust in God, he had helped her through her terrifying ordeal.

Now he was thinking about his father. Never again would Leopold see his beloved wife, who had died so far from her dear Salzburg. He would not be present at her burial and could not meditate at her tomb.

Wolfgang could not suddenly, brutally announce to Leopold that the person he cherished most in the world had died. So he wrote him a letter about the concert on 18 June, about the death of treacherous, impious Voltaire, and about his rejection of the post of organist at Versailles. In order to prepare Leopold for the worst, he said Anna Maria was seriously ill, and added:

I shall keep my courage no matter what happens, because
I know that it is God who wishes it so; God who orders

everything for our greatest good, even if we think that things are going wrong. I believe, indeed, and nobody will persuade me otherwise, that no doctor, no human being, no misfortune, no accident, can give and take away the life of a human being, only God alone. Let us put our trust in Him and console ourselves with this thought: that all goes well when it obeys the will of the All-Powerful One, for He knows best what is advantageous and useful for us, all of us, for our happiness and our salvation, as much in our lifetime as in eternity.

At the same time, he sent a message to Abbot Bullinger, a monk in Salzburg, asking him to prepare Leopold for the terrible news.

Paris, 9 July 1778

On 4 July, Anna Maria had been buried in the cemetery of Saint-Eustache, in Paris. Mme d'Epinay was most sympathetic and offered one of the rooms of her house to the young musician, who had been so sorely tried.

Five days after his mother's death, Wolfgang wrote again to his father, revealing the truth and trying to comfort him:

In these sad circumstances I have sought comfort in three realities. First, in my complete and trusting abandonment to the will of God. Second, in my presence at her gentle and beautiful death, for I was imagining how happy she had become in that moment, so much happier than we that I formed a wish to leave with her, at the same moment. Finally, in the conviction, born from this wish and aspiration, that she is not lost to us for ever, that we shall see her again and will be reunited again, more joyfully than in this world. How long it will be until then, we do not know. But

I feel no fear: when God wishes it, I shall wish it, too. Now His will is done. Let us recite a fervent Paternoster for Mother's soul and deal with other subjects, for there is a time for everything.

Turn this painful page already? Yes, for real life was not limited to earthly existence. The suffering of the living did not touch the blessed dead and the dark shadows of death did not obscure the eternal Light.

When he went out to take the air in the city he loathed, Wolfgang met Thamos.

'I could do nothing,' the Egyptian said gently. 'Your mother's body was worn out.'

'She watched over my father, over Nannerl, over me. We have been deprived of a blessed spirit.'

'Your loneliness will bring you new strength.'

'Here in Paris? If only the French language were not so abominable for music!'

'Instruments sing in a universal language, do they not? Tell me about your Sinfonia concertante.'

Wolfgang opened his heart. At last, someone who listened to him!

Paris, 10 July 1778

Madame d'Epinay handed Baron Grimm a cup of delicious coffee.

'I heeded your request, dear friend, and gave a room to that poor fellow Mozart. Seeing one's mother die in a foreign land, so far from her home: how sad! Will the unfortunate boy recover from it?'

'He would do well to return to Salzburg.'

'But did he not come to seek glory and fortune in Paris?'

'Given his intransigent nature and his meagre talent, there is

316

no chance of that. German music, and his in particular, does not suit the French taste. As a child prodigy he was entertaining. Today he is a bore. Neither Le Gros, who is an excellent judge, nor the leading composers care for him.'

'Is that your last word on the matter, Baron?'

'I am never wrong, and I assure you that this little scribbler will soon be forgotten. I have therefore written to his unbearable and deplorably stubborn father, telling him that his offspring is neither clever nor enterprising enough to make his mark in Paris. The child Wolfgang's naivety amused us, but coming from his adult lips it offends us. Leopold begged me on bended knee to look after his son's welfare, but I have no wish to waste my time. Soon, dear friend, you will be free of your parasite.'

Paris, 20 July 1778

Left to his own devices but reassured by his brief encounter with Thamos, Wolfgang abandoned himself to the joy of composing. First a smiling piano sonata in C major, in which no echo of the recent tragedy could be detected; then another, in A major, beginning with an unusual slow movement with variations on a German popular song and ended with an entertaining 'Rondo alla turca', inspired by the overture to Gluck's *Pèlerins de la Mecque* (Pilgrims to Mecca). As for the trio, it evoked the exquisite Dance of the Blessed Spirits in *Orfeo ed Euridice* by the same composer.

Wolfgang thought about his mother with a surprising feeling of peaceful happiness and liberation, and he offered her these works full of liveliness and gentle sweetness, in her own image. Anna Maria had known only sadness when she was far from the home where, throughout her life, she had dispensed cheerfulness and harmony.

That same day, for Nannerl's birthday, Wolfgang wrote a

capriccio which would give his sister a chance to loosen up her fingers.

Paris, 31 July 1778

The previous day, once again haunted by the face of his dear Aloysia, Wolfgang had written to her father, Fridolin, advising him to give more help to his exceptional daughter, who was deprived of work and roles befitting her. He should declare her ill! Then the Mannheim court would take pity and at last look more favourably upon her . . .

Impatient to see her again, Wolfgang promised to compose a work which he would give to her as soon as he returned. Avoiding mentioning his mother's death to the Weber family, who had already suffered so much misfortune, he called Aloysia '*Carissima amica*', certain that she shared his feelings.

A quite different feeling, anger, motivated Wolfgang when he walked through the door of the Duc de Guisnes's private town house.

'I heard about the death of your mother,' said the aristocrat in an affected drawl. 'All my condolences. Alas, death comes to us all. Be brave: time wipes away grief.'

'I have come to talk to you about my concerto for flute and harp, Monsieur le duc.'

'A delightful work. My friends and I much enjoyed it.'

'I have been awaiting payment for three months.'

'Art first, my dear Mozart! How trivial to mix it with questions of base materialism.'

'Music is my profession – I live by it. I would like to receive the money owed to me.'

'Do not worry, you shall have it.'

'When?'

'When . . . when it pleases me.'

'It would please me to have it right now.'

'You do not think, young man! A German oaf does not give orders to a French nobleman. Kindly leave my house.'

When Mme d'Epinay saw Mozart striding towards her, she realized at once that he was very angry.

'What is wrong?' she asked.

'Some French oafs imagine that I am still seven years old and that I can be treated like a child.'

'Unfortunately that is true,' she agreed. 'Here, you are regarded as a beginner.'

Wolfgang shut himself in his room and wrote again to his father, whose heart-rending letters tore his soul apart.

You know that, in my whole life, I had never seen anyone die before. And when it came to the first time it had to be my mother! Giving lessons, here, is no joke ... It's exhausting enough! And if you don't give a lot, you don't earn enough money. Don't think that I am saying so out of laziness; it's because it is an attitude completely contrary to my 'genius' and my way of life. You know that I am, so to speak, stuffed with music, that I make it all day long, that I like to think about it, study it, apply myself to it. Well, here I am prevented from doing so by the sort of life that is imposed upon me. When I have a few hours of freedom, I use them not to compose but to regain a little strength.

69

Geytrand mopped his brow; he hated the summer. Overcome by the heat, he was suffering with his liver and had swollen ankles. It was with relief that he went to Josef Anton's secret office – the count who also hated summer and spent it in the twilight, with the curtains closed.

'The Masonic gathering at Wolfenbuettel ended peacefully,' said Geytrand. 'Officially, Strict Observance and the Swedish Rite have ceased hostilities and become the best allies in the world. As for Prince Carl, he is to govern the enormous seventh province, bowing to the directives of the Grand Master, Ferdinand of Brunswick.'

'"Officially"?' echoed Josef Anton. 'So you don't believe it?'

'Not for a moment. Judging by some indiscreet remarks by German Knights who are furious at the prince's election, this peace has been ripped out with forceps and is peppered with restrictions which are unacceptable in the Swede's eyes. He wanted to get his hands on the province at any price, so he pretended to yield, but before long he'll confront Brunswick and try to exclude him by changing the rules of the game. Prince Carl cannot remain in a subordinate position, and the Grand Master will never yield even an inch of power to him.

Despite this convenient treaty and some fine words, a clash seems inevitable.'

'Who do you think will win?'

'I don't favour either of them, Herr Count. The two adversaries are equally determined and ferocious. The Duke of Brunswick has lost one battle, but not the war. He remains Grand Master of the entire Order, and the provincial Grand Masters owe obedience to him. Besides, the German Freemasons will never elect a Swede to lead them. Whatever happens, Freemasonry will be considerably weakened.

'Oh, and there's a new name for our records. Bode, a man close to the Grand Master, at present occupies an important place in the hierarchy of Strict Observance. He is busy drawing up the deed of alliance and has proved to be zealous and efficient. He was appointed administrator of the wealth of the widow of Minister of State von Bernstorff, and now lives in Weimar, a pleasant, peaceful city. From now on he will have no financial worries and can devote himself to his crusade against the Jesuits and the Church.'

Josef Anton opened a new file.

Salzburg, 15 August 1778

Leopold was not recovering well from Anna Maria's death. It was impossible to fill the terrible void, and only time could lessen the pain of the incurable wound. He would never remarry. Nannerl was behaving with tact and devotion, but he needed to talk to his son.

When would they see each other again? Wolfgang was still fighting to conquer Paris, but without much success. One passage in a recent letter particularly worried Leopold:

Salzburg is odious to me. Anywhere other than Salzburg, I would have more hope of living happy and content. First, people involved with music enjoy no consideration at all; second, one hears nothing there.

Soon, Leopold would have to tell his son that Baron Grimm refused to help him any more and that he must return to Salzburg. Given his state of mind, how would Wolfgang react?

On 11 August, the death of Giuseppe Lolli, Kapellmeister at the Salzburg court, had given Leopold the hope that he might finally obtain that post, but he had been disappointed yet again. The only gift from Colloredo was an increase of a hundred florins in his salary. And the deputy Kapellmeister, always so obedient and so dedicated, could no longer share his feelings with Anna Maria.

Paris, 16 August 1778

Wolfgang's pupils adored his piano variations on the songs '*Ah, vous dirai-je, maman*' and '*La Belle Française*', but he devoted most of his creative energy, his questioning, and the alternate use of brightness and drama to a new sonata in F major. In it, he reflected the complexity of the chaotic life he was passing through without understanding all its secrets, which doubtless the priests of the sun knew.

A sun which, despite the season, was sadly lacking in Paris, even though his new symphony had been played again at the Concert Spirituel.

'Be satisfied, Mozart,' said Le Gros. 'The public likes your little inventions. So continue on that path, not forgetting to give your lessons, and perhaps you will make an honourable place for yourself.'

'I long to write an opera.'

'Gluck and Piccinni dominate the scene.'

'Have you no libretti you could offer me?'

'Not one. Forget that foolish plan and confine yourself to what you do well.'

Losing patience, Le Gros cut the interview short and returned to his friend, Baron Grimm.

'That German gets on my nerves,' he confided. 'He should be content with what he is given, not constantly demand more.'

'He spends time with a detestable individual,' said the baron, 'a certain von Sickingen, who has not integrated well into Paris society and will not keep his post much longer. I might have helped that Mozart fellow if he had proved tractable. Pay no more attention to him, my dear Le Gros. His career is over.'

70

Saint-Germain-en-Laye, 28 August 1778

Ah! The delightful residence of the Maréchal de Noailles, its beautiful grounds, and above all the unhoped-for happiness of seeing Johann Christian Bach again and spending a week in his company, far from stifling Paris and its miserable intrigues.

They spent wonderful hours talking about music, and Wolfgang composed a dramatic *scena* for the castrato Giusto Tenducci, a friend of Bach. He finished nine piano variations on the air '*Lison dormait*' and a new symphony, light and brilliant, destined for the Concert Spirituel.

'Paris doesn't agree with you,' said Bach. 'Why don't you settle in London? There's a real spirit of freedom there, and your talent would be recognized.'

'My mother died recently, and I can't leave my father to his loneliness.'

'You have a great heart, Wolfgang, but you don't think of yourself enough. Here you'll never blossom. The French are superficial and hypocritical, and Baron Grimm does nothing but feed his own vanity. With his little cohort of pretentious intellectuals, infatuated with their triumphant stupidity, they decide everything. They consider you negligible, even if the Concert Spiritual does occasionally accept one of your symphonies – on condition that it doesn't offend the taste of the day. You are too pure and too wholehearted to conquer a city like Paris, and because my standing isn't high enough here I can't help you.'

Wolfgang would have loved to have a father like Bach. Together, they played music, without worrying about an audience. The wondrous realm of Rücken came back to life, and the other side of life reappeared, with its enchanting landscapes.

But rain fell on Saint-Germain-en-Laye, Johann Christian Bach returned to London, and Wolfgang made his way back to Paris.

Paris, 1 September 1778

Wolfgang reread his father's letter, especially the enclosed copy of the letter from Baron Grimm. The all-powerful critic declared that the young man from Salzburg possessed none of the qualities that the Parisian artistic milieu enjoyed. 'Too naive, not active enough, too easy to get hold of, not wily enough, neither enterprising nor audacious.' And the illustrious baron had neither the time nor the wealth necessary to consolidate Mozart's future career.

When he next saw Madame d'Epinay, she was as light-hearted as ever. 'Have you heard about our latest attraction?' she asked. 'A sort of magician has set up in place Vendôme and claims to cure all illnesses with the aid of magnetism!'

'Is he Doctor Franz Anton Mesmer?'

'Do you know him?'

'Slightly.'

'He has had such success that he's already overwhelmed.'

The doctor abandoned his patients to receive Wolfgang. After mesmerizing him at length to re-establish the circulation of energy, he stressed the need to perceive the vital fluid that served as a link between living beings.

'Your music is an expression of this fluid,' he explained. 'The more it is in harmony with it, the more it will serve as a vehicle, and the more you will touch minds and hearts. And so, Wolfgang, you will contribute decisively to the balance of our world.'

'Will you ever return to Vienna, Doctor?'

'Never, for treatment by magnetism is not recognized there. Here, as well as individual treatments I carry out collective care. Several patients, seated side by side, will form a chain and be linked by iron bands or ropes to a tub containing water, iron filings and sand. The circulation of the magnetic flux will relieve their ills.'

'Paris has brought me no luck,' said Wolfgang. 'My mother died here on 3 July, and I have not found any of the success my father was hoping for.'

'Persevere, but don't remain a prisoner. Nothing must hinder your flight.'

Paris, 11 September 1778

'Monsieur le baron,' said Wolfgang rather sharply to Grimm, 'I am extremely unhappy with Le Gros's attitude to me. He takes no interest in my work and will not allow me even to glimpse any kind of future.'

'My friend Le Gros is a remarkable professional whose opinion is decisive. You, my boy, are a mere beginner. Paris demands a great deal; your music does not possess the qualities required to seduce the capital of arts and letters. And then there is a much more urgent matter ... During your mother's illness, I lent you the modest but not negligible sum of fifteen gold louis. I should like it back.'

Pale and sickened, Wolfgang remained silent.

At his lodgings, a letter from his father awaited him. Enthusiastically, Leopold announced that Prince-Archbishop

Colloredo had agreed to take young Mozart back into his service and was offering him a steady position as an organist! What more could he hope for? Wolfgang must therefore return to Salzburg with all possible speed. Magnanimously, Leopold even gave him permission to spend time with Aloysia. Wasn't everything for the best in the best of all worlds?

Wolfgang replied that he would be happy to see his father and his sister, but added that it was no great happiness to find himself locked away in Salzburg. As his affairs were improving, he would not return immediately. A few current projects might perhaps be crowned with success . . .

71

Paris, 26 September 1778

'Haven't you left yet, Mozart?' demanded Grimm, surprised and angry.

'I was hoping—'

'How often do I have to say it? You have nothing to hope for, absolutely nothing. A German musician who is starting out and has no ambition has no chance of success in Paris. Here all doors are closed to you. I shall pay for your travel: you will board the fastest, most comfortable stagecoach, and you will disappear.'

After a difficult stay of six months, Wolfgang was not unhappy to leave Paris but dreaded returning to Salzburg. There was one final disappointment: an old, jam-packed stage-coach, the cheapest and the slowest. It would take him not five days to reach Strasbourg, but ten. Yet again, that devil Grimm had lied to him.

When his anger had passed, Wolfgang cast an eye over his companions in misfortune. Among them was Thamos! He was talking to a wine trader who thought he was addressing a merchant with important contacts in England.

At Nancy, Thamos got down and signalled to Wolfgang to follow him. They got into an excellent carriage.

Wolfgang described in detail the last episodes of his

Parisian adventure, and did not hide his disillusionment.

'And now, Salzburg ... There I'm not who I really am, I'm everything and, sometimes, nothing at all. I am not asking very much, or very little: just to be something. But really something.'

'Before that, there are several stages,' said the Egyptian, 'beginning with the one in Strasbourg, where you will give three concerts. Don't expect either a large audience or a large fee, but you will enjoy playing with highly accomplished musicians, who will be happy to welcome you.'

'You ... Have you organized everything?'

'Your Mannheim friends have contacts in Strasbourg.'

Thamos omitted to add that he had visited the lodges of Saint-Louis d'Alsace, Saint-Jean d'Heredom, L'Amitié, Le Parfait Silence and Le Candeur, not forgetting the very ancient community of builders who preserved the heritage of the medieval Master Masons.

Strasbourg, October 1778

Wolfgang needed to wash off the Parisian dross and converse with people who felt a genuine affection for him. He spent time with musicians who were Freemasons, spent laughter-filled evenings round good tables and met old Kapellmeister Richter, who at sixty-eight drank only twenty bottles of wine a day instead of forty!

On 17 October, his first concert brought in three gold louis; on the 23rd, the second brought in another three; the third concert, on the 31st, brought in only one louis, for the hall was half empty. But Wolfgang rediscovered the joy of living and finished a pretty piano sonata which he had begun in Paris and which opened on a theme by Johann Christian Bach. It was synonymous with liberation and happy times, despite the letters from his father which could not understand why his son had stopped for so long in Strasbourg.

Leopold also gave him some news which was both good and bad: the Weber family had left Mannheim for Munich, where Aloysia had been engaged by the Opera. Wolfgang was glad that her talent was receiving proper recognition, but it took her heart-rendingly far away. Contrary to his hopes, the woman he loved would not be living in Salzburg and the gilded cage would be transformed into a dank and horrible prison.

In order to calm his father's impatience, Wolfgang told him he was staying with Schertz, a rich notable who had agreed to lend him some money. And he explained the deep reasons for his stay: *Here, I am held in honour. People say that everything is so noble in me, that I am so mature, so good, that I behave so well . . .'* Would Leopold at last understand his true aspirations and the quality of his being?

Thamos's therapy was proving effective. From the wounded individual, tired and jaded by the attacks and sufferings he had faced in Paris, a new Wolfgang emerged, ready to face fresh trials.

Mannheim, 6 November 1778

On 4 November, Wolfgang resigned himself to leaving Strasbourg for another city dear to his heart, ever-musical Mannheim.

The Cannabich family welcomed him with open arms. He told his friend Christian all about his French misadventures, at last freeing himself of the burden. A page had turned; never again would he set foot in Paris.

Baron von Dalberg, *Intendant* of the Mannheim theatre, and a Freemason, was informed of Mozart's arrival by von Sickingen and invited him to dinner, where another guest was Otto von Gemmingen.

'How fares my *Semiramis*, Herr Mozart?'

'It's barely sketched out, I must confess.'

'If you're staying in Mannheim for a little while, can we work on it together?'

'With pleasure.'

The work was presented as a 'duodrama', aiming at a perfect synthesis between words and music.* Wolfgang had finally regained the dynamism of *Thamos*, thanks to a theme with many resonances linked to initiation, which he perceived without understanding them. Thinking of Aloysia, he was sure to write a magnificent title role.

Otto von Gemmingen allowed him total freedom to create, and adapted to his demands when words or phrases had to be altered in order to give pride of place to the music. Meanwhile, Baron von Dalberg arranged enough piano-teaching to cover the costs of his stay and play music with his friends as often as possible.

As Wolfgang wrote to his father on 12 November, an Academy of amateurs was being set up in Mannheim; its members – unknown to Mozart – were almost all Freemasons. In their company, he spent many happy hours.

Mannheim, 15 November 1778

'It's a complete absolute disaster,' Otto von Gemmingen told Thamos. 'The elector has ordered the orchestra to join him in Munich, where he's still trying to gain the throne of Bavaria. If the situation deteriorates, war will break out between Prussia and Austria. Mannheim's musical life will be reduced from little to absolutely nothing.'

'Wolfgang will be directly affected,' said the Egyptian.

'My Brothers were discreetly preparing the ground with Karl

* Unfortunately, no trace remains of *Semiramis*. Will someone one day find this work, so important for Mozart's spiritual progress?

Theodor in order for Mozart to obtain a stable, well-paid post, but the orchestra's move has ruined that plan. And the performance of *Semiramis* won't take place – it would be impossible to stage it in Munich, where neither Baron von Dalberg nor I have sufficient contacts. Everything now depends upon the will of Karl Theodor, who will always support Prince-Archbishop Colloredo against Mozart. What we were hoping for in Mannheim cannot take place anywhere else. I would so have loved to succeed and spare him more difficulties.'

'That is how it is,' said Thamos, 'and Wolfgang must show himself equal to the difficulties that await him. A Great Magician cannot be formed any other way.'

'He is a truly exceptional person,' said von Gemmingen. 'His sensibility is not sentimentality, but intelligence of the heart. His eyes see landscapes whose existence we do not even suspect, and I believe him capable of passing on this vision through music. But how long will the fates continue to conspire against him?'

72

Mannheim, 22 November 1778

Wolfgang had not minced his words when writing to his father: '*The archbishop will never pay me enough to be a slave in Salzburg, and I feel anguish when I see myself back in that miserable court.*' Even so, he had not expected Leopold to reply so furiously:

> *You take for gold all that, in the final analysis, is only base metal. Your love for Fräulein Weber? I am absolutely not opposed to it. I was not when her father was poor, so why should I be so today when she can provide for your happiness and not you for hers? Your entire intention is to ruin me in order to pursue your chimeras.*

The father Wolfgang loved and venerated so much actually accused his only son of wanting him dead.

With Otto von Gemmingen forced to leave Mannheim, the orchestra en route for Munich, and the Opera closed, the young man found himself once again alone and without support.

Then Thamos reappeared.

'My father demands that I return immediately to Salzburg. If I don't go, I shall have his death on my conscience. What can I hope for here?'

'Because of the political circumstances, nothing – Gemmingen himself is in danger. The elector leads the game and relies upon many allies, one of whom is Colloredo.'

'So *Semiramis* is finished?'

'Unfortunately, yes.'

'Another failure, like *Thamos*. Why can I not carry such important works through to their conclusion?'

'Because you aren't yet ready. Destiny is showing that it is stronger than you; you lack magic.'

'Salzburg won't give me any!'

'How do you know?'

'Returning there will suffocate me. I won't survive long for lack of air.'

'You survived in Paris. Here is another door to pass through, and this one is even more tightly sealed.'

'Is there no way out?'

'None.'

'I was so happy here.'

'Even without Aloysia?'

'You . . . you knew?'

Thamos smiled. 'You're of an age to be in love.'

'The age to marry! Aloysia is a wonderful singer, and we're made for each other. I shall write her beautiful arias, and she will interpret them incomparably.'

'Let us hope so, Wolfgang.'

'Do you doubt it?'

'I trust your judgement as a professional. Now, on 9 December the imperial prelate of Kaisersheim is leaving Mannheim. You will travel free of charge in one of the attending carriages, in the company of his secretary.'

'Will you come to Salzburg?'

'I shall never abandon you.'

The Great Magician

Lyon, 25 November 1778

At the age of forty-eight, Jean-Baptiste Willermoz felt in full possession of his faculties and was finally reaching the goal of his Masonic dream: to create a specific Rite which would enable its followers to attain the divine.

Strict Observance had greatly disappointed him. Such paucity of teaching, such outdated ceremonies, and so little esoteric knowledge! Without breaking the links with the Templar Order and withdrawing officially, Willermoz wanted to go much further. He had therefore organized the Masonic gathering of Les Gaules, from 25 November to 3 December, in order to reveal part of his plan to the faithful.

First, he would declare the autonomy of the French branch of Strict Observance and its original character. Second, he would abandon his plans for the material restoration of the Order of the Temple, which had vanished for ever into the mists of history.

Right from the gathering's first moments, Willermoz stated Freemasonry's major mission: to do good. As a priority, it would deal with improving the lot of widows, orphans, the sick, vagrants, and would practise charity.

'Nobody could disapprove of such generosity,' observed the Count of Thebes, a fascinating man with great natural authority. 'Since we are among Brothers, subject to the law of secrecy, will you not reveal to us the true goal of Freemasonry? Each Brother here knows the depth of your research, and I have the feeling that this gathering will be like no other.'

Flattered, Willermoz did not need to be asked twice.

'Humanity is made up of two principal categories. The first is the outcasts, to whom the seal of reconciliation with God is refused. The second is the men of desire, who are capable of practising the true divine cult, thanks to initiation. As the elect, they contribute to the final salvation of humanity. We must achieve reintegration and re-establish man created in the image of God as the master of minds.'

Willermoz's speech deeply impressed the assembly.

'Does such a programme not imply a profound reform of current Masonic structures?' asked Thamos.

'Indeed, that is vital. I propose to divide the Masonic path into two classes, one preparatory and the other secret. Knowledge of the truth will be reserved for initiates of the second class, of whose existence ordinary Freemasons will be unaware. Thus we shall create the Order of the Charitable Knights of the Holy City.'*

'What city is that?' asked a Brother.

'The city in Palestine where Jesus was crucified, the true cradle of the Order of the Temple: Jerusalem, whence we must begin again. But it is fitting to talk more of Knights than of Templars, for the military aspect must disappear to the benefit of the spiritual dimension. Moreover, the authorities are suspicious of neo-Templars, whose hostility to the Pope and the King could be considered threatening. My Brothers, I summon you to a great adventure!'

'When shall we experience this ritual?' asked Thamos.

'As soon as we have officially proclaimed the birth of the new Order.'

The whole assembly rallied to Willermoz's plan. Each of his faithful followers dreamt of becoming one of the privileged ones, as quickly as possible.

* Willermoz's Rite gave birth to the present-day Rectified Scottish Rite.

73

Lyon, 3 December 1778

The hall of the chapter of the Charitable Knights of the Holy City was plunged into darkness. A faint glimmer of light came from the one lantern placed beside the Commander, Jean-Baptiste Willermoz, so that he could read the text of the initiation ritual.

Guided by a Knight, Thamos crossed the threshold.

A flame sprang up from a dish of spirits of wine, symbolizing the awakening of the new follower's consciousness. The light that emanated from it enabled him to glimpse an altar in the shape of a tomb. So it was necessary to pass through a kind of death.

The Knights lit candles.

Thamos managed to make out something of his surroundings: the walls were covered by black hangings decorated with deaths' heads crowned with laurels and surrounded by seven tears. On either side of the door there was a skeleton. At the far end of the hall, a third skeleton was seated at a small table. On a drawing-board, it drew a triangle inscribed in a circle. At the heart of infinity, beyond death, it revealed the threefold nature of thought, source of all life. After all, the triangle expressed the first possible geometric form.

Commander Willermoz led Thamos through a long

initiation ceremony, which ended with the new Charitable Knight of the Holy City being equipped with a sword, a spear and a collar from which hung a crucifix. He was dressed in a toga and a plumed hat was placed upon his head; then he was congratulated on his accession to this highest rank.

At the end of the ceremony, Willermoz congratulated the Egyptian.

'Are you satisfied, my Brother?'

'Not completely,' replied Thamos in a low voice.

'How dare you—'

'This ritual is merely a preamble to the real Mysteries. It does not differ sufficiently from those of Strict Observance. You have devised another degree, totally secret, which exceeds the state of Knight. It is to that rank that I wish to be initiated.'

Willermoz's kindly face hardened. 'Are you a good Christian?'

'Is it enough for you that I am the disciple of Abbot Hermes, who was murdered by Muslim fanatics?'

The Commander gazed steadily at him. 'I shall initiate you into the supreme rank.'

Mannheim, 9 December 1778

As Thamos had said, there was a seat reserved for Wolfgang in one of the coaches carrying the servants of the imperial prelate of Kaisersheim, and he travelled with that dignitary's secretary and cellarer. They were not very talkative and did not bother him, leaving him to dream of how he would soon see his dear Aloysia again and ask her to become his wife.

This long series of ordeals, which had lasted since his departure from Salzburg, would therefore end in the happiest of ways: marriage with the first woman he had loved, a wonderful singer! Before them opened up a whole life during which they would work together, he as the composer and she as the interpreter of his work.

There was only one annoyance during this comfortable journey: a ten-day halt at the Cistercian monastery of Kaisersheim, where the prelate dealt with Church various matters. The place was full of nervous and aggressive soldiers; it was like a barracks. The god of armies had visibly taken possession of the area.

Several times during the night, sentries asked the same question: 'Who goes there?' and Wolfgang, who would have preferred to sleep in peace, replied: 'All's well!'

On 24 December, they set off again for Munich.

Wolfgang was obsessed by Aloysia's face, and above all by her voice. Tomorrow, Christmas Day, he would reveal to her the depth of his feelings and announce his grand plans clearly to her and her father. He would establish himself in Munich, work frenziedly there, and make his wife triumph on the stage of the Opera.

Never would he lock himself away in Salzburg. His father would agree to the marriage and to the new direction his son's career was taking.

Lyon, 24 December 1778

Thamos was initiated by Jean-Baptiste Willermoz into the highest and most secret rank, Profession, which was the crown of Freemasonry – even though Freemasonry itself was unaware of it.

Convinced of the Egyptian's sincerity, Willermoz agreed to reveal to him the Rite he had written.

'Man has lost his original purity,' he said. 'The truth is hidden to corrupt individuals, who are deprived of Light.' His tone hardened. 'Egypt raised temples to wicked, perverse gods, but fortunately Moses triumphed over the Egyptian mages.

The Hebrews, the chosen people, left the righteous path. Solomon found it again by building the temple in Jerusalem, but because of his vanity he lost wisdom. The temple was destroyed and, worse still, the Jews committed a crime by failing to recognize the Saviour. Only one initiation exists, my Brother: the message of Christ, which is restricted to an elite capable of understanding it.'

Thamos received the attributes of a Grand Professionial: a white robe with a red cross, a coat of mail, a voluminous cloak, sword, hat, boots and gold spurs.

Whereas he had expected a ritual inspired by the first days of Christianity, the Egyptian found only a banal session of religious instruction and conventional prayers, recited by Willermoz.

Then, led by him, all the Brothers entered the Operations Room in order to bring down higher spirits and control them.

For Thamos, this path was not the path of initiation, and would be of no use at all to the Great Magician.

74

Munich, 25 December 1778

Wolfgang's heart was aflame. Dressed in an elegant red suit with black buttons, he knocked at the Webers' door.

Fridolin opened it. He looked pale as he bowed. 'Oh ... it's you.'

'I'm so happy to see you again.'

'As am I, Wolfgang, as am I.'

'May I come in?'

'Of course, of course.'

The apartment was spacious and comfortably warm.

'Are you in good health, Herr Weber?'

'I am beginning to grow old.'

'At the age of forty-five? Surely not.'

'Too many difficulties, too many blows from fate ... I feel worn out.'

'You must be delighted by Aloysia's success.'

'Nothing is certain. There is nothing more arduous than a singer's career.'

'Are you enjoying Munich?'

'There are worse places,' said Fridolin.

'May I see Aloysia?'

'We weren't expecting you; she's busy.'

'Did she receive my letters?'

'Certainly.'

'Then she was expecting me.'

'Very well, wait a moment . . . Wouldn't you prefer to come back tomorrow?'

'Oh no, I want so much to talk with my dear, my very dear Aloysia, as soon as possible.'

'As you wish.'

Fridolin trudged heavily into another room; clearly Wolfgang's future father-in-law was ill. A long quarter of an hour elapsed before he reappeared.

'I shall take you to the music room.'

It was a charming place, with a fine harpsichord. Dressed in a sumptuous orange gown, her hair and make-up perfect, Aloysia was consulting a piece of sheet music.

'I'll leave you,' said her father.

The young woman did not look up.

'Aloysia . . .'

'Who is it?'

'It's Wolfgang!'

'Which Wolfgang? I know several.'

'I am Wolfgang Mozart, my dear and tender friend.'

'Wolfgang Mozart? The name means nothing to me.'

'Don't tease me like this, Aloysia. It's too cruel.'

'Tease you? But I don't even know you.'

'On the contrary, you know me very well, and must have perceived the depth of my feelings.'

'Your feelings? I don't understand.'

'I love you, Aloysia, and I want to marry you.'

The young woman looked at him haughtily. 'You must be delirious, Herr Mozart. There can be absolutely no question of it! Stop offending me immediately.'

'You . . . you don't love me?'

'Of course not. Whatever did you imagine?'

The heavens collapsed upon Wolfgang's head. 'It isn't

possible, Aloysia. Make this nightmare go away, I beg of you!'

'This conversation bores and irritates me, Herr Mozart. Leave at once, and do not come back.'

So it was not a nightmare. Aloysia did not love him, he would never marry her, and they would not build a life based on music together.

Wolfgang retained his dignity and did not burst into tears. Sitting down at the harpsichord, he sang a popular song by Goetz von Berlichingen, 'Lack mi am Arsch', 'I don't give a damn about those who don't love me', then strode out of the Webers' lodgings.

Munich, 29 December 1778

Offered accommodation by a friend, the flautist Becke, Wolfgang read his father's letters. Leopold feared that a great war would be unleashed, and that many countries would be involved, first of all Russia, Austria, Prussia and Sweden, then France, Portugal, Spain and others. '*So the great lords*', he reminded Wolfgang, '*have their minds on things very different from music and compositions.*' There was only one solution: his son must return at once to Salzburg, a quiet place which would be spared by the conflict.

And Leopold was deeply worried about the family's financial problems: *I wish only to know that we can be sure of paying our debts. I do not want what we possess to be sold at a loss after my death to pay the debts. If they are paid, I can die in peace. It is essential, and I desire it.*'

Without giving details of the drama he had just been through, Wolfgang summed it up in a few words: 'There is no room in my heart for anything but the desire to weep.' Could his father detect his despair and anguish at being locked away in Salzburg?

Leopold's new letter proved his affection. He was deeply saddened by his son's sorrows and thought only of comforting him: 'You have no reason to fear either myself or your sister, or that you will be greeted without affection or spend unhappy days.'

Rediscovering his family, a piece of his childhood, a cosy little room, a city without dramas ... Was this, then, the end of those long journeys across Europe?

Munich, 8 January 1779

Wolfgang wrote to his father:

> *I do not feel guilty of anything. I have done nothing wrong. I cannot endure Salzburg, or its inhabitants. Their language and their way of life are totally unbearable to me. I burn with the most ardent desire to embrace you once again, you and my dear sister. Ah, if only it were not in Salzburg!*

And yet he would once again have to submit to the will of Prince-Archbishop Colloredo. After so many failures, he no longer had a choice.

Before his painful return, he finished a great aria, '*Popoli di Tessaglia*', dealing with the grievous pain of Alceste as she announced the death of her husband, Admetes, to the people of Thessaly.

The work finished, he walked briskly to the Webers' residence.

Fridolin opened the door, looking even more bowed and grey-faced.

'I am leaving Munich,' Wolfgang announced. 'Before I go, I should like to give Aloysia a present.'

Fridolin fetched his daughter, who stood very stiffly at her father's side.

'I feel no resentment, Aloysia, and I wish you happiness. This aria will display your virtuosity to best effect. Goodbye.'

When Wolfgang got into the carriage for Salzburg, there was only one other traveller: Thamos the Egyptian.

'I reserved all the seats,' he explained. 'We will stop as often as you wish and we shall share a few good meals in the best inns. Good wine will help you regain your energy.'

'You know, for Aloysia—'

'Trying to console you would be pointless. You will absorb this pain, like the other sufferings, and you will be greater than it, because your destiny is different from that of other men.'

'What destiny can the prison of Salzburg have in store for me?'

'You will confront a dragon there. Either it will defeat you or you will be nourished by its strength. Thanks to the beauty and power of your music, you may succeed in directing yourself towards wisdom, if you know how to seek out the essence that lies at the centre and at the heart.'

Surely the Egyptian must be alluding to initiation into the Mysteries of the sun-priests, that still-inaccessible ideal? It was up to him, Mozart, to make it real.

Bibliography

The letters of Wolfgang and Leopold Mozart have been partially preserved and are a mine of information which we have used widely, notably by putting words from these writings into the musician's mouth.

Several partial editions of this correspondence exist, along with one complete edition, *Mozart: Briefe und Aufzeichnungen* (ed. W. A. Bauer, O. E. Deutsch and J. H. Eibl), most of which has been translated into French by G. Geffray, in seven volumes. For this first novel, see *Correspondance I, 1756–1776*, Paris, 1986; *Correspondance II, 1777–1778*, Paris, 1987; *Correspondance III, 1778–1781*, Paris, 1989.

In reference works on Mozart, you will find detailed bibliographies on the composer's life and work.